LESLIE NIELSEN

THE NAKED TRUTH

by LESLIE NIELSEN
and DAVID FISHER

Art Direction
DAVID KAESTLE

POCKET BOOKS
New York   London   Toronto   Sydney   Tokyo   Singapore

Produced by: David Kaestle, Inc.
Associate designer: Richard DeMonico
Photo retouching: Robert Rakita
Original photography: Chuck Fishman

POCKET BOOKS, a division of Simon & Schuster Inc.
1230 Avenue of the Americas, New York, NY 10020

Library of Congress Cataloging-in-Publication Number: 93-84539

ISBN: 0-671-79577-5

First Pocket Books hardcover printing July 1993

10 9 8 7 6 5 4 3 2 1

This book is gratefully dedicated to all those people who have made the motion picture industry what it is today—the only business in the world in which the trailer comes first.

1

THE FIRST CHAPTER OF MY LIFE BEGINS

T he preeminent German philosopher Friedrich Nietzsche once wrote that to truly understand the human condition, and have a good time, it was necessary to go to the movies. Years later, in his classic treatise *Die Geburt der Blues* ("The Birth of the Blues") he added the now-famous warning, "But don't buy the Jujyfruits because they stick in your teeth."

From my earliest memories I've known precisely what my nietzsche in life was: To be an actor. It is the only thing I've ever wanted to do, with the possible exception of driving against traffic in the Indianapolis 500.

I am an extremely fortunate person. Fate cast me into a wonderful role. I've been rewarded both emotionally and financially for doing that thing I most love doing. I've had the extreme privilege of working with some of the greatest directors in motion picture history: C. B. deMille, Spike Lee, Howard Hawks, Vincente Minnelli, Billy Wilder, Alfred Hitchcock, David Lean, Emilio Estevez, Steven Spielberg, and Woody. I've acted with such legendary performers as James Dean, Marlon Brando, Grace Kelly, Clint Eastwood, T. P. Panther, Robert De Niro. I've been married to four wonderful women.

I've also been honored by my colleagues with four Academy Award nominations and have twice been named Best Actor. I've won two People's Choice Awards, a Golden Globe, a Best Actor at the Cannes Film Festival, a Best in Show at Westminster, an American League batting title, I've been a three-time finalist in the Publishers' Clearinghouse Sweepstakes, I was named "Mr. Week of April 23rd" on Home Shopping Network, and finally, in August 1990, I received the highest honor any actor could be given other than participation in the gross receipts—I was awarded the coveted Nobel Prize for Good Acting.

Being selected as the recipient of that award was perhaps the greatest thrill of my life, even if it didn't come with any small gifts like a weekend for two at the luxurious Kuala Bay Hotel on Catalina Island. The prize is given for a body of work rather than a specific film, and it had last been awarded three years earlier, when it was given to Sir Charlie Chaplin posthumorously. Tears welled in my eyes as I stood on the podium and addressed the distinguished audience. "This is indeed a great honor you have bestowed upon me," I told them, "and it is very difficult for me to express how truly grateful I am. One of the primary reasons for the ascendancy of mankind over the world of animals is that animals have tails, and if you have a tail, you can't hide your emotions. So mankind always knew what animals were feeling. And if we didn't like it . . . But I tell you this tonight, and I mean it from the very bottom of my heart, if I had a tail, right now I'd be wagging it in your face.

"It's almost impossible to believe that a poor boy from Canada, a large country just north of the American border, could one day become a Nobleman. . . ."

I was born to be an actor. Perhaps my earliest memory is my mother looking down lovingly at me as I lay in my crib, telling me, "You're six years old, stop acting like a baby." As I grew older, it was my father who inspired me, constantly urging me, "Why can't you act normal like the rest of the kids?" And even later, when women entered my life, I would repeatedly be told, "Why do you always have to act like such a jerk?"

I suppose it really shouldn't be surprising that talent ran in my veins. Although I was raised in northern Canada, my family had long been in show business. My great-grandfather was reputed to have been one of the finest actors in America's Old West. Few records exist of precisely what roles he performed, but he must have been superb because every time he arrived in a new town they ordered him to get on the stage.

The first actress in our family was my great-aunt Lila, who was recognized all over for the "naughty" roles she created in still pictures. And my half-uncle was the famous actor Jean Hersholt, who portrayed kindly Dr. Christian on radio, television, and in the movies. My uncle, Jean, was one of the founders of the Academy of Motion Picture Arts and Sciences, and each year the Jean Hersholt Humanitarian Award is given in his name.

Neither my mother nor my father cared about show business. The truth is that they were both very cold people. In fact, everybody in my family was very cold. This was undoubtedly due to the fact that we lived in a unheated log cabin not far from the Arctic Circle. My father was a constable in the Royal Canadian Mounted Police. Just after I was born he was assigned to the small town of Fort Norman, up the Mackenzie River, in the Northwest Territories, which could only be reached by boat in the warmer months. Basically, the population of Fort Norman consisted of us. We used to say that it was so far north that when John Wayne's movie about gold prospectors was released there, its title had to be changed to *South to Alaska!* At times during the year, the sun shone for twenty-four hours a day, and eventually the cold and the constant light would get to people, and they would have terrible daymares.

Most of the people who came through the town were trappers. I can remember only one case my father solved. Two Eskimos had gone into the wild, and three days later only one of them returned. He immediately confessed that he had killed the other man. He had no choice, he explained, because they'd been out in the bitter cold for three days and the other man had refused to

My father, seen above, was one of the great carriageless horse drivers in the Royal Canadian Mounted Police. He was a man of tremendous integrity and wit, but to me, seen with him at left in 1928, he was just a big holdup man.

smile. Years later I would hear performers claim they'd "killed the audience," but this was the only time it actually happened. Perhaps it was that memory that impressed upon me the importance of comedy.

My mother was basically a stay-at-cabin. Her passion in life was decorating, although in that part of the world decorating consisted primarily of deciding where to hang the moose head.

I grew up with two wonderful brothers. Living in such an isolated place caused us to become very close. We played all the usual childhood games—cowboys and Eskimos, Eskimos in space—but our favorite game was hide-and-seek. It wasn't because we particularly liked hide-and-seek, but rather because we loved hearing someone say "You're getting warmer."

My brother Eric was two years older than I am, and as I often tease him, he turned out to be the big disappointment in the family. He was so smart, so talented, he had so much to give to the world, but instead he became a politician—"Old Velcro Lips," as he was called in Canada because he never smiled and rarely spoke to the media. He eventually rose to the office of deputy prime minister. We rarely speak of this when we're together. We feel it's best to try to put those sorts of things behind us and simply go on with life.

When I was about four years old, my family moved to Edmonton so we could attend a regular school. It was there that I discovered my love for the theater. My fourth-grade teacher was Mr. Stockwell, and he probably had more impact on my life than anyone other than my parents and my second wife's divorce attorney. Mr. Stockwell was a warm, caring man. He loved the theater and tried to share that love with his students. He wanted us to understand the beauty of Shakespeare, but realized we were only in elementary school, so he created Shakespearean plays specifically for our age group. My first starring role was that of Romeo in the play *Romeo and Gretel*. It was the tragic story of star-crossed young lovers who get lost in the enchanted forest, and in the big finale I commit suicide by throwing myself into the oven.

Mr. Stockwell called it a half-baked role, but as I stood on that stage bathing in the applause of the audience, I felt happier and warmer than I'd ever been in my life. It was a magical moment, and I knew then that I would spend my life learning how to act, being in the movies, going out with starlets, paying divorce lawyers large sums of money. But first, I knew, I had to finish fourth grade.

It was in Edmonton that I went to the movies for the very first time. I was five years old, and I went with my brothers on Saturday morning to see the original *Frankenstein,* starring

Boris Karloff, Colin Clive, Steven Wolf, and Mae Clarke. It was incredible to me that I could sit there in that small Canadian town and have the rest of the world brought to me. I learned many of life's most important lessons from those Saturday-morning movies: Never get involved in a showdown with a cowboy wearing a white hat. Never stand up on a battlefield and say loudly, "It's over. We won. Those cowards have gone." And never trust a character whose head has to be bolted on.

When I was seventeen years old I left home to join the Canadian Air Force. I wanted to fly like Richard Arlen in *Wings*. I

As a thirteen-year-old in Edmonton, the only two things I wanted to do in life were to be a great actor and get out of eighth grade.

knew it was dangerous, but I also knew, as John Wayne told me in *Angels at 12,000 Feet*, "Anybody can take one of these crates up, but it's only after ya been shot fulla more holes than a slice a Swiss cheese, and your landing gear's been blown away, and you're outta gasoline, and your wing is hangin' on with chewin' gum, and you're in a hurricane and your carrier's sinking and ya have to go to the bathroom, that you learn what color blood ya bleed."

I was accepted for pilot training and learned how to fly the old Cornell, a British-made single-engine trainer. I desperately wanted to be a fighter pilot, but sometimes things just don't work out; instead I became a pilot fighter. I was young and strong, I looked terrific in my uniform—I was perfect for the job. In those desperate days of World War Deuce the casualty rate among fighter pilots was unacceptably high, and ranking officers blamed part of that on a lack of confidence. These guys had seen too many of their buddies go down in flames; they were tired and scared. In order to help restore their self-confidence a top-secret, elite corps was created, and I was ordered to volunteer for this unit. Our primary assignment was to amble into the pilots' favorite drinking hole the night before they were to fly a danger-ous mission, drink a little too much flak juice, make lewd com-ments about the girls they left behind, pick fights with airmen smaller than we were, and let them throttle us. The theory was that this helped restore the pilots' self-confidence. It gave them a renewed sense of immortality. Who knows, maybe it worked.

Ironically, years later this would turn out to be invaluable training for my portrayal of the down-and-out-cold light-heavy-weight "Ten Count" O'Brien, in Howard Hawks's gritty boxing classic, *Ring Around My Heart*. Initially Hawks intended to use a stand-in for me in those memorable fight scenes in which I threw bouts to earn enough money to pay for the long-shot operation that would enable June Allyson's crippled son to walk again. But I insisted on doing them myself.

"I'm warning you," Hawks warned, "you'll get hurt."

"Maybe," I agreed, "but the audience will know my pain is real. Sure, Lancaster and Douglas use stuntmen; I'll take my own punches. I get hit, I fall down; that's acting! Sometimes integrity is a punch in the face." It all worked out very well. The movie was a mild success and I was elected Red Cross Poster Man of the Year.

When the war ended, I was just another dogperson with too many sad stories to tell and no one to listen to them. Without a college degree, without any experience, without any real skills of any kind, I knew my choices were limited. I could either become a bum, living on the streets and begging for pennies, or an actor. I grappled with the decision, but acting won, two falls out of three.

I eventually got a job at radio station CKMM, a Canadian station with five thousand watts of power. It wasn't acting, but the opportunity to be on radio was thrilling for me; where I grew up, we were thrilled to be on the telephone. I did everything that needed to be done around the station: I was an announcer, a disc jockey, I sang gospel on Sunday mornings, read commercials, slept with the boss's wife, sold airtime, kept the log, fired the furnace in the morning and rehired it in the afternoon, and I loved every minute of it. I was in show business.

Actually, I slept with the boss's wife by mistake. She was having an affair with the most popular deejay at the station, and one night he got sick and asked me to fill in for him. Only later did I find out that he'd meant he wanted me to do his show.

I knew I needed more training so I enrolled in Lorne Greene's School of Radio Broadcasting. Lorne gained stardom as Paw Cartwright in the television series "Bonanza," but during World War II Canadians knew him as "The Voice of Doom." He had such a deep, somber voice that he could say "Scattered clouds" and it would sound like "The world is coming to an end." During the early days of the war, people would sit by their radio sets in blacked-out houses listening to Lorne Greene on the CBC broadcasting the latest bad news from Europe. Then they'd say, "Boy, the war is going terrible, but doesn't Lorne have a great voice!"

I learned a great deal at his broadcasting school. The only course I flunked was Emergency Broadcasting. I was doing fine until our teacher announced a pop quiz one afternoon. "It's a simple test," he explained, "I just want to hear each of you announce, 'This is not a test.'"

I raised my hand. "Is this a test?"

"No, that's wrong. 'This is not a test.'"

I was slightly confused. "I'm sorry, I thought you said this was a test."

"It is. This is not a test. That's the test."

"Let me get this straight. If I say to you, 'This is not a test,' then I've passed the test?"

"That's right. It's a very simple test. This is not a test."

I began to realize that this radio business was a little more complicated than I'd anticipated.

At the end of my first year I was awarded a scholarship to go to New York City and study acting with the esteemed teacher Sandy Meisner at the Neighborhood Playhouse. It didn't make a whole lot of sense to me: I'd done so well in radio broadcasting school that they sent me out of the country to study another profession. I left Canada with hope, determination, and one clean shirt. But I felt extremely confident that my future was in front of me. When I reached the American border at Niagara Falls, the customs agent asked me, "Do you have anything to declare?"

"Absolutely." Turning around, I faced Canada and vowed, "One day I'm going to be a great actor."

"Move along, buddy," he replied.

New York City. The Big Apple. Gotham. Buildings the size of skyscrapers. New York City in the late 1940s was the most exciting place I'd ever been. In those days the city was alive with possible dreams: the opportunities were big and the potholes were small. Like the generations of young actors who had come there before me, I was young, ambitious, and very poor.

Mostly poor. Money was a rumor. I shared a converted coal bin on West Ninety-second Street with another actor, named Charles McLaughlin Kelly. The landlord claimed it had been converted, but we were never convinced he'd completed the job. The best thing about it was that we never needed curtains for the windows—we needed windows.

Charley Mac and I practically survived on ketchup sandwiches. We'd go into the Schrafft's on Broadway or the Horn & Hardart Automat on Forty-second Street and pour ketchup between two slices of leftover bread. The first time Charley Mac tasted one of these, he took a big bite, considered it for a few seconds, then decided, "Needs ketchup."

I came to New York in 1948 to study acting. While learning those things every young actor needs to know—how to wait on tables and how to survive on ketchup sandwiches—we put on shows everywhere, from small theaters to local bars (below). But my first great performance was convincing the landlord I could pay my rent.

When we got tired of ketchup, we'd spice it up with gobs of mayonnaise. I actually didn't like mayonnaise, but it killed the taste of the ketchup. Even after I'd started working and could afford food, I'd occasionally order a ketchup sandwich, but I'd proudly tell the waitress, "Hold the mayo."

The Neighborhood Playhouse and the Actors Studio were the mecca of young actors. So many wonderful and talented people were just beginning their careers: people like James Dean, Marlon, Eli Wallach and Anne Jackson, Nick Adams, Mark Rydell, Shelley Winters, Ben Gazzara, Roger Rabbit, Sr., Paul Newman and Joanne Woodward, even Marilyn Monroe. Maybe the most important lesson I learned at the Neighborhood Playhouse was that talent is like potatoes: it doesn't grow on trees. If you are fortunate enough to be born with talent, you have an obligation to work with it and shape it and develop it. And if you don't, you should become an agent. If that doesn't work, you should become a critic.

As Mama Rose sang in *Gypsy*, "You either got it, or you ain't." Everybody knew that James Dean had it. The first time I met Monroe I took one look at her and her talent was obvious. It took a little longer for my talent to emerge; in fact, my real talent was underplaying my talent. I was extremely talented at that.

At the Neighborhood Playhouse we studied every aspect of the craft. We had to take acrobatic lessons, mime, even dance. Our ballroom dance instructor was a conservative, internationally known artist named Martha Graham. Martha tried everything to teach me ballroom dancing, but I just wasn't very good at it. I have terribly bowed legs, and I just couldn't seem to get them moving in the same direction. One day we were trying to master the box step and I suggested we try something slightly different. Miss Graham was very upset. "Absolutely not," she said firmly. "The beauty of dance is in its tradition. The reason for doing it this way is because it's always been done this way. There's only one correct way of doing these steps, and that's the way we're going to do them."

"I'm sorry, I can't." Because of my bowed legs, I explained, I just couldn't do it. "But maybe if I moved my right leg slowly across my body, then twisted my left leg behind me, turned swiftly, then raced across the stage and leaped into the air as if I were being carried on the wings of angels . . ."

"Wait a moment," she said. "I'm beginning to see what you mean. You're talking about putting . . . movement into dance."

I could see she was intrigued. "It certainly would be different."

"It just might work," she agreed finally, her voice growing with enthusiasm, "it just might work. Let's just try it and see what happens." Suddenly she threw off the shackles of tradition. "Damn the fox-trot," she said, "full dance ahead!"

Which is how I got out of ballroom dancing.

Our lives revolved around the theater. We would take any job we could find that was even remotely connected with the business. The Off-Broadway theater was then in its infancy, and while everyone still dreamed of opening on Broadway in Tennessee Williams's latest smash hit, we were almost as happy to be working in an experimental play in a converted loft on MacDougal Street. I once did a decent *Richard III* in the back of a kosher deli on Hester Street. We worked everywhere: if we weren't able to find something on Broadway, we worked Off–Broadway. If there was nothing Off–Broadway, we worked Off–New York. If there were no parts Off–New York, we worked Off–Western Hemisphere.

17

I auditioned for almost every conceivable type of role. Once I answered an ad in *Variety* for an actor who could play a clarinet. At Actors Studio I'd played a tree, a chair, a policeman's whistle . . . I knew I could play a clarinet. I was tall and thin, so I dressed in black and stuck a big reed in my mouth. I was probably lucky I didn't get the part; the actor they hired to play the saxophone suffered a badly wrenched back.

I remember they were doing a new drama at the Prince Street Playhouse titled *A Shadow in Darkness*, and I auditioned for the role of the shadow. I had to stand behind a sheet and pretend to be a shadow. The director didn't like my work very much, explaining, "You cast too much of your own shadow. Think you could try to cast someone else's shadow?" Believe me, I was learning that there was more to acting than meets the eye.

Most of these plays were written by young writers and staged by new directors. Sometimes they had no idea what they were doing. I once went up for the lead in a conspiracy drama called *The Lincoln Conspiracy*. The stage direction read: Lincoln walks through door and discovers Mary Todd Lincoln in bed with John Wilkes Booth.

So I did.

"Cut!" the director screamed. "Cut! Cut! Cut! You're supposed to open the door first!"

I tried to be professional about it. "If that's what the author wanted," I explained, "he should have made it clear."

Eventually I started getting a few small parts. I did *Accent on Youth* in Boston with Paul Lukas, and *The Pope Tells a Whopper* with Gillian Boswell. I even toured with Sarah Churchill, the daughter of Sir Winston Churchill, when she made her American stage debut in Philip Barry's *The Philadelphia Story*. Miss Churchill was an extremely lovely, very feminine woman. Perhaps at first I was put off a bit by that big cigar, but as I got to know her, I found that she possessed her father's legendary intelligence and wit. During a backstage game of stud poker one evening I asked her if she'd had any difficulty learning to speak with a Philadelphia accent. "Oh, no, my deah boy." she said, laughing sweetly. "It's quite simple actually. To speak proper American all one must do is imitate the Oxford linguistics professor who entered a monastery and took all the vowels of silence."

Frankly, I think she must have been joking.

After completing my formal training at the Neighborhood Playhouse I often worked at the Actors Studio. Actors Studio was becoming known as the center of "the Method," a revolutionary technique created by the great Russian actor-director-producer Stanislavsky at his Moscow Art Theatre. At its core, "the Method" stressed a natural approach to acting. Actors were taught to do the part, within the discipline demanded by the character, rather than create a stylized or more formal portrayal that would be disconnected from themselves. In other words, the key to acting was to act as if you weren't acting. The biggest criticism at the Actors Studio was "You're acting." If you weren't acting, you were considered a good actor.

I was fortunate enough to be invited into the small class taught at the Studio by Mr. Stanislavsky. He was quite old by this time. I can close my eyes and see him sitting there, his large haunted eyes seemingly ready to burst from his tightly stretched skin, with a large shock of wild white hair that made him look like an old Albert Einstein. His English was not very good, but he had an incredible ability to find the essence of a character.

In class he was an absolute dictator. When he gave an order, he expected it to be carried out immediately and without discussion. One of the exercises we did in class, for example, was to imitate objects he would select. At various times I was a chair, a typewriter, a broken radio. During class one afternoon he told a talented young actor named Andrew Glenn to be a tree. Andrew had some difficulty figuring out what his motivation was. Compared to that understanding, a chair was simple: my motivation was to get sat on. But Andrew wanted to know what kind of tree he was, where he was planted, what time of year it was, how old a tree he was. He agitated Mr. Stanislavsky with endless questions until finally, when he asked, "What is the essence of this tree?," Mr. Stanislavsky threw up his hands in despair, then shouted in his broken Slavic accent, "Leaf!"

Unfortunately, Andrew did. And what might have been a successful career in the theater ended that day.

We didn't spend all of our time in the theater. In New York this was the very beginning of the beatnik era, and we spent a lot of late nights in coffeehouses and jazz clubs like the Downbeat, the Village Vanguard, and the Blue Note discussing philosophy, religion, politics, paying the rent. One night I was at the Village Gate listening as a young trumpeter named Miles Davis carried us into the morning on his horn. It was obvious to everyone who heard him that Davis was a genius; he was far, far ahead of his time. In fact, I'll tell you how far ahead of his time he was. That night he did a long riff on the song "Memories" from the show *Cats*, and that song wouldn't even be written for another thirty years.

Of all the people I knew during this period, the one who became most closely associated with the so-called Beat Generation was my friend James Dean. People remember James Dean as the incredibly intense, introspective, troubled, alienated symbol of those rebellious times. But that wasn't the Jimbo, as I called him, that I knew. The man I knew was a happy-go-lucky, without-a-care, wisecracking practical joker. No one could short-sheet a bed like he could—he could do it while someone was sleeping in it. The fact is that he became that troubled, alienated person only after we became close friends.

Jimbo was a very handsome man and had already played bit parts in several low-budget movies by the time I met him. Ironically, he always had trouble getting dates. Women just didn't find him particularly appealing. I actually felt a little sorry for him. For a time when we were living on Forty-fourth Street he was dating a lovely Italian actress studying at the Studio named Gia Angelica. He was crazy about her, crazy. One morning at about 4 A.M. the phone woke me. Jimbo was wandering the streets, threatening to commit suicide because Gia wouldn't marry him. "I'm serious," he insisted.

"What time is it?" I asked.

"Little after four o'clock."

"Okay," I said sympathetically, "do me a favor. I've got to get up at six-thirty. If you haven't committed suicide by then, call me and we'll talk about it."

"And what if I do it?"

"I guess I'll oversleep," I said. When Jimmy laughed, I knew he would be all right.

Although it's not generally known, the truth is that I'm at least partially responsible for his great success. While Jimbo obviously had a great deal of natural talent, he had difficulty expressing real emotions while performing. His characters often came across as wooden and stilted. So when Elia Kazan invited him to audition for the starring role in the movie adaptation of John Steinbeck's *East of Eden*, he panicked. "I can't do it," he cried, "I just can't do it. They want me to play some-

Few people know that my friend James Dean had great difficulty showing emotion in front of a camera. To help him "feel" hurt and anger while auditioning for East of Eden, *I volunteered to have an affair with his girlfriend, Gia Angelica, behind his back.*

one who feels pain, someone who's passionate, a real flesh-and-blood character. Why me? Why don't they ever ask me to play a part I've been rehearsing for years? I could be a great chair."

"I know you could," I agreed, trying to calm him down. "You could even be a sofa if you really wanted to. But maybe I can help you with this part. Exactly what are you supposed to do for the audition?"

He showed me his script. "It's a confrontational scene with my brother. I'm supposed to be hurt and angry." He laughed mockingly and shook his head in despair. "Me. Hurt and angry. I just can't do it."

"Now just wait a second, maybe we can figure something out." I frowned. "Hurt and angry, hurt and angry. Let's see . . ." Suddenly it came to me. I snapped my fingers. "I think I've got an idea. Let me ask you something. How would you feel, I mean really feel, if you knew that while you were at this audition, Gia and I were going out behind your back? You know, that we were alone together, hugging, kissing . . . touching private parts."

I'd touched a nerve. A troubled look crossed his brow. "Well, I guess . . . I'd be . . . hurt. You know, she's my girl, you're my good friend. Sure, I'd be hurt, hurt and angry." He smiled knowingly. "Yeah, that's right, hurt and angry."

"Okay," I said emphatically, "then that's what we'll do."

"Wha . . ." Even Jimbo couldn't contain his emotions. His eyes hinted at tears. "Would you . . . would you really do that for me?"

"Sure, kid," I said, shrugging, "no big deal."

He was speechless. For a moment I even thought he might cry. "It's just . . . I . . . No one's ever done anything like this for me before."

"Hey, we're all in this together, right?" I gave him a guy-type punch in the shoulder. "Look, I'll tell you what else I'll do. Give me every penny you have in the bank. Knowing that I'm out there spending all your money on your girlfriend'll add a real subtext of fear and anxiety."

Gia wasn't really my type. I've never been very attracted to absolutely gorgeous women with perfect bodies. But this was for a friend.

I explained my plan to her, pointing out, "If you really care about him, you'll go out with me."

"I do for Jimee" she said.

"For Jimbo," I agreed. We shook hands.

While James Dean was auditioning for Kazan, Gia and I had an intimate dinner at a candlelight bistro on Fifty-second Street, then huddled together in front of a roaring fire in a plush East Side brownstone. I have to admit I was very surprised. Gia obviously liked her "Jimee" much more than she let on, because she was willing to do anything with me that would help him get that part. Slowly and seductively, she unbuttoned her blouse, whispering softly to me, "I wouldn't do this for anyone but my Jimee."

I took her in my arms and kissed her lush lips. "He's lucky to have friends like us."

Apparently my little plan worked. Jimbo was able to overcome those emotional barriers and Kazan gave him the part. His performance made him into a star.

Eventually we both ended up in Hollywood. I was living in a rented guest cottage on the very top of Viewmont Drive, and he had a house halfway down the hill. On occasion we'd drive past each other, me in my old Buick, Jimbo in his Porsche. "That's you," he'd shout at me, "an old Buick."

His career was meteoric and tragic, ending in a terrible auto accident after making only three movies. As I said about him at the giant fund-raising gala *Variety* hosted at Spago to celebrate my sixtieth birthday, "So sad but true, only the good die young."

When I was beginning my career in New York, actors had a love-hate relationship with talent agents. We loved to hate them. We used to say that agents were to actors as foam is to beer: neither one has much substance, but without them you can't get ahead. Or: Agents are like belly buttons: there's nothing there, but everybody has to have one. Or: What do George Washington and my agent have in common? I can't get either one of them on the telephone. In those days actors actually believed that agents were selfish, greedy men, out only for themselves, squeezing every last cent out of an actor, then discarding him like tissues in a hurricane.

But through the years I've come to understand that that was only propaganda put out by the big studios to drive a wedge between agents and actors. I've realized that rather than being vilified, agents should really be used as role models for small children. They are selfless, charitable human beings, people who have dedicated their lives to the welfare of their clients, people who would gladly drain their swimming pools in August if it would help one lowly actor get one small part. Their professional title really should be agent-slash-humanitarian.

Early in my career I believed that the only thing worse than an agent was not having an agent. Without an agent an actor didn't get invited to auditions, didn't know who was casting what, and when and where they were doing it. Agents were the lowest rung on that stepladder of success. The major reason actors performed in showcases in the back of bars and delis was that they might be seen by an agent who had come in for a sandwich. In fact, that's where I met my first agent.

I was playing the lead role of Gen. Douglas MacArthur in a controversial drama, *The World War II Conspiracy*, in which the author claimed to have uncovered startling new evidence that proved World War II had never happened. After the show a tall, very pale, extremely well dressed man came back-counter to meet me. I'd noticed him during the show as he'd sat rigidly throughout the performance, plus the fact that he was wearing a tuxedo in a deli. "I enjoyed your performance this evening," he said. "I'd like to talk to you about your future."

I raised my eyebrows. "Oh?"

"I'm an independent theatrical agent." He handed me a card that was engraved so sharply that I nicked my finger on his phone number.

I looked at the card. In bold black script it read JOHN DEATH. Beneath that was the explanation—Theatrical Agent—followed by an address and telephone number. I looked at him questioningly. "Your name is Death?"

"Pronounced Deeth," he corrected. "It's a long *e*." After a second of embarrassed silence he added, "I guess it's sort of an unfortunate name. My grandfather had an unusual sense of humor. He liked walking into a room and hearing people say, 'Well, if it isn't Mr. Death.'" He frowned. "I don't know, maybe it's held me back a little."

"Well, it is an attention grabber," I said, trying to be kind. "What can I do for you?"

"Your question really should be, 'What can you do for me?' Had you asked that, I would tell you that I might be able to make you a star. That depends on your talent and determination, but when there's a part you're right for, I'll know about it and I'll get you in to see the producer or director."

For an agent, there was something very unusual about him. He knew who I was. "Well, Mr. Death—" I started.

"Deeth," he again corrected. "Remember, it's a long *e*."

"Deeth. I guess we have a deal." We shook hands. Was it my imagination, or did his hand feel unusually cold and clammy?

As he left the cold-cuts section, he said two words that sent a chill down my spine, two words I've never forgotten. He paused and looked right at me and said in a deep and ominous voice, "Trust me."

Almost immediately Death began getting me work on television. As I discovered, few casting directors would refuse to take a phone call from "Mr. Death." Television at that time wasn't so much an industry as an oddity. Unlike today, people didn't care what was on, as long as the TV set was on. The big radio advertisers and the major motion-picture studios were so afraid of it that they wouldn't allow actors under contract to appear on TV. That meant there was a lot of work for young actors. My first leading role was on a dramatic show called "Studio One." I don't really remember the role, but I do remember I was paid $7.50 a day. That doesn't sound like much, but remember, that was a long, long time ago. To put things in perspective, in 1992, when I guest-starred on the highly rated series "Golden Girls" playing Bea Arthur's husband, I was paid more than ten times as much.

Another thing I remember about that "Studio One" paycheck was that Death refused to take his 10 percent commission. That might have been when I first began to realize how truly misunderstood most agents have been.

Within months I became one of television's first stars, appearing on any show that wanted me. I did "Suspense Theater"; "You Are There," narrated by Walter Cronkite; I did "Armstrong Circle Theatre," "Philco TV Playhouse"; I did test patterns; "The Inner Sanctum"; I played center on a Spanish soccer team—anything to get on TV. I was making a great deal of money, too. One year I had leading roles on forty-six different shows and made almost $5,000.

I even began to be recognized on the street. The first time that happened I was walking out of Gimbel's when a woman stopped me and said, "I know you, I saw you on the TV. You know, you look much taller in Gimbel's than you do on the TV."

Naturally I was interested to know how my audience perceived me. "Oh, really? How tall do I appear to be on TV?"

"About five inches," she said, "but I've only got a ten-inch set. You'd be a lot taller on a sixteen-inch."

Years later the chairman of the Federal Communications Commission, Newton Minow, would describe television as "a vast wasteland," but in those days it was much smaller. Certainly a part of television's initial appeal was that everything had to be done live. Videotape didn't exist, and film was too expensive to waste on television programs. We got no second chances; whatever happened on the air, happened. In fact, many viewers watched television just to catch the mistakes, or bloopers, and when a show was done without any mistakes, they were very disappointed.

I was one of the most popular actors on TV. Although I grew to love the excitement of working live, at first I was a little nervous about it. I remember being interviewed by Dave

I was a big star in early television, one year starring in forty-six different shows. This was just before the "Golden Age of TV" began, a period affectionately remembered as "The Leaden Age."

Garroway on his "Today Show." Garroway was aware that I was new to the medium, so he reminded me, "We're on the air live from New York City."

I looked into the camera. "So that means that whatever I do or say, people are going to see. It can't be changed."

"That's the excitement of live TV. In fact, recent surveys have shown that people don't really like television; they watch in anticipation of mistakes."

We sat there staring at each other. "Boy," I finally said, "it sure is suspenseful waiting for one of us to make a mistake."

"That's live TV," Garroway added. "You never know when something worth watching might accidentally take place."

It was an entire decade of television remembered for mistakes. It was the period during which my career began. Maybe I wasn't as big a star as Milton Berle, who wore dresses, or Howdy Doody, a puppet who had his own show, or Woody the Woodpecker or even Garroway's monkey, the legendary J. Fred Muggs, but I was working regularly and I was being paid to act.

As I look back, I realize now that that was when the Dream first appeared. Most actors are plagued at some time in their career with insecurity, and I'm no different. In my case, my insecurity took the form of a dream. It was hazy in those days, and in black and white. In this dream I was awakened from a deep sleep by a persistent pounding at the door. I went to the door in my nightshirt and opened it. Then I realized I was standing there buck naked in an open nightshirt and I quickly buttoned up. Three people were at the door, dressed in what appeared to be law enforcement uniforms of some kind. Their hats were pulled down over their faces, but one of them looked vaguely familiar to me. "Can I help you?" I asked. I'm always very polite to people making guest appearances in my dreams.

"Acting Police," the smallest one said crisply. "You're under arrest. Get your things, you're coming with us."

"But . . . what for?"

"Impersonating an actor. We've seen you on television, we have all the evidence we need."

I started to sweat, yet I was very cold. I glanced to my left, no escape; then to my right, blocked. I knew I had to make a break for it. Suddenly I . . . and then I woke up.

For years I was afraid to tell anyone about that dream. But it got worse and worse until I was afraid to go to sleep at night. The more successful I became, the more threatening the Police seemed to be. Finally, I gathered enough courage to consult the noted Beverly Hills psychiatrist Dr. Robert M. Acton. Even then it took me another ten years before I was able to reveal it to him in detail. We discussed it for a long

Some people have dream lovers; I dreamed the Acting Police arrested me for impersonating an actor. They returned for years to haunt my dreams.

time, developed it, and finally he optioned the rights. He set it up at NBC, but the story editor wanted me to redream it for a woman, thinking it might be a good vehicle for Lindsay Wagner. Eventually, though, the network found out that CBS had a similar dream in development and let the option expire.

Meanwhile, in real life my childhood dream was coming true. I was making my living as a professional actor. And I loved every minute of it. Acting gave me a unique opportunity to grow as a human being, to put myself inside the minds of an extraordinary variety of real and imagined characters with different hopes and dreams and motivations, to explore my own emotions and understand the incredibly complex forces that combine to form a personality, to travel, to experience the world in a fascinating way, and finally, I got to meet a lot of pretty girls. Acting is truly a wonderful profession.

Growing up with two brothers in northern Canada, I knew almost as much about girls as I did about sunburns. Girls seemed to be so smart, they seemed to have such good taste— although I couldn't really be certain of that because they wouldn't go out with me. All I knew for sure about girls was that they wore dresses and painted their lips. At least I was sure I knew that until Milton Berle became a star by wearing a dress and painting his lips. I know all of this seems difficult to believe based on my reputation in Hollywood, but the truth is that in school I was much too shy even to speak to a girl. And believe me, I certainly wasn't known as Velvet Lips back then.

I kissed a girl for the first time when I was sixteen years old. Her name was Kathy Nelson and I was crazy about her. I'd walk down the street staring at her, holding her glove in mine. When I look back on it, we were so incredibly naive—we thought petting meant playing with her father's dog team. One day, when we were alone in the back of the classroom, she let me kiss her on the lips. It was the first time I'd ever touched the skin of a woman other than my mother. Whoa! As our lips touched, parts of my body moved that I hadn't previously known existed. My heart started playing biological reveille. A warm glow came over me. I thought that kissing was truly a miracle—it made me warm all over and didn't require the use of electricity.

We dated almost our entire junior year. Whenever I came home from a date with her, my brothers demanded all the details. "Where'd you touch her?" they wanted to know.

"Everywhere," I finally admitted.

Where? they demanded. And in what order? They wanted details.

"First, in the back of the school I held her hand," I told them. "Then in the hallway I put my arm around her. In the gymnasium I stepped on her foot . . ."

My brothers were disappointed. "Didn't you get any bare tit?" one of them asked.

I looked at him as if he were crazy. "There are no bears in high school."

My relationship with Kathy ended after the junior prom. We spent the entire night together. Although it seemed like minutes, it was almost two hours. After that her father wouldn't let me see her again.

I was just so naive. When one of my friends told me he'd lost his virginity, I offered to help him look for it.

On my seventeenth birthday, not too long before I joined the Canadian armed forces, my father decided he'd better have that special talk with me. I could see he wasn't very comfortable about the whole thing, but he knew it was his duty. We strolled through the woods and for a long time he didn't say a word. Finally he broke the silence, telling me, "You're getting old enough to know the facts of life."

"Okay."

"There's three things you should know. First, never piss into the wind. Second, don't run when you're carrying a sharp pencil. And third, you can never have too many starting pitchers."

I was stunned. That wasn't what I'd expected at all. "But, Pop," I said, "what about, you know, girls, and the birds and the bees?"

"Oh, yeah, I forgot about that part. Girls are for the birds. Be careful."

I stopped walking. "That's it? Those are the facts of life?"

He thought about that for a moment. He rubbed his palm over his mouth. "Well, lemme see. Oh, yeah, there is one other thing about women. Once a month, for no reason at all, they just start acting crazy. There's nothing you can do about it, so don't even waste your time trying."

"When's that?"

"When the bills come from the department stores."

We walked in silence back toward the house as I tried to impress upon my memory my father's words of wisdom. But suddenly he stopped, struck by the realization that he'd forgotten to tell me perhaps the most important thing.

"Life can be hard sometimes, son. And wherever you go in this world, you're gonna meet some people who try to take advantage of you. But you just remember, no matter what they tell you, no matter how hard they insist, bears definitely do shit in the woods." From that moment on I tried to follow in my father's footsteps, particularly when we were walking in the woods. But I never did figure out what he meant about running with a sharp pencil.

I made love to a woman for the first time after moving to New York City. Love? Who really knew what love was then? To me, love was just another four-letter word, like sex. If you know what I mean.

At the Neighborhood Playhouse women had to speak to me. As part of our work we had to prepare a scene for class every week. Preparing meant rehearsing with each other either at their apartment or at my coal bin. We'd pair off and pick scenes from plays or movies. Right away I noticed subtle differences in how men and women perceived the theater. The men in the class usually wanted to do scenes like the lovemaking scene on the beach between Deborah Kerr and Burt Lancaster in *From Here to Eternity*, or the bedroom scene from Henry Miller's autobiographical play, *I, Sexist*. I confess I was no different. Once I told a beautiful young actress I was working with that I thought we should do the famous voyeurism scene from Shakespeare's *King Lear*.

She knew the play. "There's no scene like that in Lear."

I had to think fast. "Oh, wait, I know," I said knowingly, "you probably read the American version. The scene I'm talking about is from the original French version."

The women in class, on the other hand, usually preferred to do scenes from plays like *Arsenic and Old Lace* in which the gentlemen callers are poisoned, or Strindberg's *Jeanne d'Axe*, in which she cuts off the head of King Peter the Thoughtless and parades around the stage with it proclaiming mightily, "I am woman, hear me roar."

We were young, we were dedicated to the theater, we had apartments of our own, and our parents were thousands of miles away. So at times we wrote our own scenes. One rainy afternoon I was rehearsing a scene from a 1930s melodrama, *Cub Reporter*, with a lovely young woman named Joanna Jones. She was from Omaha, Nebraska, had hair the color of a cornfield in the early light, and a very husky voice. She was also much older than I was—she had been born on a Monday, while I hadn't been born until Friday. She wasn't a very good actress, much too mannered, and in this scene she was supposed to say to me in a world-weary tone, "Maybe you got a new story to tell an old dame." Instead she said, "I'd like you to rip off all my clothes and lick every part of my body."

I looked at my script. At first I thought she might have had a revised edition. I couldn't find that line anywhere, so I asked her, "What page are you on?"

She tossed her script over her shoulder. "Forget the script," she said.

I was very impressed. We'd agreed to work together on this scene only a day earlier, and she'd already memorized her lines. I still couldn't find the right page. She took my script out of my hands and put her arms around me. Then I realized what she was doing—she wanted to do an improvisation.

"I want you," she said, "I want you right now."

Suddenly it dawned on me. She wasn't acting. That's why her performance was so professional. She'd said, "I want you," so I tried to figure out the real meaning of that line. She wanted me, she wanted me. I got it. She really wanted me.

I didn't know what to do. I had just started acting classes. So I made the silly mistake that all men make at one time or another in affairs of the heart. I told her the truth: "I'm a virgin."

"I don't care," she said, her hands grasping the waistband of my Bermuda shorts and tugging slightly. I knew at that moment we wouldn't be doing this scene in class.

It was an afternoon I'll never forget. When we'd finished for the first time, she was very quiet. Too quiet. The kind of quiet I'd hear in monster films seconds before the monster attacked.

Finally she asked, "Was this your first time?"

"I told you that. I told you I was a virgin."

A look of recognition came over her face. "Oh," she said knowingly, "I thought you meant you were from Richmond."

Our relationship had a lot of ups and downs that afternoon, but as we parted, she said to me, "I'd like to see more of you."

I was puzzled by that. I thought she'd already seen everything there was to see.

I was a changed man. I'd finally found out for myself what all the fuss was about. To my great surprise, sex had a lot in common with something else I'd recently discovered—Chinese food. When you finished each one, you were content, but fifteen minutes later you were ready to start all over again. Suddenly I understood why China had the largest population in the world.

Look, I like sex. I've never denied that. But most of the stories written about me in the supermarket tabloids aren't true. No matter what people say, the truth is that I have never lied to a woman just to get her to make love with me. Never. Oh, perhaps I stretched a point once in a while, but if you believe, as I do, that Charles Darwin was right and all human beings are descendants of one female African ape, then you know I am absolutely in the line of succession to the throne of England. I'm just not right up there near the top.

After that day, I found sex becoming more and more important in my life. But often, when I thought about sex, something was missing. Most of the time it was the woman. Not always, though, and sometimes even after making love to a woman I felt hollow inside. It took me a long time to understand that what was missing was a deep feeling of affection, love. Sex without love is like a chocolate ice cream cake without candles—absolutely fantastic, fabulous, wonderful, but not perfect. But I really didn't know what I was missing until I met Grace Kelly.

What is there to be said about Grace Kelly that hasn't already been written? That she was beautiful and charming and elegant? That she was sweet and kind and nursed hurt ani-

I met Grace Kelly when we did a TV show. We had little in common—she was smart, beautiful, and talented—but we became close. I took her to the beach, but she always wanted her own country.

mals? That we shared a fleeting passion? That she didn't shave the hair under her arms?

We met while working on "Armstrong Circle Theatre." I took one look at her and I knew that my eyes would never be the same. I don't remember what the show was about—it was probably about an hour—but I do remember watching her sitting in a corner knitting. She loved to knit. At that time she was best known as the socialite daughter of Jack Kelly, a former world-champion rower and a wealthy Philadelphia business-man. Although Grace had done some cigarette commercials, her acting career was just beginning.

As time passed we became friends, but from the beginning I wanted more than that. I wanted to get to know her inside and out, but she wouldn't go out with me. One day I just couldn't hold back my feelings any longer, and I confessed that I wanted to make love to her.

She pursed her lips and lowered her eyes demurely to the floor. "You're so sweet," she whispered, "but I'm chaste."

"Boy, that certainly doesn't surprise me," I told her. "Pretty as you are, men must be chasing you all day."

She resisted, but I pursued her. I couldn't get her out of my mind. And eventually she succumbed. I'll never forget the first night she slept with me. She had been working on a "Playhouse 90" and was absolutely exhausted. I took her to a lovely French bistro and ordered my favorite meal, steak tartare, medium rare. During dinner I was regaling her with tales from my eleventh-birthday party when I noticed she had fallen asleep. I didn't want to wake her, so I lowered my voice and finished the story. Later she admitted she'd loved sleeping with me.

Who knows what might have happened between us if she hadn't gotten the female lead in director Fred Zinnemann's *High Noon* and left New York for Hollywood? But the rest of the world soon discovered what I had known, and she became an Academy Award–winning actress. Four years later, while making Alfred Hitchcock's *To Catch a Thief*, she met Prince Rainier of Monaco and he asked her to marry him.

She didn't know what to do. She knew that if she married him, it would be over for good between us. But there were some negative aspects about it, too: the end of her acting career, the

In the early days of my career I was fortunate to have friends like Howdy Doody, here with me at the Copa. Unfortunately, the great Doody's drinking problem warped his mind, ending his career.

loss of her privacy. She called me from France to discuss it with me. "Princess," I said—I always called her Princess, she always called me collect—"I don't think you have a choice. He's offering you a kingdom, he's offering you your own stamp collection—"

"Many people have their own stamp collections," she interrupted.

"Not with their own picture on the stamps," I pointed out. "Look, I know it isn't easy, but you're going to have to forget about me, forget about that incredible night under the stars in Spain."

"What night under the stars in Spain?"

"That's good, Princess, you're on your way. Don't let the fact that Prince Rainier is young and handsome bother you, go for the security."

And so she marched down the aisle and out of my life. Oh, I'd hear from her once in a while. Sometimes, on lonely nights, the phone would ring and a man's voice would ask for a Margy or a Peggy, but I knew who it really was, I knew.

I look back on those early days in New York with great fondness. It was the time I came of age. Some people were not so fortunate. As the quality of television programming improved, some of the biggest stars of early television quietly disappeared from our lives. The legendary Howdy Doody, for example, who once dominated afternoon television, spent his decaying years squashed in a small box in a damp New Jersey basement. For me, though, those New York years were only the beginning. Sometimes, when I listened very carefully, I could hear the casting call of Hollywood.

2

THE FIRST CHAPTER
OF MY LIFE
(CONTINUED)

T he world of television, in which I had once played such an important role—as well as many smaller roles—was changing. Good programs were going on the air. Network executives were becoming concerned about the quality of their shows. So for the first time I thought about moving to Hollywood and working in motion pictures. It was a very difficult decision for me to make, and I sought the advice of my friends. One night, I remember, a group of us were discussing it after dinner at Max Asnas's Stage Deli, and one of the guys said, "You know, kid, years ago when I was in the same situation, the great journalist Hoss Greeley advised me, "Go west, young man, go west."

"So, Henny," I asked, "why didn't you?"

He shook his head sadly. "I couldn't take my wife."

Jack Carter agreed. "Yeah, I know your wife. I can't take her either."

Henny glared at him. "I meant she didn't want to go there with me. So I decided to stay in New York."

I understood. "But what about me?" I asked.

"Nah," Henny said, "she wouldn't go with you either."

There I was in New York, in a state of total confusion, wondering if California would be any better. So I called my uncle, Jean Hersholt, to ask his opinion. I'd mailed him kinescopes, very grainy tapes, of some of my best performances. "What do you think?" I asked. "Should I move to Hollywood?"

He sighed. "I've looked at the kinnies," he said. "With your ability, you should go far in this business."

"You mean you think I should come to California?"

I heard him take a deep breath. "Actually, I'm not sure that's far enough."

That was all the encouragement I needed. I took all the money I'd earned in television out of the bank. I figured if I was very careful, if I spent my money wisely, I could survive in Hollywood without working for at least six or seven hours. Particularly if I gave up luxuries, like eating. So four days before my twenty-fourth birthday, I took a Greyhound bus three thousand miles to Hollywood, California.

Unfortunately, Greyhound caught me and made me give it back.

Hollywood, California. Where the only three things people really care about are movies, movies, and grosses. In fact, when

President Franklin Roosevelt announced his New Deal to America, in Hollywood they thought he meant he had three pictures in development at Warners. Hollywood, my new home.

I spent my first few days there getting settled and visiting all the famous places I'd read about. I went to Grauman's Chinese Theater to see the Walk of Fame, where celebrities were honored by putting their handprints in cement. I went to the Hollywood Wax Museum. I went to Schwab's Drugstore and saw the stool on which Lana Turner had been sitting when she was discovered by a talent scout. I went to the Hollywood Bowl and rolled a solid 178. I went to all the great restaurants: the Babylonian Gardens, which had been built to be an exact replica of Nebuchadrezzar's Babylonian gardens; the Brown Derby, built in the shape of a brown derby; and the Cock and Bull.

Finally it was time to get to work. Although I had a bit of a reputation from my work in New York, I didn't think that would hurt me. I began the way young actors and actresses have begun in Hollywood since the days of the silent pictures, when the first directors shouted, "   !" I started reading the ads in the trades, the newspapers that report everything going on in the industry: *Daily Variety*, *The Hollywood Reporter*, and *Fat Chance*.

Weeks passed, and although I wasn't getting any work, I felt that I was growing professionally. In New York, I hadn't been able to get a part on Broadway, so I wasn't being seen by thousands of people. But in Hollywood I wasn't getting parts in movies, so I wasn't getting seen by millions.

I came close to getting a part on several occasions. One day I read that Metro was casting the role of an out-of-work actor for a movie entitled *Silver Screen*. Well, talk about typecasting.

43

I was perfect for that part. I got to the studio at dawn and was first on line. The moment the producers saw me they gave me the role. Later that afternoon, though, they fired me, claiming that since I was working, I was no longer right for the part.

I finally had to take a part-time job to pay my rent. The maître d' at the exclusive Beverly Hills Grill needed an experienced waiter. He hired me but the job didn't last too long. My first night there I was standing in a corner doing my job when he started screaming at me: "What are you doing? What do you think you're doing?"

I thought that was a pretty silly question. He was the one who'd hired me. "Waiting," I told him.

If I had known he was going to get so angry, I wouldn't have taken that job in the first place. I didn't have to go to a fancy restaurant to be insulted.

It's important to understand that in the early 1950s the major studios had absolute control over the movie industry. Actors and actresses had to sign unbreakable contracts that allowed the studios to dictate not only their careers, but their entire lives. Studios gave performers new names and backgrounds, created an image and personality for them, told them what movies they would make, what characters they would play, whom they would date, where they would go, where they would live, which newspaper and magazine writers they could speak to, even when they could travel. Of course, the thing that most actors hated about these contracts was that they were so hard to get.

Getting discovered was tough, as no one really knew the best place to be seen by a studio talent scout. The fountain at Schwab's became the place to be seen after Lana Turner had supposedly been discovered sitting there wearing a very tight sweater. Young actors and actresses waited hours for a seat at that fountain. Not me. I was a trained actor, schooled in my craft, and I simply refused to submit myself to that form of blatant marketing. I wore tight sweaters because I like them.

Besides, talent scouts wouldn't risk their reputations by discovering someone before they were successful. Once you were successful, it was relatively easy to be discovered. So I continued answering every casting call I might be right for. Among the parts I almost got was the title role in RKO's science-fiction thriller *The Thing*.

A good friend of mine, a talented young actor named Barry Cooper, was up for the part of the mad scientist and had a copy of the script. "They describe the Thing as 'an intellectual carrot,'" he told me excitedly. "You'd be perfect for that role."

I laughed at his joke. "It's not a roll," I corrected, "it's a carrot." But the idea intrigued me. A carrot? It would be a stretch for me, but I was confident I could do it. About the closest thing to an intellectual carrot I'd ever done was in an Off–Broadway drama in which I'd played a smart cookie. But this was very different.

I prepared for the audition as I had been taught at the Actors Studio. I tried to understand the carrot's motivations, its hopes and dreams. What did this carrot want? What was standing in the way of this carrot's getting what it wanted that had to be overcome? I tried to put myself in this carrot's place, to peel away its emotional defenses, and by the time I'd finished I'd managed to get to this carrot's roots.

The audition itself was grueling, but I thought it went very well. A few days later, though, I found out that an actor named

James Arness had won the part. As it turned out, the producers thought he had more training for it than I did. While I had been studying at acting school, he'd been cutting classes at the Culinary Institute.

But they must have liked my audition because a few weeks later I was invited to audition for the title role in the movie version of the Broadway hit *Harvey* opposite James Stewart. Harvey was an invisible six-foot-tall rabbit who could be seen only by Stewart. This was another difficult audition. As soon as the producers saw me, I failed it. The part eventually went to a character actor named Harmer Johnson, who apparently got the part by failing to show up for his audition. When the producers looked for him and he wasn't there, they liked what they didn't see. They knew they'd found the right actor.

In a sense I was glad I didn't get it. Johnson gave such a great performance that he became typecast. A few years later he was nominated for an Academy Award for his sympathetic portrayal of the Invisible Man, but after that there were few parts for him, and he eventually disappeared.

I was beginning to get a little desperate. There just didn't seem to be any parts for actors with talent of my caliber. I finally accepted the fact that I had to take work as an extra. Actors are usually advised not to do extra work because producers tend to look down on them, but I needed the paycheck. Admittedly, I had some difficulty explaining to my brother exactly what I was doing. "I'm working as an extra," I told Eric.

"An extra what?" he asked.

"Just an extra, that's all."

My brother knew very little about the movie business. "I don't understand," he said. "Extra means not necessary. That means they don't need you, right?"

"That's right."

"Well, you should be good at that. But let me ask you a question. If they call the people they don't need extras, what do they call the people they really need?"

"Accountants."

I worked as an extra in a lot of films. I was sitting in the grandstand when Stewart Granger crashed his race car in *Indy!* In *Quo Vadis?* I played a Christian slave; in fact, in the classic scene in which the Romans are all voting thumbs down, if you listen very carefully you can hear me screaming, "Recount! Recount!" I played the part of a one-eyed pirate in the Douglas Fairbanks, Jr.–Jane Russell pirate adventure *Treasure Chest*. I even did a brief walk-on as the cream-pie deliveryman in the Abbott and Costello army comedy *Mess Hall*.

The work wasn't always easy. I was one of the people riding the giant roller coaster in *This Is Cinerama*, but I was cut out of that picture. I'd eaten a big lunch just before we shot that scene, and when the roller coaster went straight down, my lunch came straight up, in full Cinerama. The director, the Hungarian filmmaker Georges Zelma, was furious, screaming at me, "You blew my scene. You blew my scene."

I said knowingly, "So that's what you call it in Hollywood."

I gained a reputation as a very professional extra because of my ability to play almost any kind of character. One day I was an American soldier attacking the beach in Audie Murphy's *Back to Tokyo*; the next day I played a Japanese soldier defending the same beach. I was an Indian warrior in Bob Hope's *Yellowfeather*. In *Plantation* I played a pregnant black slave. One of my most difficult roles was that of an orphaned twelve-year-old girl in *Lassie's Eviction*.

I had several lines in director Vincente Minnelli's musical *The Continentals*, in which I played Benjamin Franklin's hearing aide. My big scene took place in the Continental Congress on the Fourth of July, 1776. Thomas Jefferson, played by Jeff Chandler, says to Ben Franklin, very well played by Ed Begley, "It's a lovely day for a revolution, isn't it?"

To which Franklin responds, "What?"

And then I had my line. "HE SAYS, 'IT'S A LOVELY DAY FOR A REVOLUTION, ISN'T IT?'"

Even though I was desperate, I refused to lower my professional standards. And at times that meant turning down lucrative offers. For example, a producer of low-budget films offered me "big money" and above-the-title billing to star in a film that had some frontal and backal nudity in it. Another major Hollywood producer offered me three days' work in a trailer. Naturally I assumed he was referring to the coming attraction for his new feature film. It turned out he wanted me to paint his trailer.

Perhaps I wasn't a big star, but I still had my pride, and at least I was working in the motion-picture industry. I was learning what it was like to be on a movie set, and I was getting to know some of the biggest stars in Hollywood. Many of these stars, I was surprised to discover, were quite different from their public image. For example, as friendly and clever as Francis the Talking Mule was on-screen, offscreen he never said a word to anyone. Boris Karloff might have been a monster to all of his fans, but offscreen he was a shy, kind gentleman. And certainly one of the people who impressed me greatly was Ronald Reagan, with whom I worked for a few days in *Bedtime for Bonzo*.

There was one incident I'll never forget. Bonzo was very temperamental. He was the first actor I ever saw who literally bit the hand that fed him. One morning there was a terrible problem on the set. Bonzo had learned that his biggest rival in the film business, Cheetah, had landed the plum role of "Monkey" in the Tarzan musical *Swinging in the Rain*. He refused to come out of his cage, he wouldn't listen

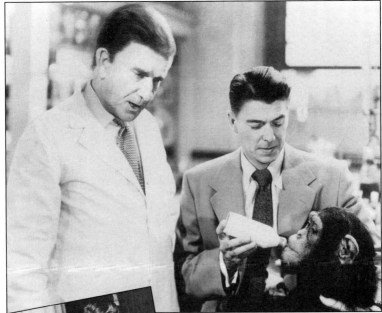

I first met Ronald Reagan when I played a bit scientist in Bedtime for Bonzo. *When his movie career had ended and he'd become president, we appeared at a charity dinner for Bonzo, who'd become homeless when his retirement house was cut down.*

to anyone. The set was shut down and the production was falling behind schedule. Finally Ronnie Reagan offered to speak to him.

I happened to be standing nearby and overheard Ronnie, in a soothing manner, trying to calm him down. "Now, Bonzo," he said, "sometimes we don't always get what we want, you know that. And I know you're upset right now, and frankly, I don't blame you. But golly, I'm not sure you're doing the right thing. That reminds me of a story about a little chimp I once knew who lived down in Dallas, Florida. Whenever this little fellow got mad at people, why, he would just climb up to the top of a big rose tree, high above everyone else where nothing could touch him, and he would make pee-pee, and it would trickle down on all the people below him. Now, maybe that little fellow up in the tree was happy, but the people down there on the ground were very unhappy. So what they did was find this sweet schoolteaching grandmother from Minneapolis, Indiana, who also happened to be a crack shot with a Remington twenty-aught-twenty. And she blew the smithereens out of that little fellow. Well, he certainly learned an important lesson, didn't he? That same sweet woman, Bette Ann Langsam, just happens to be visiting the set today. And she's been looking all over for you."

Bonzo was back at work in five minutes, and they never had another problem with him. When we wrapped for the day, I introduced myself to Reagan and told him how much I admired his diplomatic method of handling a difficult situation. He got a little embarrassed. "Oh, shucks," he said, "that's very nice of you to say."

"I'm serious," I continued. "Have you ever considered going into politics?"

He was startled. "Politics? Oh, that's a good one. Wait'll I tell Nancy about that. She doesn't even think I can remember to . . . remember to . . ." He frowned and scratched his head. "Oh, there's something I always forget, but I forget what it is."

I persisted. "Oh, details aren't important; you can always find someone to take care of the details. Just think about what I'm saying."

Suddenly he got very serious. "I will. I definitely will." Then he paused again. "Uh, what was that you were saying . . ."

"Politics, Ronnie, you should think about going into politics."

"Oh, yes, yes." He chuckled. "Well, the only thing I know anything about is". . . he paused, then got it . . ."acting. That's it, acting."

I laughed politely at his self-deprecating humor—but I stopped when I noticed he was no longer laughing. His eyes had narrowed and he seemed to be peering into some distant future. Just then we were interrupted by the lovely actress Nancy Davis, whom everyone knew he was dating. Ronnie tried to introduce us, but before he could remember her name, the studio limousine arrived and within seconds they were gone.

Ronnie Reagan's film career was in a serious decline from which it never recovered, and eventually he married Nancy Davis and became president of the United States. Bonzo went on to star in the sequel, *Bonzo Goes to College*. After finishing college, he decided to continue his education and obtained his master's degree in primate psychology. He retired from the movie business and opened a small practice, specializing in helping small animals who had gone bananas.

My brief appearance in the film as a scientist who is attempting to teach snakes how to play the game Simon Says must have attracted some attention, because Columbia Pictures offered me a screen test. I was thrilled, but very nervous. My entire career might depend on the outcome of this test. I studied every night for several weeks, until I knew everything there was to know about Columbia and its legendary founder, Harry Cohn. I took the test with a very beautiful young actress named Joanne Curtis, who might best be described as Jeffersonesque—she was well endowed by her Creator. The screen test consisted of two sections, a written part and an oral part.

The written part included several very difficult math questions. One, I remember, asked: You have been given a small percentage of the net profits of a motion picture. The cost of making this film was approximately $4,000. After six months in release this picture has grossed $120,000,000. How much more must this film gross before it goes into profits?

There was a whole section on Hollywood Etiquette. For example: You are in a restaurant with your wife. An important Columbia producer arrives alone and is clearly attracted to her. At the end of the evening he requests your permission to escort your wife home. True or false: You should respond to this by asking politely, "What wife?"

The final part of the written exam dealt with Management Skills. At Columbia Pictures, read one of the questions, conflicts are resolved by carefully examining all pertinent facts, endeavoring to obtain a consensus, and then: (a) doing whatever Harry Cohn decides; (b) doing whatever Harry Cohn decides; (c) doing whatever Harry Cohn decides; (d) all of the above.

They then put Joanne and me on-camera to see how we photographed full face, right profile, left profile, full chest. I aced this part of the test. Unfortunately, Joanne had some difficulty with it. When the director told her to turn to her right, she came very close. "That was a good try, Joanne," he said, "but now I want you to turn to your other right." When she tried again, and failed, the director suggested, "Okay, let's go for the best three out of five."

To complete the test Joanne and I had to do a brief scene together. This is actually the most important part of the exam. They gave us an abbreviated version of the final scene from *Gone With the Wind* in which Rhett Butler declares to his love, Scarlett O'Hara, "Frankly, my dear, I don't give a damn," and walks out, leaving Scarlett her monologue, ending with the famous phrase "Tomorrow is another day."

This is probably the best-known scene in motion-picture history. I knew there was no way I could compete against Clark Gable's performance, but I wanted to give it my personal interpretation. I wanted to do something to make them remember me.

I thought the scene went well. When the moment for my parting line came, I stood in the doorway looked directly at Joanne, paused several beats, then said clearly, "Frankly, my dear, I don't give a damn." Then I turned slowly, defiantly put on my hat, and skipped out the door, loudly singing the opening bars of "Dixie," "'Oooohhh, I . . . wish I was in the land of cotton . . .'"

Joanne watched me skip away, my voice fading as I pretended to be moving farther and farther away from the beloved mansion, Tara. Then she ran to the door, covered her mouth with a handkerchief held in her left hand, raised her right hand, waved to me, and shouted loudly, "See you tomorrow, Rhett."

The director was sitting behind the cameras at the back of the soundstage, so his voice came to us through speakers.

"That was fine," he said to me. "Let's do it one more time. Ah, this time, though, would you please do it in Greek."

Greek? I looked at the speaker. "What'd you say?"

"Do it in Greek, please. We want to see what you'd look like in a foreign picture."

I paused. Greek. The one subject I never thought they'd ask about. Finally I had to admit, "I don't know Greek."

The speaker was silent for several seconds. Then it crackled with whispering I couldn't interpret. I thought I heard someone laughing. But finally I heard the director sigh, and he said, "All right, then, we'll do it in the original Latin."

Thinking fast, I did the scene in Canadian. Nobody knew the difference. I didn't hear from the studio for several days as they marked the tests. It was almost a week later when a secretary called me with the news: Mr. Cohn wanted to see me.

Harry Cohn had turned a small film-distribution company he'd founded with his brother into the powerful Columbia Pictures by the force of his personality. "Harry the Horror," as he was known, could make or break a career with the snap of his fingers. He supposedly had more enemies than anyone else in Hollywood, which made him the envy of every status-conscious studio executive in town. In fact, he was so powerful that by the time I took my screen test he had already been dead for two years, but everyone was afraid to tell him so he continued running the studio. More than a year after I'd met him, an aide accidentally blurted out the fact that he was dead, to which Cohn supposedly replied, "In this business I'm not dead until the grosses tell me I am!"

I arrived at his office on Tuesday morning precisely at nine-thirty, as I had been told. But I figured I might have a long wait when his receptionist asked politely, "May I grow you a cup of coffee?"

The following Friday morning I was escorted into his large office, reaching his desk early in the afternoon. He was bellowing into the phone as I came in. "Bellow!" he shouted. "Bellow! Now you just listen to me. When I want your opinion about something, I'll tell you what it is!" He slammed down the receiver and shook his head. "These people I have to deal with. All they know how to do is say yes to me. Yes, yes, yes. Yes, yes, yes. I'm getting damned sick and tired of it. What I need around here is some new blood. You, for example, you think you have the guts to say no to me?"

"Yes," I said firmly.

"Good. I need more people like that around here." He picked up a sheet of paper, which I presumed was my screen test results, and began reading it. "Good," he muttered, "good. Good. Hmm. Hmm, hmm." My palms began sweating. Finally he laid it down, stuck a big cigar in his mouth, and looked right at me. "I've seen your screen test, kid. Lemme tell you something, I've watched a lot of screen tests in my day, but I've never seen anything quite like yours. You have that one special thing that practically guarantees success here in Hollywood . . ."

I knew my screen test had been good; I hadn't realized it had been that good.

". . . a powerful relative in the business. That means we can forget all about your screen test. So after considering your talent and your uncle, we've decided to offer you a contract with Columbia Pictures. Congratulations."

He started outlining the basic provisions of my contract, but I was too excited to listen closely. I heard him say something about my firstborn male child and all literary and cinematic rights to my life and death, but none of that sank in.

". . . okay now," he said, bringing me back to reality, "the first thing we're gonna do is figure out who you are." He cupped his chin in his palm and stared at me for a few seconds. "Well, don't worry about it. They're expecting you over at the publicity mill. They'll tell you who you're going to be." He stood up and offered his hand. "Let me give you a little advice, kid. The best way to get ahead in this business is to always be yourself, whoever we decide you are. That, and don't ever be afraid to say no if you think you're right. Got it?"

"Yes," I said.

He gave me the Columbia Pictures secret handshake. "You'll be fine," he said.

On the Columbia lot the publicity mill was right next to the rumor mill, and both of them were grinding full blast when I got there.

It was here that the studio determined who you were going to be for the rest of your career. As I was to learn, each studio had a roster of actors under contract to fill every type of role, from handsome leading man to scarred villain. Once you were cast as a certain type, those were the roles assigned to you by the studio. You didn't have to accept the roles—the choice was either accepting them or never working again as long as you lived.

I was brought into a small conference room. Five men were sitting around a mahogany table. Columbia's famed talent coordinator, Peter Snider, introduced me to each of them, then asked, "Would you turn around slowly for us, please?"

They began discussing me as if I weren't even there.

"Definitely not a Latin lover," someone decided immediately.

"Chin's too strong to be a sidekick," another one added.

"How 'bout a leading man?" the third man suggested. Everybody turned in their chairs and stared at him. "Just kidding," he said defensively, "just kidding."

"He's blond," pointed out the fourth man, who then quoted the well-known Hollywood dictum, "You can never have too many dumb blondes."

"That won't work," the first man replied, "he's not blonde enough."

"He's also a man," Snider interjected with just a tinge of irritation.

The fourth man, a small, handsome executive named Frank Biondo, spoke boldly. "So maybe it's time to stop discriminating. Where does it say that all dumb blondes have to be women? Look at him. I'll bet he can be as dumb as any woman."

I thought he was absolutely right, but no one took his suggestion seriously. Snider then suggested, "How about a debonair foreigner?" There was a murmur of interest, and he asked me, "Where you from, kid?"

"Northern Canada," I said.

"Canada, huh?" the first man repeated, then asked the group, "Is Canada considered a foreign country?"

"Not where I come from," the second executive replied.

Snider sighed. "But Jacques," he said, "you come from Montreal."

This meeting continued for quite some time as they went through the entire roster of types: leading man, hero, sidekick, Latin lover, handsome rival, all-American boy, debonair foreigner, mysterious foreigner, debonair criminal, street tough, heel, ordinary working Joe, kid, dog, comedian, animated rodent. I didn't seem to be right for any of the common types.

Then Biondo snapped his fingers, drawing everyone's attention. "Wait a second, I think I've got an idea." Everybody waited a second to see if he had an idea or not. "What's the one type that every studio executive in the business wants and nobody has?"

After several seconds of silence the third man guessed, "A gorgeous nympho with a heart of gold?" Once again, everybody glared at him. "Oh, yeah?" he said. "And maybe you can name me somebody who doesn't want one?"

"No," Biondo continued, "everybody's looking for a rebel. A guy they can't tell what to do. The public loves 'em, the press loves 'em. I can see it now . . ." He looked up at the ceiling and pretended to be writing in the air. "The man no studio could control." Then he looked around the table and said evenly, "And we'll be the first studio to own one."

"Brilliant," Snider said, "absofrigginlootly brilliant."

Biondo concluded, "We can start by assigning him to pictures we don't want him for that he can refuse to do."

It was agreed that I would become the studio rebel, the one man they couldn't control. I would be free to do everything I wanted to do. First the studio would tell me what I wanted to do; then I would be free to do it.

All I needed was a name to go with my character. I am admitting now, for the first time publicly, that Leslie Nielsen is not my real name. My real name isn't important. It isn't a lot of other names either. I changed my name when I signed with Columbia Pictures because at just about this time another actor with the same name as mine was starring in a series of low-budget films. These movies were so low-budget they were shot with home-movie cameras and distributed individually. So as not to confuse me with this other actor, who was definitely not me, even though there was some slight resemblance around the head and body, I adopted a stage name.

In those days every actor changed his or her name. Names came from everywhere. One day a young actor named Aaron Chwatt walked into a studio wearing a particularly ugly jacket, and several hours later Red Buttons walked out. On another occasion a beautiful young woman name Velma Fronk met a studio executive who'd just had his pants altered by a pretty seamstress named Elizabeth, and Velma Fronk became Elizabeth Taylor. Roy Scherer, Jr., recalled playing boyhood games among the huge boulders along the Hudson River in upstate New York, so he became Rock Hudson. Singer Leonard Slye stopped into a fast-food outlet for a roast beef sandwich on his way to the studio, and a few hours later he took the name of the restaurant to become Roy Rogers.

There was quite a bit of debate over exactly what to call me. "I don't care what it is," I said, "just give me a good moniker."

"We can't do that," the second man protested. "Monica's a girl's name."

Once we got that straightened out, they tried to find something that would fit my personality, something strong, something athletic, something me. "How 'bout Trip?" Snider suggested.

No one liked that. Then they searched for a common name, something that might be found around the house. "Art?" the first man said. "Big Bill?" Jacques said, adding, "There's always a big bill around my house. "Philco?" someone else offered.

After more than three hours of this, Biondo exploded. Suddenly, he threw a pile of papers up into the air and started shouting, "I can't take this anymore. Why do we have to give him any name?"

"It helps with the billing," Snider pointed out. "It's tough to promote an actor who doesn't have a name."

"That's not what I mean," Biondo persisted. "Why do we have to make up anything? Why do we have to create myths? Why do we have to invent phony names and personalities and backgrounds for actors? I've had it with all this phoniness, all this fantasy. It's time we told the truth about actors, that they're human beings with the same defects and problems we all have. What we need to do in Hollywood is to tell the truth, the real truth, not the truth we make up. We need to tell less lies and get on with . . ."

He stopped, struck absolutely silent by a thought.

"That's it," he continued softly, "that's the name. Less lies . . . Lesslies . . . Leslie, that's his name. It's . . . it's so . . . honest. It's the best real name we've ever made up."

Within minutes Biondo had also come up with my last name. "What's the one thing that everybody in this business wants?"

"Here we go again," the third man said, then guessed, "A gorgeous nympho with a heart of gold?"

"A big house?" Snider guessed. "Leslie Bighouse."

"No," Biondo replied, "what they really want is a great Nielsen rating for their television shows . . ."

The third man mumbled, "I'll bet there're a few people who'd prefer a nympho."

Biondo ignored him. ". . . so we'll call him . . . Leslie Nielsen. That way we can easily sell every movie he makes to the TV networks because they'll be assured of getting a good Nielsen rating."

Believe it or not, that's how I came to be—Leslie Nielsen, studio rebel. Finally I had a name and a character; now all I needed was a career. Thus far my motion-picture career had gone very well, but eventually I had to be in a motion picture.

The movie industry operates unlike any other business. The bigger star you become, the fewer pictures you can make. If an actor makes too many movies he or she becomes overexposed and the public won't pay to see their movies; but the fewer movies they make, the more anxious the public is to see them. The biggest stars make no movies at all. As everyone knows, Marilyn Monroe, Elvis Presley, and James Dean haven't made a movie in years—yet they're more popular now than at any time during their careers. The only possible way Elizabeth Taylor could ruin her career as the motion pictures' biggest star would be to make a movie. Conversely, there was the devastating effect of the so-called Michael Caine Rule, passed by the Screen Actors Guild, which mandated that Michael Caine had to be in every movie made. Although the Brian Dennehy/Wilford Brimley Amendment allowed either actor to substitute for Caine, the result was the same: Caine's brilliant career suffered terribly because the audience could see him.

The studio wasn't going to make that same mistake with me. Columbia decided that the best way to build my career as a movie star was to keep me out of movies. They wanted to create excitement about me by publicizing the fact that I refused to appear in the movies they wanted me to make. The bigger the movie I wasn't in, the bigger star I would become. Remember the classic fight scene in *From Here to Eternity*?

I wasn't in that. The spectacular chariot race in the CinemaScope picture *The Robe*? I wasn't in that one either. Perhaps the best film I didn't appear in during this period was *The Caine Mutiny*, in which I didn't costar with Humphrey Bogart and Jose Ferrer. I honestly believe that the only reason I didn't receive an Academy Award nomination for my work in this film is that I wasn't in it.

As the mystique surrounding me continued to grow, so did my price for not working. According to Hedda Hopper, for not appearing in *A Streetcar Named Desire* I hadn't been paid only $10,000. But less than a year later I wasn't being paid $25,000 for not working with Clark Gable and Ava Gardner in *Mogambo*.

Maybe I wasn't the only actor not making movies at the time, but I was one of the most successful. Eventually, though, the studio decided that the time had come for me to risk my career—and make a movie. The question was: What picture?

The studio briefly considered starring me in a B-picture. At that time the studios were making both A-pictures, movies with well-known actors and large budgets, and B-pictures, movies that often had plots similar to successful A-pictures but featured less well-known actors and were made with small budgets. *Forbidden Planet*, for example, was an A-picture; the B-movie version of that would have been *Forbidden Planet: No Landing 8 A.M.–6 P.M. Monday–Friday*. Many smaller studios specialized in B-pictures. Regent Studios actually used to advertise, "We're First at Being Second!" Naturally several other studios disputed that, with Crown Pictures even claiming in a famous full-page ad in *Variety*, "We were first at being second first!"

Columbia finally decided that I should play a small but pivotal role in an A-picture, a role that would give me visibility without overexposing my talent. Apparently they wanted to keep that a secret. They cast me as a medical student in the Dean Martin and Jerry Lewis comedy with music, *A Pair o' Docs*. Of course at that time no realized it would become the classic that it has. Like all plots, this one was just another variation of Shakespeare's work: Martin and Lewis played students about to graduate from medical school who accidentally misplace their cadaver. If they don't hand in their body of work at the end of the semester, they'll fail dissection and won't graduate. Completely unknown to them, however, the cadaver was that of the Boss of a Mafia family murdered and left in a vacant lot without identification, and there was still a large price on his head. Early in the movie, in fact, Jerry actually finds the price tag but doesn't know what it means. But he does realize something is wrong when he finds twelve bullets in the heart, causing him very definitely to suspect this man had not died of natural causes. The action centered around Dean and Jerry's misadventures trying to recover the body, which was being held for ransom by a rival mob family, while another mob family was trying to kill Jerry because he had found the bullets. June Allyson played the girl. It was in this movie that Dean introduced the popular standard "I Ain't Got Nobody." I played a handsome, rich, yet unspoiled student who helps solve the problem by convincing Jerry to impersonate the reclusive mob boss from Detroit, Mr. Bigg, which leads to the bloody shoot-out unforgettably described by critic Pauline Kael as "the movies' most corpus delectable," thus enabling Dean and Jerry to steal back the cadaver and return it to the school just in time to get full credit.

Supposedly Harry Cohn was so impressed by my performance that he considered changing the billing to "Martin,

Lewis, and Nielsen," but eventually decided to save me for bigger pictures.

During the making of this movie I came to truly appreciate the unique talents of both Dean Martin and Jerry Lewis. Without question, no actor in the long history of motion pictures has done more to improve the image of buck teeth than Jerry Lewis. Among the many things that impressed me about Jerry was how hard he worked to make things seem real. He'd spend hours alone in his dressing room perfecting his trademark nasal whine until no one could tell it wasn't natural.

Off the set I spent quite a bit of time with both of them. Much to my surprise, in private Jerry Lewis was a quiet, dignified man who lived to read the words of the great philosophers, while Dean was the real comedian. Somehow, though, they made magic when they were together, and unlike many other legendary movie teams, each of them greatly appreciated the other's talent. It's always been a mystery to me why they broke up. They certainly gave no hint of dissatisfaction when I worked with them.

One night, for example, I was supposed to have dinner with Dean, but he'd spent the day filming the scene in which he saves Jerry's life, after Jerry had been drugged into stupidity, by carrying him down three flights of stairs, and he canceled because his back was killing him. Instead Jerry and I had dinner at Musso and Frank's on Hollywood Boulevard. Jerry was in a great mood, rhapsodizing about Dean's singing voice. "I sing a little, you know," he said, "but Dean . . ." He shook his head in admiration. "I'm so jealous. He has such a magnificent voice. Every time I hear him sing, I just want to scream, 'Listen America, listen to that voice.' I tell you, Leslie, I'd kill to have a voice like that."

I got my first big break when I appeared with Dean Martin and Jerry Lewis in the last picture they made together, the classic comedy A Pair o' Docs. *To this day no one has ever figured out exactly what it was that came between them.*

"Boy, Jer," I said—I always called him Jer—"that's really beautiful. And I think Dean feels the same way about you."

"Really?" he asked, smiling. "He told you that?"

"Well, not exactly," I admitted, "but the only reason he isn't here with us tonight is because he's tired of carrying you on his back."

"He what?"

"Yep, he told me it felt like he'd been carrying you forever."

Jer just sat there silently. I think he was genuinely touched by Dean's sentiment. But there was one thing I'd always wondered about, so I took advantage of this quiet moment to ask him this question. "Maybe it's none of my business, but . . . you know, a lot of people wonder, how did you and Dean decide that his name would come first in the billing?"

It must have been their secret, because Jer didn't say a word.

A few nights later I was having dinner with Dean, and I told him how highly Jer thought of him. "Oh, Deano"—I always called him Deano—"he said some things you just wouldn't believe."

"Like what?" Dean wondered.

"Nice things. I remember, he told me that every time he hears you singing he feels like screaming."

"Oh, he did, huh?"

"Absolutely. And then he told me that he was jealous of you."

"Really?" Dean seemed just as touched as Jerry had been.

"Uh-huh. And then he said that every time he hears your voice he feels like he could kill."

"Yeah, yeah? That's what he said, huh?" Dean was getting more enthusiastic every time I opened my mouth.

They seemed to genuinely like each other, so I was shocked when I heard months later that they'd decided to split up. Fortunately, both of them went on to greater success. Dean Martin, who many people believed would have a difficult time succeeding without Jerry, became one of television's most popular stars when he teamed with Dan Rowan to create "Rowan & Martin's Laugh-In." Then, of course, he went on to manage the New York Yankees five times before retiring to marry the lovely and talented actress Victoria Tennant.

Lewis, who'd once doubted his singing ability, had a huge popular hit with the rollicking rock-and-roll anthem "Great Balls o' Fire." Then he settled in Paris, achieving international recognition as auteur and acteur Jeré Lewis, finally receiving the Arc de Triomphe, the French Oscar, for his work as producteur, directeur, and staur as the befuddled iconoclast in the existential comedy *L' Individual Stupide.*

My work in *A Pair o' Docs* got considerable attention. There was even some talk of an Oscar nomination, and for the first time my name began appearing in the important movie-news columns. To help promote the picture I did an in-depth interview with the legendary film journalist Hedda Hopper. We sat poolside over lunch at the Beverly Hills Hotel. She was extremely flattering, telling me, "I thought you were very funny in the film. How did it feel to hear people laughing at you?"

"Oh," I said, "I'm used to that."

She looked surprised. "I didn't know you'd been in other comedies."

"Oh, I haven't."

That seemed to surprise her. "Um . . . well, let me ask you, where do you get your timing?"

"I have an old Bulova. Still works pretty good, though."

"Uh . . . um, well, then, did either Jerry or Dean give any tips when you were working with them?"

"Absolutely, they're both very generous men. I mean, practically every time I did anything for Dean he'd give me a buck."

She laughed and said, "So comedy comes for you wherever and whenever."

"Wherever."

Having made one comedy in a row, the studio wanted me to appear in a different type of film. So for my first starring role

67

they cast me as the demented Professor Albert Einstein in the horror-thriller *Pi Aren't Squared?* It was based on a fascinating premise: What if Einstein had been driven insane by the discovery that he'd added wrong, forgetting to carry the five, thus invalidating his entire theory of relativity; and rather than serving mankind by inventing the atomic bomb, he'd instead turned his genius to a life of crime? In this story he's invented an infernal combustion engine capable of creating the largest vacuum in history, and he threatens to suck up the entire world if he is not paid $2 million. But disaster strikes when he puts too much of nothing inside the vacuum, causing it to overflow.

In my first starring role I played Albert Einstein in Pi Aren't Squared? *It took five hours each morning to apply several layers of makeup.*

There is nothing all over, growing bigger and bigger, sucking up everything in its path. In my climactic sequence I finally come to my senses and realize that I am the only one who can save the world from the monster I've created. The scene began when my assistant, played beautifully by William Lundigan, burst into my lab and said ominously, "It's reached the edge of the city."

Until that moment I'd successfully hidden my crime from the only woman I'd ever loved, Ida Lupino. "What's he talking about, darling?" she asked.

I knew I had to tell her the truth. "Nothing," I said.

"Please tell me," she said sweetly. "Whatever it is, we'll face it together."

"Honestly, it's nothing," I confessed.

"But if you won't tell me, how can I help you?"

I put my hands on her shoulders and looked into her eyes. "You must believe me when I tell you it's nothing."

One tear welled in her eye and rolled slowly down that little crack between her cheek and her nose. "Oh, Al," she whispered, "someday I hope you'll find someone you trust." Then she turned and ran out of the lab. My evil genius had caused me to lose the woman I'd loved. I managed to save the world with only seconds to spare when I discovered that the vacuum could be filled with auto emissions. The movie finished with a heroic montage of ordinary people around the world starting up their cars and letting them run, filling the vacuum until it disappeared.

While *Pi Aren't Squared?* was not critically acclaimed, it was a big commercial success. For the first time, people in Hollywood began to recognize me. In New York, I'd been able to walk down Broadway without anyone knowing who I was. But less than two years later people were stopping me on Rodeo Drive and telling me, "I know who you are. You're that guy . . . you're what's-his-face, right?"

Of course I had to admit that I was.

But it didn't take me long to discover the dark side of fame. While most people are friendly and polite, there is always one wise guy who gives the entire human race a bad name. I was dining with friends in a quiet restaurant one night when a very large man who'd obviously had too much to drink stumbled over to my table. Pointing a finger at me, he said, "I know you. I saw you in that movie. You're Robert Mitchum, right?"

Robert Mitchum? How flattering. "Well," I said politely, "that's nice of you to say, but I'm not Robert Mitchum."

He took a swig from the beer bottle he was carrying and examined me closely. "You calling me a liar?"

"Oh, no, of course not." I could see this was getting out of hand. "But I'm not Robert Mitchum."

"All right. Just who do you think you are?"

That was an interesting question. Did he mean, was I being sarcastic, or did he want me to take a guess at my identity? "I'm Leslie Nielsen," I admitted.

"Yeah? Since when?"

I told him the truth. "For almost two years."

He didn't like that. "Whaddaya, think you're funny?"

"I guess that depends on the critic you read," I said modestly. "Look, friend, I really am Leslie Nielsen."

"No, you're not," he said firmly. "I saw her in *An American in Paris*. You can't be her, her hair was much darker than yours."

"That's Leslie Caron," I corrected him.

"So you are calling me a liar, huh?" It was then I discovered that the old adage "The bigger they are, the harder they fall," doesn't actually apply to people six feet, six inches tall and 275 pounds. Apparently the proper adage to apply to someone that large seems to be, "The bigger they are, the harder they hit."

When I came to, I thought I was seeing stars, but it turned out to be Wendell Corey and Elisha Cook, Jr., both great character actors but not really stars, who happened to be dining at that restaurant.

Columbia was very unhappy about the negative publicity. They didn't want to have a rebel they couldn't control. So for getting involved in a barroom fight, they suspended me for six months. I was very upset about that, and I went to see the head of legal affairs at Columbia, the legendary Hollywood attorney Richard Langsam, to discuss the matter. "Can they really do that to me?" I asked.

"Let me draw you a picture," he replied. A few minutes later he handed me a lovely sketch of a sunset over a mountain, which I still have. "Now," he said as he finished, "let's talk about your case. The right of a studio to penalize an employee for misconduct was firmly established by Walt Disney, when he suspended Snow White after she'd been caught in her drawing room with some character who'd just escaped from the pen."

I knew exactly what he was talking about. White had sued the studio, but the Supreme Court had upheld Disney in the landmark "suspended animation case." There was nothing I could do but accept the penalty. I was very upset. But had I known what was about to happen, I would certainly have changed my mind—I would have changed it into one that thought the studio was absolutely correct.

3

A NEW ERROR IN MY LIFE BEGINS

H ad I not been on suspension, the studio would have
assigned me to play the title role in director Nick
Ray's *Rebel Without a Cause*. But production was
scheduled to start before my suspension was over and they
couldn't wait, so they began looking for a so-called Leslie
Nielsen type. Ironically, a month earlier the readers of *Modern
Screen* magazine had named James Dean, my old friend from
New York, the winner of the Leslie Nielsen Look-Alike Contest,
so I suggested him for the part. That meant I was still available
two months later when Alfred Hitchcock called.

Hitchcock had been searching for a male lead for his new thriller, *The Sleepwalker*. When he saw my performance as Einstein, he thought I might be perfect for the part. We met at the famed Polo Lounge in the Beverly Hills Hotel, and he admitted being afraid I might be too big for the role.

"Oh, no," I said humbly, "I don't care if it's a small part, I think it would be a very important step in my career."

"Actually," he explained, "I meant I was looking for someone shorter." But after we'd spoken for a while I'd shrunk in his estimation. He told me how impressed he'd been by my portrayal of Einstein. "Rarely have I seen an actor able to project that glassy-eyed stare that seems to come so naturally to you."

The script for *The Sleepwalker* was truly a masterpiece. Supposedly, it was the only screenplay written by William Shakespeare. So, obviously it had been ghostwritten. There was a lot of speculation that it had actually been written by one of the Hollywood Ten—a group of producers, directors, and writers who had been blacklisted by the movie industry because of their political beliefs, and who were known to be writing scripts under assumed names, but this was vehemently denied by the film's producers, Abraham Lincoln and Thomas Jefferson.

The Sleepwalker starred James Stewart and Lana Turner. I played the title role and Lee Liberace played the piano. Supposedly, I lived next door to Liberace in a quiet suburban neighborhood. Each night after I fell asleep, Liberace's beautiful music entranced me—and while in that trance I was compelled to stalk Lana Turner, who lived several blocks away. Stewart played a cheap detective who'd met Turner when she'd begged him to recover her stolen seventeenth-century chaise longue. He did, but he did a terrible job, using a ridiculous flo-

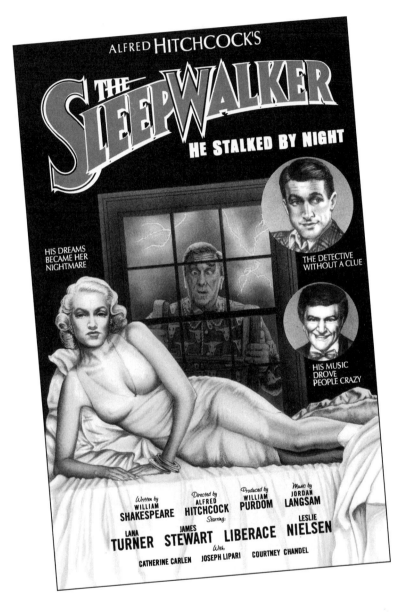

Alfred Hitchcock always claimed that after watching me act for only a few seconds he knew I was perfect for the title role in his masterpiece, The Sleepwalker. *It made me a star. Critics raved about my performance, calling me "every woman's nightmare," and my colleagues honored me with my first Oscar nomination.*

ral print and completely messing up the seams. When Turner desperately tries to convince everyone she is being stalked by a zombielike creature, Stewart is the only person who believes her. He finally tracks me down, only to discover that I was as innocent as Turner, although certainly not as attractive. At the last second he saves her life, shocking me out of my deep sleep by shooting me five times.

In the chilling final scene, as my coffin is being carried out of the church, the diabolical Liberace is seen playing the funeral march on a giant organ.

This was a difficult part for me. I knew how important it was to my career. I spent many, many sleepless nights worrying about how to prepare for this role, and that turned out to be exactly the right way to prepare for this role. I played it as if I'd spent many, many sleepless nights. I sort of stumbled along, my eyes half-opened or half-closed, depending on whether you're an optometrist or a pessimist. My lines were relatively easy to remember: "I'm tired," "I'm exhausted," "I don't remember," "I am not a crook," "I was not in Paris that October," "Has anyone ever told you, detective, that you look just like James Stewart?"

The most difficult part of my performance was looking through a window at Lana Turner as she slowly got undressed and acting as if I were asleep.

Hitchcock loved my work. Although his disdain for talented actors was very well known in Hollywood, for some reason we got along very well. I asked him once about those stories I'd read that he thought actors were like children. "Not true," he snapped, "not true at all. Actually, actors are more like lampshades. The director turns on the light and his genius is filtered through them. Yet they get the credit for creating the beauty."

He paused to take a deep breath.

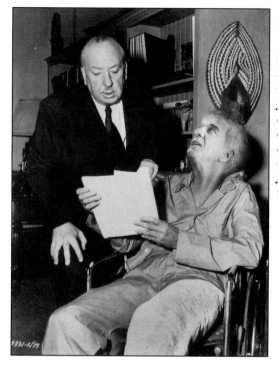

Hitchcock had a well-known disdain for talented actors, but we always got along well. I think his feelings about actors changed after he took my suggestion and learned how actors feel by appearing in his own films.

"Actually, though," he continued in that deep and somber voice that resonated with a thousand years of British culture, "actors are more like infected wounds: they must be treated with respect. In fact, actors are most like the crud squashed into those depressions on the bottoms of sneakers after you've walked through a field of muddy cow droppings; they're unavoidable."

I started to protest, but he ignored me.

"No, wait, wait, actors are really most like a maggot's excrement after it's feasted on a bloated water buffalo." He paused, and sighed. "But not nearly as intelligent, you understand." Then he looked upon me benignly. "Nothing personal, of course. I suspect you're far more intelligent than maggot droppings." As an afterthought he speculated that when he'd finished his directorial career, he might like to run a major studio.

On occasion, after we'd wrapped for the day, Hitch and I would sit by the prop ocean on Columbia's backlot, watching the artificial water rolling gently up the plastic sand, and he would discuss his philosophy of filmmaking.

"Many people don't know this," I remember him telling me, "but the word *suspense* is derived from the Yiddish word *suspenders,* meaning it holds up the entire plot." Then he added in an absolutely awful British-Yiddish accent, "Widout de suspenders, everything goes plotz."

The thing that surprised me most about Alfred Hitchcock was how little he actually knew about acting. One night we were shooting the scene outside Lana Turner's bedroom window. It was a close-up of me watching Lana Turner through her bedroom window. I was staring at Lana when my nose started itching. So I scratched it. Hitch just went crazy.

"Cut!" he screamed, leaping from his director's chair. "Cut, cut, cut." He came running toward me. "What was that?" he yelled, imitating me scratching my nose. "You call that acting?"

"Absolutely not," I said, "of course not. That's not acting. That's called scratching my nose. Acting is when you say words written by somebody else and pretend you thought of them yourself. I gotta tell you, Hitch, after all the movies you've made, I'm really surprised you don't know that."

He was shocked, and flustered. "Bu . . . bu . . . but . . ."

I laughed. "No, sorry, that's not acting either, Hitch, that's just a pretty bad imitation of Jimmy Stewart." Suddenly I was hit with a tremendous inspiration. "You know, Hitch, if you really want to learn about acting, you should appear in your own pictures. Just little parts; you can play a guy getting off a bus, or ordering in a restaurant or begging for a few pennies."

The idea obviously intrigued him. "You really believe so?"

"Sure. And believe me, no one would ever notice you, or my name isn't Leslie Nielsen." Of course, my name really wasn't Leslie Nielsen, but that was just a detail.

Who knew that Hitchcock would turn out to be such a big ham? Oh, sure, he was always a little overweight, but within a few years he was hosting his own TV show.

Certainly one of the most enjoyable aspects of making *The Sleepwalker* was the opportunity to work with such legendary stars as James Stewart, Liberace, and the gorgeous Lana Turner. All that glamour, those magnificent costumes, the elaborate makeup and stylish hairdos, the hordes of men hanging around the set—that Liberace was really something special.

Obviously we'd all heard the rumors about his personal life. I remember Lana asked me one morning as we waited for the cameras to be set up, "Do you think it's true that he likes men?"

"Well," I admitted, "he's always been very nice to me."

Then she learned closer and whispered, "I heard he's a cross-dresser."

I was shocked. "You mean he's a priest!"

Lee had heard all the stories about his private life, but refused to let them bother him. "Oh, don't worry about me, I can handle anything that comes my way."

I got about as close to Lana Turner as any man could ever get, say about thirty-eight inches away. Lana was probably the most popular pinup girl in American history, and she was more beautiful in real life than she was on my bedroom wall. Or in my kitchen. Even though we became friendly, I never asked her out because I didn't want to ruin my fantasy; my fantasy was that she would go out with me. But unlike her image as a sex symbol, which had carefully been created by the studio, she was really a stay-at-home. She stayed at Artie Shaw's home, at Bob Topping's home, Lex Barker's home, Steve Crane's home. When I think back on it, I'm not sure I ever met anyone who believed in the sanctity of marriage as strongly as she did. In fact, she believed in it so much that she got married seven different times.

I believe it was while we were making *The Sleepwalker* that she began dating a gangster named Johnny Stompanato. I met him only a few times, but he never tried to hide the fact that he was a criminal. He even used to boast about his membership in the Los Angeles Racquets Club. Lana and Johnny had a tempestuous relationship, and one night as they argued bitterly, Lana's teenaged daughter stabbed Stompanato in the stomach to protect her mother. Everyone was stunned when it happened; Harry Cohn said it was the first time in memory that someone in Hollywood had been stabbed in the front.

The Sleepwalker was both a critical and commercial success, and I received the best reviews of my brief film career. Judith Crist wrote in *The New York Times*, "Leslie Nielsen is as bad as anyone I've ever seen in the movies. Of course, I've never been to a theater in Times Square." *Variety* claimed my performance would "do more for coffee than anything since the invention of the percolator." And radio critic Mary Billiard said, "Leslie Nielsen is every woman's nightmare." I was so proud.

The studio offered me several exciting projects, so my career was going very well. My social life, on the other hand, left a lot to be desired—dates, for example.

There were so many beautiful women in Hollywood I had a difficult time picking which one to be turned down by. The biggest problem I faced being in the movie business was that I kept meeting gorgeous young starlets. Unfortunately, I discovered that they were called starlets because they let stars do anything they wanted to do with them. I wasn't a star, and I found out pretty quickly that there are no such things as character actorlets, or sidekicklets.

Most of the girls I went out with aspired to be starlets. They were called twinkies. Although many people thought that these girls weren't very smart, as far as I was concerned, they were all Superwomen—they could see right through me. I tried all my best lines: "I know Cary Grant personally," "I have James Dean's private phone number," "I can get you Gable's autograph," but I really didn't have a lot of success with women.

When I complained about my social life to Lana Turner, she introduced me to legendary Hollywood swashbuckler Errol Flynn, who offered to show me the ropes. Several nights later I got all dressed up for a night on the town, and we drove to a secluded spot in the Hollywood hills and he showed them to me. It turned out they weren't really ropes so much as long cords, and they were hanging from the top of the second *L* in the massive HOLLYWOOD sign overlooking the city. "There they are," Flynn said, clapping me on the back, "the Hollywood ropes. Nobody except everybody in the movie industry knows about them. It's our little secret. And every star in Hollywood has made it to the top."

This was not what I expected. "But what about girls?"

"Oh, they get to use a ladder," Flynn said, laughing. I knew he was kidding, because there was no lady up there.

Fortunately, after the release of *The Sleepwalker* I began getting invited to some of the more fashionable Hollywood parties. I wasn't actually on the so-called A-list, the list of the most important people in the industry; or the B-list, the people who get invited when the most important people aren't available; or even the "short list," which consisted mostly of Mickey Rooney. The truth is, I was on the "wait list." I had to wait until people on the original list turned down the invitation—then I got invited.

It was at the often lavish parties that I began meeting many of the other young actors and actresses in Hollywood. It was at a cocktail party at Bing Crosby's magnificent home in Bel Air, for example, that I first met Shirley MacLaine. I was sipping an hors d'oeuvre when I noticed this absolutely adorable young redhead standing alone in a corner, looking every bit as nervous as I felt. I went over to her and made one of the great mistakes of my life. I asked her, "Haven't we met somewhere before?"

Who knew that was such a complicated question? Four years later we were only into the fifteenth century. "Have you ever wandered in the desert for forty years?" she asked. When I replied that I didn't remember that precisely, she said that we might have been woodsmen together in the land that later became known as Great Britain, but at that time was known simply as Not-So-Terrific Britain.

Shirley and I eventually became good friends, and through her I met her brother, the legendary Hollywood unbuckler, Warren Beatty. When I first met Warren, he was just a shy little kid who could barely ask a beautiful woman to take off all her clothes and roll around with him in a tub of scented oils. Years later he had become the best-known sex symbol in America. I got to know him quite well when we were making *Bonnie and Clyde*. Warren volunteered to teach me the ins and outs of Hollywood, and sometimes we'd go out together. I can tell you from experience, Warren Beatty had the smoothest pickup line of any man I've ever known. He'd see a lovely woman and approach her, smiling that sheepish-yet-wolfish smile, and ask in a soft voice, "Excuse me, but what's the most orgasms you've ever had in an hour?"

Although I was certainly not the ladies' man that Beatty was, I was nice-looking and polite, and occasionally at one of these parties I would meet a woman who seemed interested in me. One woman I shall never forget I met at the regular Sunday-afternoon croquet party at Ingmar and Ingrid Bergman's beautiful mansion in Holmboy Hills. Her name was Paulette Satur and she was an actress. She was very pretty and sweet and we passed the whole afternoon together. She was just so easy to talk to. Finally as the party was starting to break up, she smiled and asked me, "Would you like to come back to my place? I'm having a ménage à trois Stooges."

Call me Warren! I couldn't wait to get back to her apartment. I drove her home to a small apartment on Havenhurst, and when we got there, sure enough, Curly, Moe, and Larry were waiting. And they'd started without us. Chocolate syrup was dripping from the walls, chocolate icing was on the furniture, chocolate cake on the floor. I took one look around this place and it was obvious Paulette was too sweet for me. We did have a good time, though. I'd never met a Stooge before, and they were all very friendly. Moe was the most boisterous of the trio; he told me he was Lincolnesque—he acted with mallets toward all. Every time someone walked into the room, Curly and Larry would shout in unison, "One Moe time," and Moe would hit the newcomer on the head with his plastic mallet.

Probably the biggest star I dated during those early years in Hollywood was the inimitable Shelley Winters. Of course, she's much bigger now. But at that time she had already established herself as one of the most talented and sexy young actresses in the business. I was quite flattered that she paid any attention to me at all. I think one of the reasons we got along so well is that we had both been trained in the New York theater. You could always tell the difference between the formally trained actors and movie stars in Hollywood, because the movie stars would sit around gossiping about who was sleeping with who, while those of us with professional training in our craft would sit around discussing who was sleeping with whom.

I can't honestly claim that Shelley and I ever slept together. When we were alone together, the last thing we wanted to do was sleep. But years later, in her frank and often startling autobiography, she told the entire story of our relationship. She admitted that even after we'd stopped seeing each other, the pull was so strong that each New Year's Eve she would visit me for a brief lovers' tryst before we went our separate ways for the evening.

The oddest thing about that, though, was that in her book she made precisely the same mistake as the man I'd fought in the restaurant—she also thought I was Robert Mitchum.

After *The Sleepwalker* I decided to do the science-fiction thriller *Forbidden Planet,* in which I got my first co-starring billing, along with Walter Pidgeon, Anne Francis, Earl Holliman, Francis Geller and Louise Geller, who later starred in the Bobbsey Twins series, making their screen debuts, and Robby the Robot. *Forbidden Planet* was the futuristic version of Shakespeare's *The Tempest.* In this story I commanded a spacecraft sent to a distant planet to find out what had happened to a previous expedition that had landed there and disappeared. I discovered that Pidgeon and his daughter, the only survivors of that mission, had built a one-man empire with the assistance of Robby the Robot. In this movie Robby, who can accurately claim to be the first heavy-metal performer, created the classic character on which years later George Lucas would base C-3PO in his *Star Wars* trilogy.

In the science-fiction classic Forbidden Planet *I took a wrong turn at Mars and ended up on Walter Pidgeon's incredible planet, beginning my meteoric rise to stardom.*

Robby was unlike any other actor I'd ever worked with. Offscreen he was as tough as nails, but very, very nice. Contrary to those rumors he didn't really have a heart of gold, it was actually gold-plating, but if someone was in trouble, he'd give 'em the sheet metal off his back. We got along quite well; he said he liked me because we both had relatives in the business—his grandfather had played the Tin Man. During the making of *Forbidden Planet* the biggest problem we had with him was that he tried to screw everything he saw—everything. Admittedly, it wasn't really his fault, his index finger was an electric screwdriver.

People have often asked me what it was like to work with a robot. For me, it was much like working with a child, or an animal. I've always explained that it never mattered to me whom or what I was working with as long as that person or object came to the set prepared to work and knew his or its lines, or in Robby's case, his beeps.

The only thing that is unforgivable in this business is not knowing your lines. That wastes the time of everyone else in the production. Now, forgetting lines is a very different thing; at one time or another every actor has forgotten his or her lines, and that's just part of the business. Of course, as I was to learn years later when I struggled with my own serious problems, the worst thing of all was forgetting that you didn't know them.

It was while we were filming *Planet* that I was called off the set and told that I'd received an Academy Award nomination as Best Supporting Actor for my work in *The Sleepwalker*. Champagne was delivered to the set and we stopped shooting for the rest of the day. That first Oscar nomination is always the most thrilling. I was surprised, pleased, and excited. The competition in my category was tough: Jack Lemmon for his portrayal of Ensign Pulver in *Mister Roberts*, Sal Mineo as a confused teenager in *Rebel Without a Cause*, Arthur Kennedy for *Trial*, and the legendary character actor Joseph Verola for his work in *Marty*. Still, I felt I had a strong chance to win.

The next morning I met with the head of the publicity department at Columbia, Emily Perschetz, to find out what to do. "This is all so new to me," I explained, "I hardly know how to act."

"I know," she said, "many moviegoers are aware of that."

"But what do I do?"

"You need a plan, a strategy. The first thing you've got to do is tell the press that you don't deserve the Oscar and you don't want it."

"Excuse me?"

"That's very important. If you admit that you want it, nobody'll vote for you. But if you tell them that you don't deserve it because every other nominee was better than you, then you've at least got a shot."

"All right," I agreed, "I don't want to win. What else can I do to win?"

"How're you feeling?"

"I'm very excited, nothing like this has ever happened—"

"No, no, I mean healthwise. Anything wrong with you?"

"Oh, I'm fine, I'm in great shape."

She frowned. "That's too bad. It would help if you could have some kind of operation before the voting. The sympathy vote is very important." She paused, considering alternatives. "I don't suppose there's anybody close to you who could die in the next few weeks, is there? Temporarily, I mean."

"No, I don't think so."

She sighed and mused wistfully, "Why does RKO get all the deformities?"

I tried to help her. "On second thought, I probably don't need my appendix."

"No." She shook her head firmly. "Wouldn't work. Nobody in this business has ever read a book. They wouldn't even know what an appendix is." She inhaled and held her breath, her cheeks bulging out as if she were storing chestnuts in them. "This isn't going to be easy."

None of this so-called strategy made sense to me. "What about my performance? Doesn't that count?"

"Only in sex. This is business."

"Well, isn't there anything else I can do? I can probably get my mother to come out here."

Emily's face brightened. "Anything wrong with her?"

"Nothing, but . . ."

She waved the suggestion away. "Forget it, everybody's got a mother."

"Hey, wait, that's it," I said, getting into the spirit of the campaign. "I can come out very strongly in favor of motherhood. They'll love me for it."

"They'll hate you for it," she countered. "They don't want people using the Oscar to promote a cause. Every cause is controversial, and around Oscar time, causes are death."

"Well, then, I'll come out strongly against death. That's not controversial. Who can possibly be in favor of death?"

"Every other nominee in your category. I really don't think you understand how cutthroat this competition is."

The studio finally decided to run a sophisticated, low-key campaign, built around the slogan "Leslie Nielsen for Best Supporting Actor. He's terrifying!" The ads ran in all the trade papers; unfortunately, the only offer they got was from the Brooklyn Dodgers, who offered to trade Carl Erskine even up, and everybody knew that his pitching career was just about over.

The studio was very supportive. I even got an unusually warm congratulatory note from Harry Cohn. "Dear to whom it may concern," he wrote, concluding with the reminder, "The ceremony will be televised around the world and seen by more than a hundred million people, so don't touch your private parts until commercial breaks."

There were two things I needed to do to prepare for the ceremony: write an acceptance speech and get a date. Although everyone happily assured me that I had no chance of winning, that no one ever wins an Oscar the first time they're nominated unless they can prove they have a fatal disease, I still had to write a speech not to give. So I spent several days working on it, until I was satisfied that it was completely spontaneous. It actually turned out to be a pretty good speech, ranking right up there among speeches never delivered, such as Custer's Victory Address.

"I never expected to win so I didn't even prepare a speech . . ." my speech began. I began by paying homage to my competitors: "I feel privileged just to have been nominated with four such talented actors, any one of whom is far more deserving of this award than I am."

That's what I wrote, but what I really wanted to say was, "Sure they are. And maybe one day the pope'll be Polish and Elizabeth Taylor will marry a lounge singer from the Catskills."

What I wrote was, "I'd really wish I could cut this up into five equal pieces and share it with you guys."

What I wanted to say was, "Even think about touching this baby and I'll make you uglier than an Edsel."

And for my big finish I wrote, "This means you love me, you really love me."

When what I really wanted to say was, "I love me, I really love me."

Finding the right woman to take to the ceremony was a little more complicated. I really had no one to invite, so I thought the studio might be able to arrange an escort for the evening. I stopped by the publicity office and explained my problem to Emily Perschetz. "Look," I said, "I need a date for the Oscars."

"Oh, no problem," she said, "it's April fourteenth."

I wondered how she could make jokes about something so important to me, so I snapped back. "What, is everybody around here a comedian?"

"Absolutely not." Now she seemed angry. "I'll have you know that Sir Laurence Olivier is making a movie on soundstage five, and he's one of our greatest dramatic actors."

"Look, I'm sorry, I didn't mean to lose my temper. I'm just a little nervous. But I think it's very important that I have a beautiful girl on my arm that evening."

"You're right," she agreed. "Have you considered a tattoo?"

I still don't know why she was upset, but she finally made an appointment for me with the head of illegal affairs at Columbia, Nicky Fabian. Fabian was a former producer who was acknowledged in the industry as the expert in the supporting-actress category, apparently because he'd supported more actresses than anyone else in show business. Nicky arranged a date for me for the Oscars ceremony with a beautiful young actress named Sue King.

As it turned out, her name was very appropriate. Sue King was my first wife. Believe me, if I had known then what I know now, things would have been very different. To start with, I would have married my third wife first, because when she divorced me she got everything I owned, so my first wife, who married me only for my money, would never have married me. Then I would never have even met my second wife, who was working for the lawyer I used to divorce Sue King.

I suspect I should have known from the moment I picked up Sue King that she wasn't right for me. As we walked to our limousine, she looked at me with that absolutely gorgeous smile and said, "You're rich, right?"

"No, I'm Leslie. I thought you knew that." Well, at least she wasn't calling me Robert Mitchum.

She was one of the most beautiful women I'd ever seen, as well as the most publicity conscious. It didn't take me long to see that she had trouble written all over her. "Excuse me," I finally asked, "do you realize you have little tiny words written all over you?" She even had little dots over her eyes. Apparently she was a pretty bad speller, too.

The press didn't seem to notice. Perhaps that's because of what she was wearing. I don't want to say she exuded sex, but she was the only woman at the Oscars wrapped in a plain brown envelope.

I shall never forget that night. People have often asked me what goes on in the mind of an Academy Award nominee while he or she is waiting for that big moment. The answer is many things. While they were filling time giving away some of the less important awards like Best Actor and Best Director, I passed the time playing mind games. That didn't work out very well at all; I lost almost $500. Then I started doing that silly thing everyone does when they want something very badly: I started negotiating with God. If You let me win the Academy Award, I'll . . . I'll never take the name of the Lord in vain. Or, for that matter, Mrs. Olivier. If You let me win the Academy Award, I'll . . . never again play tennis on Sundays. Actually, I didn't play tennis at all, but we were still early in negotiations. As the time came near for the award to be announced, I started offering a better deal. If You let me win the Academy Award . . . I'll be generous to everyone poorer than me, and let me point out, if I do win this award, there'll soon be many more people poorer than me than there are now. Finally, I stopped. This was absurd. Who did I think I was, a mere actor, to negotiate with the Almighty? Clearly that was a job for William Morris.

I also spent a lot of time reminding myself that the TV cameras would probably be focusing on the nominees when the award was announced. To prove I was a good sport I had to smile broadly and applaud vigorously when I lost. I tried to think of things that would make me smile; a quiet beach on a summer's afternoon; a fine wine chilled to precisely fifty degrees; Mamie Eisenhower roller-skating down Broadway in her underwear. Suddenly, I stopped. And I remembered that ancient wisdom that has been handed down from generation to generation on posters in boys' locker rooms: if you think you're going to lose, then you will lose. Think positive, I told myself, think positive, think positive. And sure enough, by the time they were ready to award the Oscar for Best Supporting Actor, I was positive I was going to lose.

The award was given by Edmond O'Brien, who'd won it the previous year for *The Barefoot Contessa,* and two-time Best Actress Bette Davis. Being invited to present an important Oscar is an honor usually bestowed on Hollywood's elite, those actors and actresses with distinguished careers and reputations, or large breasts, who have a movie or perfume to promote. O'Brien's new picture, *1984,* was about to be released, and Miss Davis asked him to predict what the world might really be like in that year. "Oh, much like today's world," he explained, "except we're ruled by a handsome actor serving as a front man for a committee, and the people can take pills to create any feeling they desire."

"Well," chuckled Miss Davis, "we certainly know that isn't going to happen. But if we don't move along with this award, this show might still be on the air."

They announced the nominees. I held my breath. I reminded myself to smile no matter what happened.

Miss Davis fumbled with the envelope. "And the winner is . . . Dear me, I can't seem to get this envelope opened." Everyone tittered. I started turning light blue from holding my breath. "The winner is Jack Lemmon!"

I smiled. I applauded. I cheered. I vowed I would never again shop at the accounting firm of Price Waterhouse, which had tabulated the votes. I felt as if Rocky Marciano had just punched me in the gut so hard I could sing soprano in a eunuch marching band. Jack Lemmon bounded happily to the stage and raised his arms to quiet the cheering crowd. "Whew!" he said. "This is some upset!"

Yeah, sure, Jack, I thought, and if you're upset; imagine how I feel.

The rest of the ceremony was a blur of tears. As we drove home that night, I was lost in thought. Sue King asked me why I was so quiet. "I just can't figure it out," I admitted. "What is it that Jack Lemmon has that I don't?'

She considered that for a few seconds, then guessed, "The Oscar?"

But none of that is why I shall never forget this night. It was what happened after the ceremony that made it so memorable. We went back to my place and I opened the envelope and started looking for trouble in all the wrong places. We did things that we would never have been allowed to do in the movies. If we'd dared, not only would we have been ejected from the theater, we would probably have been arrested. We spent the night making wild, passionate love.

Early the next morning I went to see Nicky Fabian. "I thought you told me she was sexually inhibited," I said.

"Inhabited," he corrected. "I said she was sexually inhabited."

Two weeks later we were married. Sue King and I, I mean—Nicky was already married. A lot of people get married too early, and I certainly did not want to make that faux pas, so I insisted the ceremony begin after nine P.M. I admit it, the marriage was a mistake. I was foolish, I was madly in love with her, I allowed her beauty to make me overlook what was so obvious to everyone else. I should have known better. During the ceremony, for example, when the justice of the peace asked Sue, "Do you take this man to . . ."

She could just as well have raised her hand and said, "You can stop right there, Judge. I'm gonna take him for everything he's got."

The truth is that she was much too young for me. That's something I should have realized right after the ceremony. As we left the chapel, her friends showered us with Rice Krispies.

Our marriage was never very good. Right from the beginning she gave me hints that she didn't really love me. Sometimes, when we were together, she would hand me picture postcards from foreign countries on which she had written, "Wish you were here."

My attorney told me I needed grounds to start a divorce proceeding. "How about mental cruelty?" I suggested.

"Maybe. What'd she do?"

"She tried to beat my brains in." At least she hadn't taken my sense of humor, which turned out to be just about all I got to keep in our divorce settlement.

Perhaps she was young and shallow and not too bright and interested only in money and fame, but it could have been much worse. I could have gone to the Academy Awards ceremony without a date.

We were married for such a brief time, sometimes it seems as if it never really happened. But in fact, when I look back upon it, I still think, those were the day.

She disappeared from my life for many years. It had been some time since I'd even thought about her when someone told me she'd written a book about our marriage. It was titled *The Feminine Mistake*.

My heart wasn't completely broken when our marriage ended. It was more like a pulled muscle. But I felt a need to get away, to go somewhere I'd never been before, to cleanse myself and start anew.

It was at just about this time that the legendary director Cecil B. deMille was completing his remake of his legendary epic *The Ten Commandments*, adapted from the Bible. Suddenly every studio wanted to make legendary biblical pictures. Apparently what had happened was that in the aftermath of the McCarthy hearings and the movie blacklist, the studios recognized that they had a moral obligation to the American public to produce wholesome family entertainment, movies that could be spiritually uplifting as well as educational and entertaining—that, and the fact that Paramount discovered that the Bible was the most read book in the world and was in the public domain. In Hollywood, this was considered the greatest discovery since Walt Disney had pointed out that animated characters didn't have contracts. Supposedly the race to make biblical epics began when the legendary producer Sam Goldwyn announced, "There are profits to be found in the Bible."

Goldwyn was a brilliant producer. When he found out that deMille was remaking *The Ten Commandments,* he began making plans to produce an independent sequel, *Commandments II: 11–20*. When informed that the Bible enumerated no such commandments, he decided it was an impossible problem—so he assigned it to Special Effects.

It seemed as if every studio had a biblical picture either in development or production. Twentieth Century-Fox had made *The Robe* and its sequel, *Demetrius and the Gladiators*. Universal had made *Sign of the Pagan* and was developing the tender story of Mary Magdalene as a vehicle for Doris Day, tentatively titled *The First Virgin*. Paramount had a script for the autobiographical shocker *Moses: My Story!* And MGM was planning a legendary epic spectacular about the troubled relationship between Jesus and his father, entitled *The Son Also Rises*. Many people in the film community thought that was going too far.

Harry Cohn's primary complaint about the Bible was that it didn't have enough sex. "Once you put a little shmatte on Eve," he wondered, "what've you got left?" Eventually he hit upon the remarkable idea of producing an entire film based on each of the commandments, or, as he phrased it so beautifully, "one sin per picture." As far as he was concerned, that would enable him to make morally uplifting films with plenty of cleavage.

The first picture in the series was scheduled to be *Coveting!*, which was loosely based on the Tenth Commandment: "Thou shalt not covet thy neighbor's house nor his wife nor his manservant nor his maidservant nor his ox nor his ass nor anything that is thy neighbor's." When Cohn was asked if this film was capitalizing on *The Ten Commandments,* he pointed out that nowhere in the Tenth Commandment was Paramount even mentioned.

Coveting! was going to be shot in Technicolor entirely on location in Hungary. It was set in a small village just outside Bethlehem called Leaventown and took place just after the initial publication of the Bible, when it was still a controversial bestseller and arguments were raging whether it should be on the fiction or nonfiction best-seller list. Cohn gathered a somewhat-star international cast. I signed to play the Coveter, and the legendary Marlene Dietrich was cast as my neighbor's wife. James Mason was my strange neighbor who seemed to be pushing Marlene and me together for his own amusement, while Jane Wyman played my dutiful wife. Arthur Treacher was going to play the manservant—clearly no one would covet him—while Una Merkel would be the maidservant. Anthony Perkins was a troubled shepherd who lived across the street, Lillian Gish was his busybody mother, and Patty McCormick was the little girl who claimed to have seen Dietrich and me coveting. Jay C. Flippen was making a so-called "special guest appearance" as the Ox. A lot of veteran character actors auditioned for the role of James Mason's ass, but the part finally went to newcomer Rob Satine. The Italian director Roberto Forgione was signed to direct.

Most of the cast arrived in Budapest to rehearse about three weeks before we were scheduled to begin shooting. This was actually the first time I'd been out of the country, if you don't count being born and raised in Canada. Budapest was a lovely city; two cities, actually, divided by a meandering river. On one side of the river is the historic city of Buda, while on the other side is the city of Florence, Italy.

It was really quite an honor for me to be cast as the romantic lead opposite Dietrich. Although she was in her mid fifties at this time, she was still an unusually beautiful and sensuous woman. In order to make her look young enough to play opposite the rest of the cast, we were going to shoot with special lighting. In fact, as far as anyone knew, this was the first time a film was going to be shot with fifteen-watt bulbs.

As I'd never made a picture on location before, I was just a little nervous. I'd heard all about the "location romances" that often occurred among members of the cast and crew while a picture was being shot, but obviously I'd never been involved in one of them. Truthfully, I'd never even been involved in a "West Pico Boulevard" romance. But I must admit, the prospect excited me.

I'd heard it said about Marlene Dietrich that she truly loved mankind—one at a time. Her affairs with her leading men were legendary: Maurice Chevalier, James Stewart, a three-year affair with John Wayne, Yul Brynner, Doug Fairbanks, Jr., Paul Bunyon, Gary Cooper, John Gilbert, Kirk Douglas, the French star Jean Gabin, and many more. Supposedly her sexual appetite was insatiable, which may have been why she'd agreed to make this film in Hungary. Once, so the story goes, when she was making *Rancho Notorious,* she was being extremely temperamental. Finally director Fritz Lang exploded and screamed at her, "That's enough, Marlene! Why don't you just get a grip on yourself!"

She didn't even hesitate. "Yes," she said, "dat's a very good idea. Have vun sent to my dressing room immediately."

Naturally I was looking forward to meeting her. Forgione liked to have his cast read through the script several times before he began blocking the scenes. We met in a large, drab office at the Ministry of Culture. The tables had been pushed against the wall, and folding chairs had been arranged in a circle. Marlene was politely late: just late enough to establish the fact that she was the star and we would wait for her, but not late enough to irritate anyone. Her legs were long and perfect, even better than they'd been in *Blue Angel.*

"So," she said bluntly when we were introduced, "you vill be ze one who vill covet me, ya?"

"Ya," I said, "and it vill be my pleasure."

"Yes," she agreed, looking me over slowly, "it vill be."

The rehearsal went acceptably well, and as we left the drab office, I found myself walking next to her.

"I like you," she told me. "Dat is good for you. You vill come to my room tonight and you vill bring vit you a big banana!"

A banana! Marlene Dietrich wanted me to bring a banana to her room. That was incredible. I had absolutely no idea what that meant, but it certainly sounded exciting. "Why, certainly," I said coolly, "but may I ask why?"

She smiled seductively. "Because I like catered affairs."

I brought her several bunches. When I entered her room that night, she was wearing a long black skirt, sheer silk stockings, and very high, sharpened spiked heels. She kissed me gently on the cheek, then placed her long right leg on the very edge of a chair and began slowly raising her skirt, showing me just a few inches of perfectly proportioned leg. Then she lifted her skirt a few more inches, then a few more inches after that, then some more, and a few more . . . she had the longest leg I'd ever seen . . . a few more inches, then another two inches, then maybe another inch . . . I sat down and began peeling a banana . . . a couple more inches, a few more inches, three inches, she paused and took a deep breath, then returned to work, raising her skirt a few more inches, finally revealing a black garter, and inside that garter was a stopwatch. In one graceful, sweeping motion, she took out the stopwatch and purred, "You have forty-five seconds. Go!"

I slowly finished eating the banana, then asked confidently, "And what do I need the extra fifteen seconds for?"

Seconds later we had become lovers. After a moment of exquisite silence, she asked, "Has any voman every told you zat you are ze sexiest man alive?"

"No," I admitted.

"Goot. I despise liars."

I loved her sense of humor and felt so privileged to be with her. To commemorate the moment, we shared a chilled wine from the wine region of France. "Ahhh," I said after the cool, sweet fruit of the grape slid smoothly down my throat, "my favorite. White."

Then she handed me my membership card. "Congratulations," she vispered, "you have joined ze very exclusive club." I signed it on the back as she directed. My only complaint was that I would have liked to have had a lower number.

From that night on she called me, affectionately, "my little Veiner," and I called her "Miss Dietrich." Our affair was passionate, but oh-so-brief. It ended when I became the "Father of the Hungarian Revolution."

In 1956, Hungary was a totalitarian state ruled by the local Communist Party. In fact, the Russian government of Nikita Khrushchev was actually in charge, and the country was in shambles. Hungary was appropriately named, everyone there was hungary—while the Russians were misnamed, because they never seemed to be in a hurry to get anything done. Our hotel, the Internationale, was considered to be the best hotel in the country; supposedly we were privileged because we had cold and cold running water. But nothing there worked, including most of the employees.

Coveting! was to be the first major motion picture filmed behind the Iron Curtain, and I think every member of the cast and crew could feel the oppression around us. We were followed everywhere we went. All of our hotel rooms were bugged—mostly by little black flying things with thin wings. I suspect they were eavesdropping on us, too. The first night I spent with Marlene I thought I heard the chandelier booing.

As guests of the Ministry of Culture we were requested to attend certain special events. One evening, for example, we were taken to the People's Stadiumplex to see the national championship soccer match between the Red Wave, the

NOVEMBER 1956

SCREEN STARS

Dietrich and Nielsen Hungary for Each Other?

I had my first location affair in Budapest, where I performed with Marlene Dietrich, in the biblical epic Coveting! *When she asked me to bring a big banana to her room, I didn't expect to make magazine headlines, or start the Hungarian Revolution.*

Communist-sponsored team, and the Capitalist Blood Suckers. It was the most one-sided game I'd ever seen; in fact, there was only one side on the field—the Red Wave. But the Red Wave swept down the field, passing crisply, diving for balls, just as if there were another team on the field.

The few Hungarian people we met were very nice, but clearly they were afraid to have too much contact with us. Many times while I was there, I was reminded of the classic scene from the Marx Brothers comedy *Duck Soup,* in which Harpo, who never said a word in any of their movies, was being grilled by Sylvanian police-force cooks because he wouldn't talk. Actually, he wasn't so much being grilled as barbecued. As Harpo's eyes widen, one cook asks the second, "How do you want to do this?" And the second cook sneers, "With relish."

That's when Groucho shows up, disguised as the duck, to save Harpo, convincing the cooks to drink a sleeping potion by telling them, "I think this is the sauce of all your problems."

Only for the proud Hungarian people, Groucho wasn't going to show up and save them. So I wasn't very happy about being there when the minister of culture asked me to do a live interview on Radio Unfree Hungary. The interview was conducted by Klara Gubacs, who also served as the interpreter. Her first question did not get the interview off to a very good start. "So tell us, Mr. Leslie Nielsen, what do you think of our workers' paradise here, eh?"

I decided to be completely honest. "Miss Gubacs," I replied, "this country is revolting."

She translated my answer: *"Az orszaz forradalom megkezdodott."* Apparently, in Hungarian that means, "The country is in revolt," or more precisely, "The revolution has begun."

The next thing I knew, Gubacs was kissing me, which seemed a little bit strange because we'd just met. Moments later I heard gunshots and people started running out of the building into the street, screaming over and over, "*Az orszaz forradalom megkezdodott.*" Gubacs was describing the scene on the radio, but I finally managed to get her attention. "Pardon me," I interrupted, "but do you have any more questions?"

"You've said everything," she yelled joyfully. As I left the studio, she grabbed my arm and shouted, "Tell Americans, tanks."

"It was nothing," I replied, "you're certainly welcome."

When I got back to the hotel, everyone was packing. "Get your stuff," I was told, "the revolution has started."

Within two hours Marlene and I were in the back of an old truck being driven out of the country, hidden under bags of potatoes. I was snuggled against her. "Are you all right?" I asked.

She whispered, "I love it wven men fight over me."

The Hungarian people later honored me as "the Father of the Revolution." I was very proud of that, until the Communist government hired Marvin Mitchelson and tried to sue me for support payments.

The studio canceled the movie. Harry Cohn was furious with me. "You're an actor!" he wired angrily. "Act like one!" He told me to spend some time in Europe finding myself. I thought that was a very good idea; unfortunately I had a difficult time getting lost. I've been blessed with an unusually good sense of direction. No matter where I went, I always knew where I was. In fact, although my official studio biography from this period read, "Suddenly, he found himself alone in Paris," the truth is I knew exactly where I was the entire trip. I couldn't fool me. Besides, even if I had gotten lost, all I had to do was look at my train ticket. Printed right on it in big letters was the magic word: PARIS.

The day the train pulled into Orly Station was one of the most thrilling days of my life. I was in Paris. Gay Paree. Le Windy Cité. I didn't know very much about Paris, except that when I was growing up I'd often used their famous plaster. But I felt as if Paris were embedded in my soul. I spent my first few days there sight-seeing. I visited the magnificent "Eyeful" Tower, which, frankly, was nice but could have used some aluminum siding. I saw the great School of Orthopedic Medicine, the Sorebone. And I met the French people.

The French are different from you and me, assuming, of course, that you're not French, in which case the French are different from me, and the Americans are different from you.

I had been in Paris several days when I received a message that a young French director named Roger Vadim was making a movie in St. Tropez and needed an American actor to play the role of an American actor. It sounded like a part I could play. I still had my telegram from Mr. Cohn proving I was an actor, and I agreed to meet with Vadim to discuss this movie.

We met at a small café on the Champs-Élysées. The French say that if you sit on the Champs-Élysées long enough, everyone you know will eventually stroll by, perhaps en route to Hollywood and Vine, so as we spoke, I kept an eye out for my Aunt Blossom, whom I hadn't seen in nearly five years. "So what type of film are you making?" I asked Vadim. "I've got an image to protect, you know." I was concerned that the studio would find out about this film and raise an objection.

Vadim was charming and intense and handsome. "Allow me to explain to *vous*. You saw the great film *The Robe*, yes?"

"Of course. Loved Burton in it."

He agreed. "Think of this as *Disrobe*."

"Oh, I get it. *This Robe.* Another Bible picture." I knew the studio couldn't possibly have any objections to that.

"Oh, yes, *c'est vrai, c'est vrai.* A Bible picture. It is about the creation. It is called *And God Created Woman.*"

I knew this would make Mr. Cohn happy. My only condition was that there be no nudity in the film, and Mr. Vadim agreed to that.

When Vadim admitted that the picture was actually going to star his wife, a young woman named Brigitte Bardot, I figured it was sort of an expensive vanity production, an artsy home movie. But I was in France with nothing to do, and being paid to spend a few days on the beach in St. Tropez sounded as if it might be fun.

St. Tropez is a small resort town in the south of France. The town was named after most other French towns, so there weren't a lot of great names left. We weren't working from a script; Vadim was going to set the scene, then let us react naturally. I was standing on the beach, waiting to begin, when this absolutely gorgeous woman appeared. As I stood there, she very calmly took off all her clothes. Then she stood there, naked, waiting for direction.

That was my introduction to Brigitte Bardot. She was the most beautiful woman I had ever seen. She was so beautiful she made my next wife jealous. I could not take my eyes off her. Seeing her standing there, just a few feet away from me, totally naked, raised in me the same mixed feelings of excitement and false promise that I now get from being named a finalist in the Publishers' Clearinghouse $10,000,000 Sweepstakes.

As I looked at her, I mean really looked at her, standing there, suddenly it became as clear to me as a cellophane wrapper from a cigarette pack floating in a glass of water. It: The Naked Truth.

Below the skin, I understood, truly we are all the same. We have the same hearts and lungs and funny little organs that look as if they were designed by Picasso. We all bleed when smashed over the head by an ax-wielding maniac. We all have the same needs, the same desires, we are all searching for love and comfort and shelter and a big red convertible. Below the skin we are all the same.

But from the skin up, that's an entirely different matter. From the skin up, one person looks like Brigitte Bardot and everybody else looks not as good. And that's the naked truth. Life isn't a fairway. The dice are loaded. The stakes aren't even. We all come into the world naked and must learn to shop for ourselves. We have to take a good look at what we have been given, recognize the fact that is who we are, and do with that the most it is possible to achieve.

What intelligent breasts Bardot was wearing.

When I saw her standing there without any clothes on, something more practical occurred to me: she really was naked. I'd expressly told Vadim I could not appear in a picture that contained nudity. "Hold it," I said, "just hold it. Mr. Vadim, I told you I couldn't do a picture with nudity."

He looked surprised. "Nudity? There is no nudity here."

I indicated Bardot with a tilt of my head. "And what do you call that?"

"That? Ah, that. But she is not nude."

"Yes, she is. There is dressed and there is not dressed. She is not dressed."

He laughed. "Oh, you Americans. You see, she is not nude. She is wearing the new French fashion. The no-piece bathing suit."

Initially, admittedly, I didn't believe him. But then he asked Bardot to turn around, and sure enough, right there at the bot-

I discovered the first Naked Truth when I costarred with Brigitte Bardot in And God Created Woman. *I'd never done a no-costume drama and I was nervous, but director Roger Vadim promised to make me look good if I played ball with him. So I did.*

tom of the neck, there was the label. Just a little more evidence of how appearances can be deceiving.

As Vadim worked with the crew setting up for the scene, Bardot and I had an opportunity to get to know each other. She was as intelligent as she was beautiful, completely fluent in a foreign language. To my surprise, she seemed quite at ease wearing only that no-piece suit. "How . . . don't . . . I mean," I asked, "don't you feel embarrassed . . . wearing, you know, such a small bathing suit?"

"*Mais* no," she said. "It is nothing."

"Exactly," I told her, "that's why I asked."

My scene, as directed by Vadim, did not require great acting ability. I played the role of a forlorn American actor sitting on a French beach, staring into the sea. Suddenly, the sun flashed brightly on the calm waters, and rising out of that shower of sparkles came this magnificent woman. Wordlessly, she took me in her arms and we made love, rolling passionately on the beach. When we finished, she stood up, turned, and walked back into the water, leaving me staring once again into the sea. When Vadim explained this scene to me, I finally understood why the French refer to the movies as the "sinema."

I guess it was while doing this movie that I first got the reputation of being difficult. And I was difficult, I can't deny that. As an actor with respect for his craft, I will insist on doing a scene over and over and over again until I feel that it is absolutely right. And this was one of those scenes. I'm a bit of a perfectionist, and I wanted this scene to be perfect. So we did five takes, then ten . . . Something kept going wrong. A piece of sand on Brigitte's back. A fly whizzing by. My toe itched. So I insisted we do it again, and again, and again. I spent hours rolling around on that beach with Bardot, the hot sun beating down upon us. But did I complain? I did not. As my father had often uuld to me, "There are only two ways of doing something—my way and the right way." I've always felt the same way. And I wasn't going to be satisfied with this scene until we got it absolutely right. Just another sacrifice I made for my profession.

Through the years I've been asked many times what it feels like to do a love scene on-camera. While it looks simple, even pleasurable, it's actually very difficult, because you only have ten seconds after you press the Delay button on the camera to hop back into bed and start making love before the shutter goes off.

Love scenes in the movies are much easier because someone else runs the camera.

By the end of that afternoon Brigitte and I had become very close. As we dressed to go home, she whispered, so no one else could hear, "Would you please come to *moi* room *ce soir, chéri?*"

"*Fay wrai,*" I replied, using the little French I'd learned. Of course I would be there.

Ah, women. Creatures of infinite differences, yet so much the same. I got to her room at precisely *ce soir,* bringing with me several bunches of cherries, as she had requested. As it turned out, the afternoon must have been too much for her, because she had something besides *amour* in mind. Brigitte loved animals and birds, and in her room she had two rare North American parrots. "They are *très* unhappee," she pouted to me. "Maybe you cheer them up by speaking to them in their language, yes?"

I didn't know too much parrot, but I agreed to try. "Hi. Hi," I said. "How. How. Are. Are. You? You?" That seemed to get their attention, so I decided to tell them a few of my favorite parrot jokes. "Let me ask you, what does a parrot need to go into show business?"

They didn't even hazard a guess.

"A good talon agent. All right, I got an easier one: Where do parrots go to gamble?" I waited. No answer. I told them, "Parrotdice."

"Okay, did you hear about the parrot who got arrested for beaking and entering?" They hadn't. "Here's one: What's a parrot's favorite fish?"

They shrugged their tail feathers.

"Perch. Hey, I got a million of 'em. Whaddaya give to the parrot who has everything?" They didn't know. "Penicillin. Here's an old one: What did the handsome parrot do with his money?"

They look at each other questioningly.

"I'll tell you—he gave it to a Polly with a good caws."

Then I told them several knock-knock jokes, or, as they refer to them, woodpecker jokes. I told every bird joke I knew. They were really pretty naive. They hadn't even heard the one about the clay pigeon who got fired and went to pieces. By the time I dparted that night those parrots were up and cawing. Personally, I think all they needed was a little love and attention.

We finished shooting the next afternoon, and the following morning I returned to Paris. I saw Brigitte for the final time in the hotel coffee shop. Although we'd spent two days making reel love, we'd never had the chance to get to know each other. And so there remained something unspoken between us. Who knows what might have happened if we'd met at a different time, in another place, if I had been somebody else? Who knows what might have happened if we'd only had time to be together? Who knows what kind of music our hearts might have played together? Perhaps a love song, maybe a little calypso. But I do know this, and I will remember this forever—as I was leaving, our hands brushed lightly, no more than a slight touch, and she looked at me with eyes that asked the unanswerable question.

"Cheer up, kid," I said, punching her lightly on the chin, "whatever happens, remember this: we'll always have parrots."

4

THE CHOICE TO PLAY BOND: MOORE OR LES

Hollywood was changing rapidly. The old ways of doing business were no longer applicable. The studio system with all its rigid controls over actors and theaters was breaking down. Those magnificent movie palaces across the nation were closing forever. Perhaps old Hollywood's epitaph was written by the legendary producer of *Gone With the Wind,* David O. Selznick, who, as he lay dying, gasped his famous last words, "Tomorrow *isn't* another day?"

On a more positive note, America had more bowling alleys than ever before.

My seven-year contract with the studio was due to expire soon after I returned from Europe. I knew our negotiations for a new deal would be difficult, but they were even tougher than I'd expected. I began getting the feeling that Columbia was playing hardball when my letters to the studio were returned unopened, stamped MOVED, NO FORWARDING ADDRESS. The Harry Cohn era was over. Amazingly, Cohn had been right all along. After his big-budget musical version of *Uncle Tom's Cabin*, titled *Uncle Tommy's Mansion*, flopped dismally at the box office, he realized he was dead. His legendary casting couch was bronzed, which unfortunately made it cold and slippery to sit on, then shipped to the Smithsonian Institution as a relic of Hollywood's glory days. Other once-powerful studio executives were sent to different institutions. Finally, Columbia made it very clear to me that when my contract expired, they would not be renewing it—they had my personalized parking space packed up and delivered to my home.

My initial reaction was terror. How could I possibly survive without the security of that $187.50 check every two weeks? But as I got used to the idea that I would be free to do whatever projects I selected, I started getting excited. The fact is that I had become a well-respected actor. My career was as rock solid as the very land on which the city of Los Angeles had been built. When I'd gotten back from Europe, there was a pile of scripts waiting for me to read.

The first thing I needed to do was get a new agent. At that time there were several major talent agencies beginning to emerge as important players in the film business: the giant MCA, the venerable William Morris Agency, the hot Bob's Actors and Grill, the new Ashley Famous. I had to decide among them.

The legendary comedian Fred Allen once said about agents, "Picking an agent is like picking a scab, but not nearly as much fun." I interviewed several different agents and was told by each of them why I should sign with their agency. Thomas Fenton, Jr., of Ashley promised me he would always be truthful with me, no matter how difficult that might be, although he did ask me not to tell anyone else he'd made that promise. Lew Wasserman of MCA said, "Come with us. Take the blindfold test." I was particularly impressed with the honesty of Fred Warren of Bob's Actors, who told me, "I'm gonna tell you the real truth. Sometimes I'm gonna lie to you. Now that's the truth. Would I lie to you?" ICM's Bill Chapman held my hand and looked deep into my eyes as he told me, "I don't want to be just your agent. Anybody can be your agent. I want to be more than that, I want to be your friend."

"But I've got to pay you ten percent of everything I earn, right?"

"Hey, you don't want people to think you hang around with poor people."

I finally decided to sign with John Sheldon Weisman at William Morris. William Morris had started out before the turn of the century as a small booking agency for vaudeville acts, but burst into the big time when it obtained all U.S. merchandising rights to World War II. Almost single-handedly William Morris made World War II the most popular war in American history and earned a fortune selling T-shirts, hats, campaign buttons, medals, and making deals for personal appearances in various theaters of operation by American generals. There are some people who firmly believe that, had another agency represented the war, it would have closed two years earlier.

Weisman was considered one of the toughest agents in the business. He's given credit in Hollywood for pioneering the practice of giving gift certificates to celebrity psychiatrists as holiday gifts. "It's a big, wide, wonderful world out there," he told me over lunch at Big Bill's to celebrate our contract, "but only if you stay on the straight and narrow. You've got to pick every project as if it's the last movie you're ever going to make, 'cause if you pick the wrong one, it just might be. Shane Connors was sitting right where you're sitting a few years ago and I told him the same thing, but he didn't believe me."

"Who?"

"See! You think I say these things for my health? I don't. For my health I say things like 'Ahhh!' and 'It hurts when you touch right there.' What we do is wait until the right project comes along, something that allows us to showcase your ability. Something real, something meaningful."

In the meantime, Weisman wanted me to find a business manager, someone to handle all my finances. At his suggestion, I met with a personal adviser named Donald Cronson. "I made thirty million for my clients last year," he boasted.

That certainly was impressive. "Really?"

He looked at me as if I were crazy. "Of course not. That's just a figure of speech. You think maybe I should have picked a lower figure?" He explained that he believed in conservative investments with long-term yields to maximize capital gains that were not susceptible to the whims of the bulls and bears in the money markets.

"I have no idea what you're talking about," I admitted.

He put his beefy arm around my shoulder. "And that's precisely why you need me." Cronson's first suggestion was that I incorporate, that I form my own production company. That way, when a producer wanted to hire me, he would instead hire my entire company, which in turn would hire me, assuming that I was available. In reality, I would be paying myself my own salary. The thing I liked best about this plan was that it offered real security; I knew I'd never fire myself as long as I didn't break my rules. The way Cronson explained it, somehow I would be making more money paying myself as chief executive officer, president, and employee than I would as just an actor, although the producer would be paying the same amount of money. "I'm not sure I really understand this," I told Cronson. "How do I make more money by paying myself with my own money than I do by having someone else pay me directly?"

"And that's precisely why you need me."

My company needed a name. His first suggestion, U.S. Steal, had been taken by a savings and loan, so I decided to name my company What's-His-Name Productions, Inc. I figured that every time a producer or casting agent told an assistant, "Get what's-his-name on the phone," they would just naturally call me.

In addition to my agent and business manager, I considered hiring a personal manager. I wasn't precisely sure what personal managers did, but everybody seemed to have one. The only manager I really admired was the legendary Charles "Casey" Stengel, but he was busy managing the New York Yankees. He declined my offer, telling me, "All a manager can do is not what other people have already done to make him necessary." So I took his advice and decided not to hire a personal manager.

Finally, I needed a publicity agent. One of the lessons I learned in Hollywood was that as an actor, it's not who you are, but rather who people think you are. I couldn't count the number of times producers and maître d's had asked me, "Just who do you think you are?" I needed someone to get my name in the newspaper columns and movie magazines, to reinforce the positive image I projected, to remind producers and casting agents that I was available. At Weisman's suggestion, I hired the very best man in the business, the legendary Barry Dagnal, who'd once represented the Canadian royal family. He had become world famous for his definition of a great publicity man, the so-called Dagnal principle: A great publicity man is someone you've never heard of.

My team was in place. Now it was time to get back to work. We had several offers, but Weisman didn't feel comfortable with any of them. Director Josh Logan wanted me to team with Marlon in the Japanese romance *Sayonara,* based on Jim Michener's fine novel, but Weisman thought it might be a little too ethnic for me, so we nixed it. Producer Sam Spiegel offered me the leading role of Lt. Kimball in David Lean's World War II flick, *Bridge on the River Kwai,* based on Pete Boulle's book, but Weisman felt it wasn't contemporary enough for me, so we rejected it. Orson Welles was desperate for me to costar opposite Janet Leigh in his psychodrama *A Touch of Evil,* and although Marlene had a small part in it, Weisman believed it was too obscure and negative for me, so we booted it.

I was getting very anxious to get back to work. One afternoon I was puttering in my small garden when Weisman phoned. I put down my putter and took his call. "I finally found the right project for you," he announced excitedly. "It's everything we've been waiting for. It's a gritty, hard-hitting drama about two good people struggling to find happiness in a world gone mad."

"Whoa!" It sounded perfect. "What's it called?"

"*Tammy and the Bachelor.* It was written for Presley, but when they heard you were available, they dropped him faster than a cement overcoat. You play the bachelor, a veteran pilot."

Preparing for a role can be extremely difficult. To understand the complex range of emotions motivating my character in Tammy and the Bachelor, *costarring Debbie Reynolds, I was forced to go out every night for weeks with a different beautiful woman.*

A pilot. Dashing. Heroic. Confident. I liked that thought. "So I'd have to take flying lessons?"

Weisman hesitated. "Actually, you'd have to take crashing lessons."

Tammy was an examination of contemporary relationships as seen through the lives of two people brought together by tragic circumstances. I costarred with Deborah Reynolds. I played a cynical bachelor who crashes into her life. Debbie, as she was then known, played an innocent country girl who, while attempting to nurse me back to health after my plane crash, discovers the lighter side of tragedy. At that time Debbie was America's sweetheart, and her marriage to handsome singer Eddie Fisher had captivated the nation. Debbie had previously starred in several pieces of musical fluff, including *The*

Affairs of Dobie Gillis and *Singin' in the Rain*. *Tammy* was to be her breakthrough movie as a serious dramatic actress.

To prepare for this picture I attended a special flight-crash school, in which we were taught such subjects as "ditching" and "screaming for help." The experience I gained making this picture, as well as my portrayal of the doomed pilot, would years later convince nervous producers to trust me with the lead role in my comeback film, the classic psychodrama *Airplane!*

In addition to surviving crash school, I had to learn how to be a cynical bachelor. I'd always believed it's vitally important for an actor to live his role whenever possible, to feel what the character feels. So I fixed myself to become the archetypal cynical bachelor, dating a different woman every night, telling each of them "I love you," then being gone when they awoke the next morning. I learned how to be cold and distant, to say whatever a woman wanted to hear so that I might have my way with her, even to enjoy casual, meaningless sex. And I hated every minute of it. Well, perhaps not every minute. But by the time we began shooting, I had become a bachelor.

Gene Kelly once said about Debbie Reynolds, "When she opens the refrigerator and the light goes on, she does twenty minutes." It took a lot of courage for her to accept this role because it required more fake emotion from her than anything else she had ever done. Perhaps her most difficult moments as a dramatic actress took place during the climactic scene in which I die in her arms. In this scene both Deborah and I knew I was dying. My body was racked with pain and we were saying our final good-byes. Many actresses cannot cry on cue, so ultra-slim tubes are run through their nasal passages into their tear ducts to generate tears when necessary, but Deborah didn't need any tricks. She was a tremendous cryer. As I said my last few words, she began crying. "Of all the houses in all the world," I said through my pain, "if I had to crash my plane into just one of them, I'm glad it was yours. Sorry about your family."

"Hush," she whispered.

"Lucky for us you were in the barn screwing the milkma . . ."

" . . . can," she said urgently, "milk*can*. Does it hurt?"

"Only . . . only when . . . I breathe."

"Then stop breathing and you'll be all right." The tears began welling in her eyes. "Here, let me kiss your sweet lips one final time."

I was having a very difficult time breathing. "No . . ." I pleaded, ". . . hard . . . breathe . . ."

She leaned down and clamped her lips over mine, pulling my face close to her. She kissed me hard and long; my eyes bulged, my cheeks puffed up like a balloon being inflated. "I love you," she whispered as she smothered me in her kisses, "I love you."

"Mmmmmphffffttt . . ." I said, closing my eyes forever. Then, as she held my limp body in her arms and rocked me, she started crying. And crying. And crying. She was some cryer. I was supposed to remain absolutely still—I was even wearing death padding so no one could see me breathing—but Deborah kept dripping those big wet tears onto my face and I couldn't help blinking. I mean, water was running down onto my shirt. I was soaking wet. My nose was getting bloated. Unfortunately, every time I blinked we had to start the scene again.

The director, Nick Rossi, was furious. After the fifth or sixth take he screamed at me, "I swear, if you don't stay dead, I'll kill you!"

"What do you expect from me?" I protested. "How can I stay dead when she's trying to drown me?"

Tammy was an emotionally draining movie. Rossi was an extremely demanding director, always wanting his actors to give him more, more, more. Even today I can close my eyes and hear him saying in that massive voice, "Give me fifty bucks more or I'm gonna sell those photographs to *Confidential*."

Eddie Fisher was on the set almost every day, and we became quite friendly. Late at night several members of the cast and crew would sit around the soundstage klieg light and Eddie would sing a medley of his biggest hits, ranging from "Oh My! Papa!" to the classic "That's Amoral!" Sometimes, after everyone else had gone to sleep, Eddie and I would talk for hours about our lives. I remember telling him that my experience as a cynical bachelor had made me aware of how lucky he was to have found the right girl for him at such a young age. And how fortunate he was, that with all the beautiful women in Hollywood, with so many of them willing to jump into the arms of someone like him, so young and handsome and successful and nice, that he had been able to commit himself to be with one girl for the rest of his life, through decades and decades and decades of life.

"Well . . . actually," he mumbled, "I hadn't thought . . ."

I told him how much I admired him for being able to resist the temptations of the hundreds, even thousands, of gorgeous young women yearning for his comfort, in exchange for the security of growing old with Debbie.

I think my praise made him uncomfortable. He loosened his collar and cleared his throat. "For . . . ever, huh?" He took a deep breath. "Long . . . time, forever, isn't it?"

And I told him how deeply I respected his decision to give up a life filled with meaningless sex, sharing his bed with a different beautiful woman every night, sometimes twice a night, to know that as long as he lived, he would come home every night, every single night, night after night, to the same dependable, reliable, comfortable woman. "The truth is," I confessed, "I'm just not sure I could do what you've done."

"I . . . I . . . fo . . . fo . . . fo . . . forev . . . ev . . . ev . . . ev . . . ?" he said.

"You're a very lucky man," I concluded.

It was in *Tammy* that I had the opportunity to sing for the first time in my career. Debbie and I recorded the title ballad, "Tammy's in Love," which eventually became the number-one song in America. Originally, MGM had been skeptical that I could replace Elvis and asked me to audition for the studio's musical director, the legendary John Hill. "Let me hear you sing a few notes," Hill requested.

" 'Course," I said, then sang, "I'll be back in a few minutes." Then I sang another popular note: "There was a call for you, but he didn't leave his name."

Hill admitted that he'd never heard a voice quite like mine, describing it as "otherworldly." Then he told me he wanted to see if I could carry a tune, suggesting, "Why don't you carry it out to your car, close all the windows, and sing."

Although his comment didn't lead to a singing career, the record was considered revolutionary when it was released. It was one of the first 45 rpm's aimed directly at the handicapped listener. If you played it normally, you would hear Debbie singing in her lovely voice. But if you suffered from hearing dyslexia, you played it backward and you would hear me singing the same song—although at the time there were some rumors that I'd included a subliminal message (Sendmemoney) in my version (doitnow), that simply wasn't true.

Ironically, years later I worked with the lovely Priscilla Presley in the action-adventure police movies, the classic *Naked Gun* series. Priscilla had been married to Elvis at this time, and she confided to me that he had never really recovered from being replaced in *Tammy*. "For him," she remembered sadly, "this was going to be his chance to prove that he was more than just the greatest rock and roller of all time—this was his opportunity to prove he could act. After they gave his part to you, he knew he was doomed to spend the rest of his life starring in silly movies like *Fun in Acapulco* and *Viva Las Vegas* and performing for Kiwanis Clubs in the big rooms at the Holiday Inn."

"I had no idea," I said, shaking my head in disbelief.

"How could you? Oh, Leslie, it was awful. He became a totally different person. After he saw you in *Tammy* he came home and started drinking to try to forget it. He became embittered, angry, sullen; nothing was good enough for him. He tried to drown his sorrows in drugs and ice cream sundaes. In just a few short years he went from being the handsomest man I'd ever seen to the poster boy for inflation."

"Who could of—"

"It was like they stuck a pump in his ear and blew him up. When they said he was bigger than the Mormon Tabernacle Choir, they meant physically. He used to call Orson Welles 'Skinny.'" She paused to compose herself. "He despised you so much he refused to say your name. And when your name came up in conversation, he would act as if he'd never heard of you. It was the greatest performance of his life. Can you believe that?"

Well, I had seen some of his movies. "No," I said kindly. It's a strange world. To think, I was the man who drove Elvis to ice cream sundaes. Sometimes I wonder about the strange turns life takes. And I wonder, might Elvis still be alive today if only scientists had been quicker to discover the miracle of fat-free ice cream?

While awaiting the release of *Tammy* and *And God Created Woman,* Dagnal went to work recasting my image. "You've been a rebel long enough," he explained. "It's time to try something different, something really brave. I think it's time for you to rebel against rebellion."

"What do you mean?"

"I think you should become anti-antiestablishment."

"You mean sort of like leading the revolution against revolution?"

"That's it. White shirts, tie and jacket, short hair. You are what you wear. The ultimate rebellion."

We were sitting by Dagnal's dollar-sign-shaped swimming pool, sipping exotic drinks with little tiny umbrellas in them, the reflection of his mansion shimmering in the water. The more I thought about his suggestion, the more sense it made. What could be newer than a return to the old? "How would we start?"

Many people believed studio moguls were vampires who sucked the blood of actors. But when Worldwide Pictures head Richard DeMonico died, SAG members raised money to purchase a solid-gold stake, which was given to him at his funeral.

"We've got to change your image. Maybe the first thing we do is put you in the right car."

Car? Car? I wasn't sure what he meant by that. I really didn't speak Hollywood. In the movie industry, everything is not what it seems to be. A *vehicle,* for example, is a movie or play that gets you to the next step in your career. A *package* is a group of people, writers, a director, actors who are *attached* to a *vehicle.* A *monster* is a very successful vehicle. *Legs* are what a vehicle has to have, meaning it retains its popularity for a long period of time, which in the movie business is more than one weekend, if it is to become a monster. A *contract* is an agreement between lawyers to disagree so that each of them can charge their clients, or *lollipops,* substantial amounts of money, *undisclosed income.* But a *car?* I'd never heard the term *car* used. "What's a *car?*" I asked.

"You've seen them all over," Dagnal replied. "They're the things you ride around in, you know, with four tires and a steering wheel."

I understood. "You mean a car car. I get it. But I already have a car."

He shook his head at my ignorance. "No, you don't. You got a car, not a . . . car. See, in this business a car is a symbol. You are what you drive."

"I thought I was what I wore." This certainly was a confusing business.

"You are, as long as you're wearing it in the right car. See, there's a code, the Hollywood code. Different types of cars project totally different messages. Like, if you're the kind of actor that wants to be in tearjerkers, you drive a Saab. You want to be a lover, get a bus. You want to play the other man, the guy who loves 'em and leaves 'em? Drive a Cadillac. See how it works? Like, John Wayne. What kind of car do you think the Duke drives?"

Good question. "Well," I ventured, "he was in all those John Ford movies . . ."

"Nah. The Duke has no patience for phonies, he wants to get right to the truth. That's why he drives a bulldozer. Drives away the bull, see? Now what about you? What ya driving now?"

I was almost embarrassed to tell him. "A Studebaker."

"Great. You can star in all the cooking pictures. Get rid of it, it's time to get something new." He tapped a tune on his lip with his index finger while he thought about it. "I think we go for elegance. I think we go for the Rolls."

A Rolls-Royce? "I can't afford a Rolls," I protested.

"You can't not afford one. You want a car you can afford, get a Ford, that's why they call them that. You drive a Rolls, people respect you. Fact is, nobody really likes driving a Rolls; it's overpriced, it's a terrible car. They only drive them for the good of their careers."

A small fish leaped out of his pool and caught the sunlight. "But I thought a Rolls was a great car. They say that when you're driving one, the only sound you hear is the ticking of the clock."

"That's right. Loudest damn clock you ever heard. TICK, TOCK. TICK, TOCK. You use that car to drive yourself crazy. But you need that car." He glanced at a notebook sitting on his lap. "Next thing we've got to do is start getting your name in the columns. Out here, you are who you go out with."

I would never understand the movie business. "I thought I was what I drive."

"You are, and what you're wearing when you drive, where you drive to, and who gets out of the car when you park. Your car drives up to a restaurant and the door opens and Cary

Grant gets out, people are gonna respect you. So what we got to do is find the right girl for you . . . Wait, wait, wait, it's coming to me." His mouth suddenly split open in a huge grin. "How'd you like to go out with Elizabeth Taylor?"

How would I like to go out with Elizabeth Taylor? Elizabeth Taylor, whose last husband, the legendary showman-producer Michael Todd, had been killed in a plane crash several months earlier? How would I like to go out with the most beautiful woman in Hollywood? That Elizabeth Taylor? Even the thought of that made me nervous. "Thanks," I said "but she's not really my type."

Dagnal slapped his forehead with the palm of his hand. "Hey, Midwest, wake up in there. This is Hollywood. She doesn't have to be your type. It's a great story. The husband dies in a plane crash, you played a pilot who crashed his plane. It's a perfect match. It'll take just one phone call."

"You're right," I decided. "Okay, go ahead and call her."

"Her? Who? Oh . . . oh, why would I call her? We don't need her, I'll just call Louella and offer her the exclusive." He leaned back in his chair and sipped his tiny umbrella, satisfied. "I think the two of you'll make a great couple."

"You mean Louella Parsons will introduce us?" Obviously it would be difficult to go out with Elizabeth if we never met. Although certainly less expensive.

He scrunched up his forehead in thought, reminding me of pale venetian blinds. "Intro . . . Oh, I get it. Listen, Midwest, I'm sorry I've got to be the one to break this news to you, but you know those things you read in the columns and fan magazines? Well, sometimes they're not exactly true.

"See," Barry explained, "there's the r-e-a-l truth, and there's the r-e-e-l truth. They're both true, except for the r-e-e-l truth."

"What are you trying to tell me?"

"How can I explain this to you? All right, here. You've heard of Hollywood, right?" He didn't wait for my answer. " 'Course you have. But have you ever seen it? Ever seen a picture of the beautiful Hollywood skyline? How many tall buildings are there? Who's the mayor of Hollywood? Who's the congressman from Hollywood?

"There is no Hollywood," he said bluntly. "That's why they call it the Land of Dreams. Some cute real estate operators dreamed it up. It's a few signs, a postmark, a byline, a freeway. They make a fortune in postcards."

I tried to make a joke out of it. "Sure, and I suppose there's no Oz either."

There are some things you don't joke about. "Sure there is. It's in Culver City, on MGM's backlot, right where it's always been."

I was beginning to comprehend what he was trying to tell me. "So I don't have to go out with Elizabeth Taylor to go out with her?"

My affair with Elizabeth Taylor was created by gossip columnists. But if I'd known how vital it would be to my career, I would have not had this affair years earlier.

"You know Paul Newman and Joanne Woodward? Best marriage in Hollywood, right?"

"Wrong?" I guessed.

"Right. They'd been married two years before they even met. They accidentally bumped into each other at a party at Jack Haley's house. Believe me, relationships last a lot longer this way."

Dagnal took care of everything. About three weeks later Louella Parsons broke the story in the *Examiner:* "Two people who know all about plane crashes seem to have found each other. Seen consoling the beauteous widow Taylor at the recent charity auction for Breast Enhancement was the noted actor Leslie Nielsen. It was heartwarming to see La Liz laughing the night away on the charming Mr. Nielsen's arm."

It was the most exciting date I'd never had. A lot of people called me when they read this item to find out all the details, and naturally I denied even meeting her, just as any gentleman would do.

It marked the beginning of a passionate Hollywood relationship. Before I knew it, we were being seen holding hands in Hollywood's most fashionable restaurants. None of the major newspaper columnists or magazines could allow their competition to scoop them on this story, so it continued to grow. Both Liz and I repeatedly denied we even knew each other, or, as Hedda wrote, we "coyly denied the well-known affair."

Our relationship became the hottest story in filmdom. I don't think I realized how big the story was until our separate pictures appeared side by side on the cover of *Modern Screen*. *Photoplay* ran a readers' poll: "Is it too soon after Mike's death for Liz to marry Leslie?" In *Silver Screen* I made Liz happy again, pulling her back from the abyss of despair. Unfortunately,

I learned in *Movie Star Digest* that Kim Novak was furious with Liz for stealing me away from her, but that she had valiantly decided that Liz had "earned" the right to happiness.

Right in the middle of all of this *And God Created Woman* was released in the United States. Naturally I was the focus of the publicity campaign. The picture was advertised with the promise, "More of Les than you've ever seen before." And there were rumors that Liz had seen this picture in Europe and liked what she'd seen so much that she'd called me for our first date. Years later Brigitte told me that this publicity had helped make her a star in America.

It seemed as if every time I left my small house the celebrity photographers, the so-called paparazzi, were waiting outside for me. At first I was thrilled that anyone outside my immediate family wanted to take my picture, but then Dagnal warned me that I had to do everything possible to avoid these photographers. "Why?" I wondered. "They're just trying to do their job."

I could hear him slap his forehead with the phone. "You're a trial, kid. Here's how it works. If they can take your picture, they don't want it. It's simple economics. The more pictures of you around, the less they're worth, so these guys can't afford to wait around for you. The easier you make it, the less they want it. You avoid them, you're worth more money, so they'll do anything to take your picture. Lemme ask you this: They climbing over the back fence yet?"

"No, of course not."

"Damn. All right, try stringing some barbed wire across the top. That might draw them to it."

All this publicity was making me a much more important movie star than I could ever have become simply by making movies.

In the midst of it all I spoke to Elizabeth Taylor for the first time. This type of publicity was nothing new to her, and she was very gracious about the whole thing. "Isn't life strange?" she wondered.

"*Life?*" I said. "You should see what they're saying about us in *Popular Science.*"

"It really is ridiculous, though," she told me. "Here we are supposedly getting married and we really don't even know each other."

"Isn't that always the case?" I agreed.

We decided that as soon as our affair was over we would meet in person.

The only real problem I had was that my affair with Elizabeth—or "Poodles," as I supposedly called her—was ruining my social life. Very few women in Hollywood were willing to go out with me while I was still seeing Liz. And when I tried to explain that I'd never even met her, I was accused of being "just like a man." What could I say to that—"Oh, yeah? Well, I'm not a man"? And Dagnal constantly reminded me that if I was seen with another woman, "cheating" on Elizabeth, my career might be jeopardized.

Meanwhile, my relationship with Liz had started going sour. It was terrible. Just when I read in the *Los Angeles Times* that I was making her happier than she'd been since Mike Todd's death, *Variety* had the whole story of our fight at Ciro's, claiming that she'd dumped a plate of "Ciro's delicious pasta *fertilizzante*" in my lap. Reading that story, I felt I deserved it. I was heartbroken to read in *The Hollywood Reporter* that I was heartbroken. I tried to soothe my broken heart in *Redbook* with my first wife, including three pages of color photographs, but it did absolutely no good. As Dr. Joyce Brothers explained in her nationally syndicated column, "Although many distressed persons attempt to fill the void created by the end of a deep emotional relationship by getting involved with another person, this rarely is successful and is more often a sign of emotional immaturity, which cannot be resolved without professional assistance."

Luckily, I won back Elizabeth with flowers and a promise in *True Romances*. And for a few days we were happy. Happy! I helped her stick to the simplest diet she'd ever found in *Cosmopolitan*. We sneaked away on a secret rendezvous to the ruins of a ten-thousand-year-old alien colony in *Confidential*. In *Jeweler's Monthly* I gave her a three-carat marquis diamond engagement ring, although she referred to it as a "friendship ring." Finally, a Hollywood miracle: the *National Enquirer* proudly announced that Liz was pregnant with our love child. I knew I was ecstatic because I read it everywhere. Informed sources told *Yeshiva Monthly* that we had agreed to raise our child in the Jewish faith to honor Liz's conversion when she'd married Mike Todd.

The story had gotten so huge that *Mad* ran a parody claiming that Liz and I had never even met. It was hysterical.

Then, tragedy struck. We lost the baby in *Hospital Weekly*. After that, just as predicted in *Manic Depressive's Newsletter,* we blamed each other. Things were never the same between us. Hedda wrote that I had been seen in a rear booth at Schwab's with a girl young enough to be my lover. Louella countered with the exclusive story that Liz was furious about the rumors she'd been reading in other columns. Winchell blamed the whole thing on Communist infiltration. Our relationship was running out of stories. Everything was going wrong. I began receiving more and more threatening letters, warning me that if I broke her heart again I would suffer a wide variety of terrible consequences, including being forced to make a movie at Disney Studios.

I had to get out of the relationship, but I didn't know how to do it. I pleaded with Dagnal, but he remained calm about the whole thing. Sure, it wasn't his career that was falling apart. "Relax," he advised, "just relax. There's only one way out of this thing."

"Anything," I told him, "anything."

He exhaled. "She's gonna have to dump you."

"What?" I was stunned. "How can she do that to me? After everything I've done . . . I mean, what about me? What about my feelings?" From somewhere deep in my heart came a feeling I hadn't anticipated: I was starting to get jealous. "You can tell me," I said. 'There's someone else, isn't there?"

"There will be," Dagnal admitted. "That's probably the best way to go. It'll take the heat off you. But it's got to be somebody big, somebody important. Somebody no one would expect. Any ideas?"

Who could it be? Someone no one would expect to be involved with Elizabeth Taylor. A name popped into my mind: Adlai Stevenson. Too obvious, I decided. Perhaps a debonair foreigner. Chiang Kai-shek, the leader of Nationalist China? It might work. Liz's passion for Chinese food was well known. It was one of the reasons she'd converted to Judaism. And if Grace Kelly had her own country, why not Elizabeth Taylor? It seemed like a good idea, Liz and Chiang. Finally, I rejected it, he was too married. Suddenly, in a blinding flash of inspiration, it came to me. Each of us, in our lives, at one time or another does something of which we are ashamed. And for me, this was that moment. In my defense, though, at the time I thought I was doing this person a big favor. "How about Eddie Fisher?" I suggested.

It seemed like a good idea at the time. I figured the publicity would be good for his career. I knew his marriage to Debbie was secure. I assumed everyone would deny it completely and in a few days the story would be wrapping fish.

Liz was right, life is strange. The rumors started and I was off the hook. I read all the stories in all the newspapers and magazines about Liz and Eddie, Eddie and Liz, but there was one thing about them I hadn't expected—they were true. I think that fooled even the media. Liz and Eddie eventually married, for better, for worse, and for their careers.

And me? All the publicity in the world isn't worth the paper it's written on. Unless, of course, it's written on the back of large bills. So it was time for me to try to convert all the publicity I'd received into something tangible. Fortunately, I had piles of scripts from which to choose. Picking the right project is the most important and most difficult decision an actor has to make. Careers have been made, and destroyed, on the basis of that single decision. For example, the actress Linda Lovelace became a star when she elected to play the lead in the medical thriller *Deep Throat* rather than in the adventure-comedy *Pubic Enemy*.

I read hundreds of scripts, I spent days conferring with my agent, I cut myself shaving, and finally I decided to accept producers Harry Saltzman and Cubby Broccoli's offer to bring to life novelist Ian Fleming's British secret agent James Bond, in the first of the Bond pictures, *Agent 007*. The film introduced the debonair Bond to movie audiences and set the tone for the rest of the series. It was in *Agent 007* that Bond earned his famed "license to kill." Originally, Saltzman and Broccoli were concerned that people wouldn't accept the premise that a government would issue a license to kill, so Bond began with a license to bruise and drive like a crazy person.

Many of the elements that became standard features of the Bond movies that followed were seen for the first time in *007*. The first villain was the suitably fiendish Nazi-Communist-Mafia-Republican-big-businessman, Mr. Profitt, played with great glee by Raymond Burr. Profitt planned to conquer the United States by gaining control of the Civil Service System, and he took sadistic pleasure in burying his enemies alive under tons of paperwork. To thwart him, Bond was forced to fight his way through the most formidable of all his opponents—the American bureaucracy. Assisting him in his attempt to destroy Profitt was the businessman's executive secretary, the luscious Miss Sucke, played by Tia Roberts. With her guidance, Bond successfully fights his way through Immigration, the Internal Revenue Service, the entire U.S. postal system, and finally the monstrous New York City Motor Vehicle Bureau, where he gets his license amended to permit killing, but only when he's wearing corrective lenses.

It was in *007* that we introduced the persnickety inventor "Q," played so marvelously by Bertrand Russell, making his big-screen debut, who created a wild variety of weapons and escape devices for Bond. Among Q's first creations was a handgun that could quickly be converted into a fountain pen, enabling me to write poison-pen letters; an ordinary-looking handkerchief that, when I placed it over my mouth completely, disguised and muffled my voice; and two folding twenty-five-pound cinder blocks that when tied together with a string became a deadly bola.

But the most popular of Q's inventions was the specially equipped Aston-Martin sports car, which was capable of con-

Creating the character of James Bond was an exciting and difficult task. I played Bond as suave, debonair, cultured, confident, worldly, sophisticated, and irresistible to women, as well as a professional killer. I consider it one of the greatest performances of my career.

versing with me. This was a long time ago, when automobiles still knew how to speak proper English. This car gave me basic operating instructions like "Door ajar," "Fasten ejection seat belt," "Trunk open," and "Hot babe at nine o'clock." In addition, the car also gave me warnings, such as "Hey, watch the paint job, huh!" and "Next time you put cheap gas in my tank you'll walk home." But it was at its finest in the classic chase scene, in which I was being pursued by a fleet of gypsy cabs, informing me of my progress: "Bandit approaching forty-five yards to rear, activate passenger-side nuclear weapon," "Doors blown off by small-arms fire," "Entire top ripped off by driving under eighteen-wheeler," "Rear chassis obliterated by hand grenade," and "Windshield-wiper fluid dangerously low."

From the beginning we knew that much of the success of these movies would depend on the ingenuity of the special effects, particularly during Bond's escapes. Saltzman and Broccoli hired the best stuntmen in the business and had them perform some extraordinarily difficult and dangerous feats, such as jumping out of an airplane between the rotor blades of a helicopter without a parachute, getting decapitated by a train, being shot out of a submarine's torpedo tube, making love to Shelley Winters, and riding the New York City subway.

All of these production values were extremely important to the success of the film, but what made them really work was Bond's character. His character had to hold everything together. Bond had to be handsome and charming, suave and debonair, lovable yet vicious, boyish yet mannish, big yet tall, serious yet funny; and certainly more important than anything else we did in this film, he had to continually figure out new ways of convincing incredibly sexy women to take off most of their clothes. In fact, we believed we could forget all the other stuff as long as we got the clothes off.

Director Terry Young wanted me to make my first on-screen appearance dressed immaculately in black tie, popping out of a huge cake at a terrorist's birthday party, and spraying the guests with a sleeping gas that put everyone to sleep. We argued about that. I felt strongly that since this was the first time the audience met Bond, the scene had to be believable, and no one would believe that he would be wearing black tie while he was working. Eventually we compromised; instead of black tie I wore a nice paisley print that hadn't been cleaned in years.

Finally, it was in *Agent 007* that Bond introduced the sexual double entendre that became his trademark, the seemingly innocent line that the audience knew actually meant something quite different. We used to call it the "Something big's come up" line. I guess the first of those lines was my oft-quoted dinner invitation to Miss Sucke. Although I asked rather straightforwardly, "Miss Sucke, feel like eating something?," it was obvious to the audience that what I was really saying was, "Woman, you come to house, cook dinner, wash dishes."

The picture had huge grosses. With that success Saltzman and Broccoli desperately wanted me to sign to play Bond in three additional pictures, but I turned them down. I was well aware that typecasting as a particular character had ruined many careers—for years, for example, Shirley Temple had been forced to play a little girl—and I didn't want to get caught in that trap. As my replacement, I suggested the handsome Texas governor, John Connally, figuring that if actors like Ronald Reagan and George Murphy could go into politics, a politician like John Connally could become an actor. Unfortunately, Saltzman must have had a hearing problem because he signed

Scottish actor Sean Connery. I was shocked when I heard the news. I called Saltzman immediately. "Connally," I screamed at him, "I said John Connally! Now look what you're stuck with." Sean Connery played the role of James Bond with moderate success in several films before being replaced in *Casino Royale* by the intellectual hunk Woody Allen.

Of all the performers who used *Agent 007* as a springboard to an entire career, perhaps the most unexpected was the Aston-Martin, which had extensive fiberglass surgery and went on to play the title car in the TV series "Knight Rider."

Agent 007 was the fourth-highest-grossing film of the year. It secured my position as one of America's top male box-office attractions. With my fee for a picture approaching $300,000, plus a percentage of the profits, I decided I'd earned some time off. I just wanted to relax.

The difficulty with that was that I'd been working so hard for so long that I didn't know how not to work. My father had often said that the most difficult thing about doing nothing was that you didn't know when you were finished. I had the opposite problem: I had to learn how to do nothing. Unfortunately, I had no idea how to start stopping. I would have stopped at nothing, if only I knew how.

Life is funny. Not the kind of ha-ha funny as often portrayed in sophomoric movies in which a decent, noble human being in a wheelchair is humiliated by being accidentally pushed down the steps of the upper deck of a baseball stadium and falls upon Queen Elizabeth, but rather the more sophisticated type of humor in which a homeless person finds a discarded lottery ticket in the gutter and wins $20,000,000 and is so shocked that he has a heart attack and rolls down the steps of the upper deck of a baseball stadium and falls upon Queen

Elizabeth. Although both types of humor would fall flat on Queen Elizabeth, there is a significant difference

Real life is nothing like the movies. For example, in real life you don't have to pay to get in, while the movies have coming attractions so you can decide if you want to see them or not. I suspect that if I had been able to see the coming attractions of my life, I would probably have stayed home and watched television.

Here I was, a major motion-picture star, earning more money than I had ever imagined in my life, sleeping late, working with beautiful women, and being treated as if I were royalty, but was I happy? Was I truly happy? Was I happy deep down inside, where those chemical reactions take place that make those gurgling sounds in your stomach just when you're trying to impress some babe? You bet I was. Are you crazy? I was thrilled. Who wouldn't be? At times we've all read interviews with very wealthy or successful people in which they complained that other people couldn't understand how difficult their life was, that while on the surface of their swimming pools things looked wonderful, underneath, where the filters get clogged by strange bugs and the pool boy adds too much chlorine, life is very murky. I'd finally reached the point where I understood why they said such things—because they didn't want people coming to their house and swimming in their pool! It's a great strategy: "You really don't want to be so rich that you'll never have to go to work for ten hours a day in the sweltering assembly plant for the rest of your life because you'd spend all your time worrying about losing your money." Believe me, you never hear poor people complaining about the problems caused by having too much money.

So I was happy, and that's why I began worrying when the Dream returned. The dreaded actor's nightmare. I would be fast asleep . . . Well, things were going so well for me that I could afford to take my time sleeping, so I was actually slow asleep, when suddenly and completely unexpectedly, there came the dreaded knock at the door.

I'd made great progress over the years and the Dream reflected that. Rather than in black and white, the Dream was now in CinemaScope with Sound-A-Round! And instead of going to the door in my nightshirt and opening it, I had my butler opening it for me. But I rebuttoned it myself and opened the door. As before, three men were standing there. One of them flashed his badge. "Acting chief of police," he said.

I knew who they were: the Acting Police. "Where have you guys been for the last decade?" I asked.

"Very busy," the smallest one replied. "You think you're the only bad actor in Hollywood?"

"You wouldn't believe it," the second one confided. "We been working two shifts, daydreams and nightmares. Anyway, get your things, you're coming with us."

The acting chief ordered the second man, "Read him his rights."

"Yeah, right, I forgot," the second man said, taking out a large document. "In consideration of the payment of one dollar, you hereby, now and forever, irrevocably convey all rights in any and all forms of written and electronic media, or any other forms of expression, to the material herein referred to as 'The Dream,' as well an any other stories or characters deriving from this . . ."

I woke up in a cold sweat. Why, I wondered, why had the dream returned? Why now, when I was so happy, so successful? "It's an anxiety dream," Dagnal explained. "Best thing to do is see a professional therapist."

He recommended the legendary Dr. Ken Vills, psychiatrist to the stars. I called to make an appointment, and after we'd discussed my reasons for wanting to see him, I asked, "How much is your fee?"

"Three hundred dollars an hour."

"Three hundred dollars an hour!" I couldn't believe it. "Wow," I said, "I'd have to be crazy to pay a psychiatrist that much money."

"Neat, isn't it?" he replied, chuckling.

As it turned out, that appointment wasn't necessary. A few minutes later my old friend Dean Martin called and offered me a six-month trial membership in the famed Hollywood Rat Pack.

5

THE CHAPTER WITHOUT A TITLE

The Rat Pack was Hollywood's most exclusive club. It was one of the very few gangs, in fact, that got to hang out on the corners of streets named after its members. The club was run by the legendary singer, the chairman of the board, Frank Sinatra. Actor Peter Lawford was the vice-president—probably because he knew more about it than anyone else in Hollywood. My friend Dean Martin was the undersecretary because that was his favorite position. The legendary legend Sammy Davis, Jr., was in charge of defense, and Joey Bishop was the chaplain.

This invitation to pledge the Rat Pack came at a perfect time for me. I was feeling very much alone. Not only wasn't there a special woman in my life, but I had very few close male friends. The truth is that most actors have few close friends, perhaps because we're usually traveling or competing with each other for parts. For a long time I actually thought that "male bonding" was the sticky stuff found on the back of envelopes. In my entire life I'd never belonged to a real club. In fact, I'm probably the only person ever to be blackballed by the Book-of-the-Month Club.

My pledge class consisted of the attorney general of the United States, Robert Kennedy; insult comedian Don Rickles; opening act Pat Cooper; and me. The Rat Pack was unlike any other club I'd ever heard of; for example, while other clubs met in their clubhouse, we met in our clubmansion. The club rules were explained to us at the first meeting of my pledge class. I can still remember Secretary of Defense Sammy Davis, Jr., warning us about the elaborate security system: "I don't wanna see anybody climbing over da fence."

And Peter Lawford very carefully outlined the club policy about sexual harassment: "Basically, we're in favor of it."

There was a lot of media interest in club activities, and we were instructed to tell anyone who asked us about it that the Rat Pack was actually a "health club." Or, as Lawford put it, "If you know what's good for your health, you'll keep your mouth shut." We all had to take the solemn oath of Omeleta, in which we vowed never to reveal the club secrets about egg fights. And finally we were told that under no circumstances should we ever mention singer Vic Anguilo to Chairman Sinatra.

Meetings ended with everyone joining hands and singing the club song, "His Way."

The club name, the Rat Pack, was derived from the pack rat, an animal with the odd trait of leaving something behind every time it took something. We tried to do the same thing. For example, one night we decided to stage a panty raid at Marilyn Monroe's house. We took a pair of her panties, and in return, we left behind Robert Kennedy. Look, I've heard all the stories about Marilyn and Robert Kennedy. Supposedly they had a big affair, but personally I don't believe it. I knew both of them very well, and if they had had an affair, I'm positive I would have received an invitation. I went to all the parties. However, there is also no doubt that Marilyn and Bobby were very close friends. In fact, I remember the night that Bobby Kennedy came into the mansion wearing bright red lipstick, eyeliner, and some very attractive light powder. "What happened to you?" I asked.

"It's silly," he said, trying to dismiss it. "Marilyn and I had a big fight last night, and I was feeling very bad about it. So I went over there this morning and said, 'Let's make up.' And we did."

I was especially fond of Rickles. He was the only one permitted to kid Frank. "Frank really is a benevolent guy," he said at one of our meetings. "In fact, he's started a brand-new foundation. All of his old enemies are going to be in it. And as soon as the foundation is completed, he's going to build a big building on top of it." Once he offered me some good advice: "Don't let me scare you, but if you ever have a falling-out with Frank, make sure you're on the ground floor."

Sinatra was our leader in every way. He was one of the very few people I've ever known who was bigger in real life than in reputation. There are a lot of good practical jokers in the world; Frank was an impractical joker. He would do things for a laugh most other people couldn't even imagine. One night, for example, we were all at dinner when Pat Cooper got an emergency phone call from the police informing him that his apartment in one of those high-rise buildings on Wilshire Boulevard

I knew I'd made it in Hollywood when I received an invitation to join the legendary fun-raising group, the Rat Pack. Here, in our 1961 Yearbook photo, are (left) Chairman Frank Sinatra, Dean Martin, me, Peter Lawford, Joey Bishop, and (center) Sammy Davis, Jr. Absent that day were Don Rickles, Henry Silva, and Robert Kennedy, Jr.

had been robbed. Pat was very upset, he kept a lot of things of great sentimental value there, so Frank decided we should all go with him. It was the most incredible sight I'd ever seen: right between the fourth and sixth floors I could see this huge gap where the apartment must have been. The police were absolutely right, the apartment had definitely been robbed. It was completely gone. Pat looked at that big hole in the building and said in amazement, "It looks like they got everything."

How Frank got that apartment past the doorman remains a mystery to this very day.

I spent some of the most memorable days and nights of my life with the Rat Pack. The newspapers made us sound like a wild group, doing nothing but drinking and partying, but it really wasn't that way at all. Every one of us was a dedicated professional, hardworking, and we always tried to be in bed and then home by midnight.

Because we were all in show business, members were constantly coming and going to fulfill commitments. Even I left for a few weeks to make a cameo appearance in a motion picture. Although the days of the gladiator movies were over and would not be revived until Anthony Hopkins portrayed Hannibal "the Cannibal" Lecter in *Silence of the Lambs,* biblical films were still quite popular. The legendary director George "Kingfish" Stevens hired me to play a small but pivotal role in his epic production, *The Greatest Story Ever Told.*

In *Great Story* Chuck Heston played John the Baptist, John Wayne was a Roman soldier, Paulie Herman was a fireproof-cross manufacturer, and Stevens cast me as the elegant Phillip the Tablemeister, the maître d' at the Last Supper. I had only one line, but it's often quoted in those collections of great movie lines. When Christ and his disciples arrive at my fashionable eatery, The Upper Room, He tells me He'd made a reservation for dinner. After checking my book, I respond, "Here it is. Christ, party of thirteen. Wait in the bar and I'll have a table for you in just a few minutes."

Some clubs made home movies; the Rat Pack made full-length motion pictures. I returned to Hollywood just in time to play a supporting role in *Ocean's Twelve,* a caper movie starring Frank and most of the guys in the club. It was the story of an attempt to simultaneously rob five Las Vegas casinos. We spent six weeks on location in Vegas. In the film I played a master electrician whose mission it was to short-circuit all the alarm systems and traffic lights in the city: New York has Con Ed, I worked for Con Vegas. It was the first time I'd played a Con man.

The film was really just an excuse to have a good time and we finished and got back to Hollywood just in time for Christmas. I guess I'd become so friendly with Frank that I'd forgotten some of the club rules, particularly the rule about never mentioning Vic Anguilo. Truth is, at that time, I didn't even know who Vic Anguilo was. I wanted to get my pal Frank something very special for Christmas, so I searched and searched until I finally found the perfect gift for someone who appreciated great music as much as he did: I bought him an antique Victrola and a rare set of RCA Victor recordings of the *Victory at Sea* symphony as conducted by Victor Borge at the famed Old Vic Theatre. I just hoped nobody else thought of the same thing.

Frank was furious. He reacted as if I'd given him a Vic Damone album. In fact, he was so angry, I got very nervous, remembering what Dean Martin had once told me: "Frank is a very special guy. If he likes you, he'll kill you with kindness. And if he doesn't, he'll use a gun."

Apparently he didn't like my present. "How could you do this to me?" he cried. "You were supposed to be my friend. What'd we tell you about anything that reminds me of Vic Anguilo, huh? What'd we tell you?"

I lowered my head and asked in a voice barely louder than a whisper, "I guess that means you don't want me to give your mother that vicuña coat?"

He ordered me out of the clubmansion. As I left, I heard Sammy Davis's booming voice ringing in my ears, "And don't try to sneak back in over da fence!"

I was banished from the Rat Pack. I felt terrible; I felt cold and sticky, like pasta without sauce.

When *Ocean's Twelve* was released, I knew for sure that Frank hadn't forgiven me. Most people remember that movie as *Ocean's Eleven*. My entire performance had been cut out of the picture; every scene, every sentence was gone. It was as if I hadn't even been there when the film was made. Obviously, they had to change elements of the plot. So I guess I wasn't surprised when famed film critic Jeffrey Lyons called the film "electrifying! One of the week's ten best!" Sure it was electrifying—without me in the picture there was no one to short-circuit the lights.

Frank did all that to me just because of a Christmas present. He must really dislike Victor Borge. So I guess I can call myself just another one of Frank Sinatra's victims; I just wouldn't call myself that to his face.

Ironically, *Ocean's Eleven* was not the only picture in which my performance ended up on the cutting-room floor, and certainly not the most important. One afternoon several weeks later I checked my answering service and was told, "Your agent phoned. He wants you to call him immediately."

I did just that. When he answered the phone, I said, "Well, Mr. Immediately, what do you want?"

He ignored my little joke. "We just got a terrific offer," he announced. "David Lean wants you for his new picture. It's called *Lawrence of Arabia* and it's the story of an emotionally tortured Englishman who leads the entire Arab world to freedom."

"I understand," I said. "What role do they want me for?"

"What difference does it make? It's going to be a big picture. They want you to star opposite Peter O'Toole. They've already signed Alec Guinness, Tony Quinn, Joe Ferrer, Jack Hawkins, Anthony Quayle, and Omar Sharif. But you'll be closer to O'Toole than anyone else in the film."

"Sounds great, but what's the part?"

I then heard the single most ominous sound in the entire motion-picture industry: a silent agent. After an extended silence, Weisman finally mumbled something that sounded like, "You play his hmmmmsexual lover."

"Excuse me, Immediately, what'd you say?"

He clogged his throat, then mumbled again, "You play his hmmmmsexual lover."

"Uh, let me get this straight—"

"Poor choice of words there, Leslie," he interrupted.

"David Lean wants me to play Lawrence of Arabia's hmmmmsexual lover?"

In those days no one in the movie business dared use the word *hmmmmsexual*. As far as the movies were concerned, there were many different types of men: He-men, G-men, policemen, workmen, even cowboys. But no hmmmmsexual men.

"It's a great part," he continued. "You'd play the American journalist Frederick Stevens. The Hearst papers send him to

Arabia to track down this crazy Englishman who's leading the Arabs. The next thing you know, boom, they're an item. It's a great story. Believe me, if Lawrence had been smart enough to stay alive until now, the rights to this alone would have made him a rich man."

"I don't know," I said cautiously, "it's a real stretch for me."

"A stretch!" he yelled. "A stretch! It's a goddamn thousand-yard rubber band. It's brave, it's real, it's raw, it's controversial, it's box-office boffo."

I remained hesitant. "I just don't know. I've got my whole career to think of. I mean, what if I play this part and people believe it?"

"You're an actor, they're supposed to believe it."

"No, no, no. I mean, what if I play this part and people believe, you know, that I'm a . . . I'm a . . . hmmmmmmmmmm . . . you know?"

He really wanted me to accept this role. "Com'on, what're you talking? People are a lot more sophisticated than that. If people believed acting was real, Cagney'd be in prison. You think people who saw *Some Like It Hot* think Jack Lemmon wears a dress in real life? You think anybody believes Bela Lugosi goes around sucking blood at night? You think anybody actually believes Jayne Mansfield wears breasts like that when she cleans the house? You think anybody believes Duke Wayne is really this macho hero?"

I was stunned. "You mean John Wayne—"

"All right, maybe they believe in the Duke, but nobody believes the rest of it." I could hear the frustration in his voice. "Okay, let's look at it this way. Liz and Dick. Bogie and Bacall. Tracy and Hepburn. O'Toole and Nielsen. What's the difference?"

"They all have women except for O'Toole and Nielsen?" I guessed.

"See? See? You don't see anything at all, do you? Wake up in there, Cher-for-brains. When I say what's the difference, what I'm really saying is that there is no difference. Don't you speak Hollywood? Now, I'm gonna be completely honest with you . . ."

There it was, the second most ominous sound in the entire motion-picture industry: an agent warning you that he was about to be honest.

". . . I've known a lot of actors in my life, and actors aren't like real people. Acting is not like a real job, actors don't work ten to one like everybody else. Acting is a lifestyle. A choice. You live it. And when you choose to become an actor you make this sacred pact with yourself to portray the whole world in all of its many shades and nuances. You vow to leap into roles that enable you to reflect the varied and beautiful differences between people, to educate and enlighten and entertain and even challenge the audience, to force people to think. That's what being an actor is all about. And there comes a time in an actor's life, if he's very lucky, when he's offered the opportunity to put it all out there, to show everything he's got, to stand up for what he believes in. Either you believe that or you don't, but this is the time for you to make that decision."

I almost stood up and cheered. He was absolutely right. This was my chance to show what I believed in. "Okay," I agreed, "how much do I believe in it?"

"They've offered four hundred thou, but I can jerk them up to five."

"I beleeeeve!" I shouted into the phone. "I beleeeeeeve."

"Then you'll do it?" he yelled right back at me. "You'll do it?"

"I will do it," I said firmly and proudly. "One condition, though. I'll take the chance, I'll stick my neck out. But that's all I'm sticking out."

Accepting the role of Frederick Stevens was a decision I've never regretted. I actually appeared in only nine scenes, but my relationship with Lawrence was his motivation for leading the Arab cause. He did it for me. Although most of my scenes were scheduled to be filmed on a soundstage in Spain, David Lean wanted his whole cast to spend time in the Saudi Arabian desert. He wanted us to understand the texture of the production. I was there almost two full days before I met Peter O'Toole. Lean told me that O'Toole had decided to live by himself in a Bedouin tent, trying to get deeply into his role.

"Oh, really?" I asked nervously. "And . . . just how deeply into his role does he intend to go?"

My second night there I was escorted into O'Toole's large tent. A pit had been dug into the dirt floor, and a whole pig was being roasted on a skewer, filling the tent with thick smoke and bringing tears to my eyes. In a corner a hooded figure strummed a whiny stringed instrument. As O'Toole and I shook hands, our eyes met. Through the smoke I could see that he had the deepest blue eyes I'd ever seen in my life. They seemed to bore into my soul. Even many years later, when someone claimed that O'Toole was the most boring man they'd ever met, I knew exactly what they meant. Peter smiled enigmatically. "*Salaam,*" he said, bowing slightly, "I understand you are to be my lover."

"Well, you know, I think it's my best part."

"I'm sure it is. And tell me, how would you like to rehearse?"

In Lawrence of Arabia *I portrayed journalist Frederick Stevens, who went to the desert to cover a war and instead had a meaningful relationship with Lawrence. In this controversial scene, which was later cut, Lawrence has just confessed his love to Stevens.*

His eyes had locked on to mine. "Uh . . . on the telephone?" I suggested.

In fact, there were no actual love scenes between us in the script. Everything was suggested very subtly: a glance, a smile in return, a fierce chess match played to a draw, a shared moment of amusement, a rubbing of the groin area, an index finger rolled between a joined thumb and forefinger, black-and-white photographs, detailed diagrams, and finally the scene in which we consummate our relationship, which consisted of Peter putting his arm around my shoulders and guiding me into his tent.

O'Toole was one of the most intelligent actors I've ever worked with. And it was obvious he was entranced by the desert. At night we would sit in a large circle with the tribesmen working as extras on the film, surrounded by life that had learned to survive on the barren, waterless plain, while above us countless stars cluttered a portion of the sky, twinkling with the tragic beauty of fireflies caught in a small child's jar. It was a very humbling place. One such night O'Toole broke a long silence by asking me, "Do you wonder why we're making this film?"

Out there, in the unforgiving desert, it was something I'd often thought about. "I believe so," I said quietly, so as not to disturb the spirits that wander the desert. "I think this is the story of one man's quest to discover his nature, and to do so he must first exorcise himself of everything he knows and that which makes him comfortable. It's an epic search, a man choosing to live in a world in which he is an alien in order to find the core of his own heart. It's a classic story of love and loyalty, adventure and courage, played out against the ultimate neutral background of the desert. And yet it's also the story of a man bedeviled by his own femininity and the inner battle for peace and contentment. A story in which the desert is the hero and the villain, the blessing and the curse, it is that which Lawrence makes it, using only those human skills of intelligence and bravery with which he has been endowed. It's a timeless story, in which lives are but pawns in the hands of this giving, yet ultimately selfish man. It's the story of the British Empire, and its decline, because that which it stood for most was simply the perpetuation of its own existence. It's the story . . ."

While filming Lawrence of Arabia *I got to know Peter O'Toole quite well. I felt the film was about man's search for himself, but he claimed it was made to increase cold-drink sales in theaters.*

O'Toole was shaking his head. "Nah."

"It's not?" I questioned.

"Soft drinks," he whispered firmly.

"Soft drinks?"

"Soft drinks," he stated flatly. "Most people don't know it, but the profit center in movie theaters is the concession stand. Most theaters barely break even on ticket sales. Sure, they make a little something on the popcorn, but the real money is in soft drinks. That's why they give you those big buckets of popcorn with plenty of salt on them. Sells soda."

"Soft drinks?"

"Have you never wondered why theaters don't have water fountains? And if they do have them, why don't they work? And if they have them and they work, why only lukewarm water dribbles out of them? And this . . ." He scooped up a handful of sand and let it drain through his fingers. "This . . . it's impossible to spend three hours watching a film that takes place in the desert without getting incredibly thirsty. No, they care nothing about Lawrence, they care about selling soda. The movies are not a great art form, but a cold business. And that, my good friend, that is the naked truth."

I was startled. *That* was the naked truth? What about Brigitte Bardot's body? Was there no truth to that? I wondered.

O'Toole could see the doubt in my eyes. "If I'm incorrect," he challenged, "why have they not made an epic picture about Admiral Perry's trek to the North Pole? They haven't and they won't because with all that snow and ice the audience won't get thirsty and the picture would fail."

"Well," I said, trying to lighten the mood, "with what this picture is costing, they'd better sell a lot of soda."

He smiled knowingly, "Oh, they will, they most certainly will. You see, the great filmmakers are gone, the soda sellers have gained control. And they are expert in this business of selling soda."

It was a night I've never forgotten. The night I learned that there is more than one naked truth. I knew then that there were at least two, but were there more?

Lawrence of Arabia was an extraordinarily difficult shoot. O'Toole suffered several serious injuries because he insisted on performing his own stunts. The days in the desert were long and inhumanly hot. The nights were bitterly cold. And sand was everywhere. Sand got into everything: our clothes, our food, the cameras. Ever since those weeks in the desert I've harbored homicidal thoughts about the sandman.

When I returned to Hollywood, I found a letter from my publicity agent asking me to call him ASAP. It seemed silly, but I did as he asked. I called his office: "Okay, Barry, you're a sap!"

"What?"

"You're a sap. So what do you want?"

"I've got some great news for you. Word is that *Larab* is gonna be big, so we have to take advantage of it. I've already gotten started, I called Lloyds of London—you know, the insurance company?"

"*Larab?*"

"*Lawrence of Arabia. Larab.* Remember, words take time, time is money. Anyway, L of L's done good business insuring various important parts of actors' bodies, based on the premise that if anything happened to that part their career would be over. Betty Grable insured her legs, Mickey Rooney was insured against growing, Diana Dors was insured against shrinking, Merman insured her voice, Crawford insured her temper . . . So I got them to issue a policy for you."

What a great idea for publicity. "So what part did you insure? My mind, right?"

"Hey, good guess. Wrong, but a good guess."

"Lemme see. My face, right? My face is my fortune. I get a lot of work because I've got that all-American Canadian look and—"

"Not your face. Fact is, when I asked them about that, they suggested you take out a liability policy."

"Not my mind, not my face? I know. My broad shoulders, because of their incredibly sculpted look, that strong—"

"Sorry."

I could hear that he was enjoying this. "My massive chest?"

"Nope."

"Oh, I got it; my firm, hard stomach. A real man's stomach."

"Keep going, you're in the right direction."

Suddenly, I knew. He had insured . . . my manhood. "Oh, no. No way."

"I had no choice. It was the only part that hadn't been taken. I figured, with your role in *Larab*, it'd be perfect. And we got a great deal on it, too."

My manhood? How could they possibly get publicity out of that? But there was nothing I could do about it; what was done was done. "All right," I agreed reluctantly, "how much did we insure it for?" Grable's legs had been covered for $1,000,000. Merman's voice was worth $2,000,000.

"Twenty bucks," he said quietly and so quickly I didn't think I'd heard correctly.

"How much?"

"Twenty bucks, okay?" he repeated loudly and, I thought, defensively.

"Twenty bucks? That's all the insurance you could get on my manhood?"

"And five dollars deductible."

That was terrible. I mean, twenty dollars? I really didn't know how to respond. "Well, all right, I mean, well, what kind of insurance did we get? You know, what am I . . . what's it protected against?"

"Floods," he said. "And only for replacement value, minus wear and tear."

This was the worst insurance policy I'd ever heard of. "So that's it, it's done?"

"Soon as you send them the photographs."

"Photographs!" I couldn't believe it.

"Yeah, from all angles. They need to see it in pristine condition. That way if you ever file a claim—"

"This is ridiculous."

"—and they want you to use a ruler, so that if there's water damage and you claim shrinkage . . ."

I've heard it said that any publicity is good publicity, as long as they spell your name right. I think I heard it said by Teresa Wright. I told Barry to cancel the policy. I don't need that kind of publicity, I said, and I'm not going to lower my personal standards just to get a few lines in a newspaper column. "As far as I'm concerned," I told him, "honesty is the best policy."

"Maybe," he agreed, "but you can't collect on it for flood damage."

I couldn't get too angry with him; I understood what he was trying to do. He was concerned that my portrayal of Lawrence's lover would damage my reputation when the film was released, so he was trying to take the offensive. Personally, I wasn't worried about that at all. I agreed with my agent, I believed that audiences were sophisticated enough to realize that simply because you played a character in a motion picture, you didn't become that person. So I didn't even give it a second thought. Instead, I got married.

It wasn't a quick decision. I'd been seriously considering it for hours and hours. Her name was Courtney Burke, and I'd met her while I was divorcing Sue King. She worked for my divorce attorney. She was everything Sue King wasn't: smart, plain-looking, and flat-chested. It wouldn't be accurate to describe our romance as love at first sight; to be accurate, probably not even love at the first couple of thousand sights.

We were friends long before we became lovers, and I liked her very much. In retrospect, we ruined a good friendship by getting married. I knew she was special from the very first night we had dinner. I'll never forget how she looked in my eyes across the counter and said those magical words that every man yearns to hear: "I really don't intend to get married as long as I live."

Among the many things I liked about her was that she was down to earth. Well, in Hollywood it's more down to wall-to-wall carpeting. But she wasn't the slightest bit impressed by stardom or celebrities. Most of the time we'd just spend quiet evenings in her house, eating cold pizza and warm ice cream—she never was much of a cook—and playing games like Special Scrabble, which was made especially for bad spellers, and Nationalist Chinese Checkers, which looked just like regular Chinese checkers but was played on a much smaller board.

At first I took her for granted. It was only when I was in the desert, boiling in the daytime, freezing in the nights, getting eaten by gnats and mosquitoes and strange flying things, worrying about poisonous snakes, living with filthy camels, using an outhouse, wearing soggy clothes, eating sand-encrusted food out of rusted tin cans, that I finally began to appreciate her. She was always so trusting: When she beat me at Special Scrabble, for example, she was always willing to accept my check without requiring two forms of identification.

I don't know precisely what it was that made me finally realize that we should be married. Perhaps it was that worried call from my publicity agent, but I prefer to believe it was that warm feeling of security that I got from Courtney when she told me, "I don't care if everybody is right, that once people see you playing this role you'll never work again in this life, and if you're reincarnated as an actor, in your next life either. I'll always love you."

How could I resist a woman like that? We drove directly to Disneyland, and under maritime law permitting a captain to perform marriages on his vessel, we were married by Captain Hook aboard his pirate ship, the *Jolly Roger*. After the ceremony I was dizzy from happiness, either from the wedding or from the ride on the Mad Hatter's Teacup. Everything was wonderful.

She started changing right after the ceremony. She had been wearing a beige summer dress and changed into a brown pantsuit, and from that point on she never stopped. I guess the first real hint I got that things were going to be different came when I asked her where she wanted to go on our honeymoon. She told me she wanted to go sailing. Well, that was unexpected. In all the time we'd spent together she'd never shown the slightest interest in boating. "That'd be fun," I agreed. "Where would you like to sail?"

"I. Magnin's, Lord and Taylor's, maybe Gucci, wherever they're having a sale."

The world premiere of *Lawrence of Arabia* was held at the legendary Egyptian Theatre. This was the first traditional Hollywood premiere I'd ever attended, and admittedly, I was very excited by the prospect of seeing myself on the giant screen. Although a large crowd of people surrounded the theater, this must have been a very bad neighborhood, because every few seconds huge searchlights swept the area.

As we walked up the red carpet, an elderly autograph seeker leaned over the red velvet rope and thrust a pen and a slip of paper at me. "Would you sign this for me, please?" she pleaded.

Naturally, I was delighted. I asked, "What would you like me to write?"

"Oh, just sign your name."

That seemed silly to me, but I did as she asked. I wrote "Your name" and handed it back to her. People can be very strange.

Courtney and I had just settled into our seats when the lights dimmed. My new bride squeezed my hand tightly and asked, "Nervous?"

"Sure, this is a bad neighborhood to be in in the dark. Didn't you see those searchlights?" Just then the majestic theme filled the theater and the first showing of *Lawrence of Arabia* began.

O'Toole had been absolutely correct; within moments of the start of the picture I got very thirsty and went to the refreshment stand to get a cold drink. And as soon as I saw the long line of people at the stand not watching the movie, I knew it was going to be a big success.

I watched more than half the picture before I realized that something was missing from it: me. I'd been cut out of the movie. Gone. Air Nielsen. As I watched that film, I suddenly understood the loneliness and vulnerability of an infected appendix. Worse, without the presence of my character, the film didn't make any sense at all. Without my character, Lawrence lacked the motivation to conquer the Arab world. Whom did he do it for? Omar Sharif?

David Lean did attempt to create some sort of silly relationship between O'Toole and Sharif, who played a chic Arab. It didn't work at all, although as I watched those segments of the film, I have to admit feeling an occasional pang of jealousy. How could Lawrence have even looked at him when my character was available?

Later, David Lean explained to me that he believed my scenes with Lawrence were much too graphic for American audiences. To prove it, he sent me copies of the graphs, as well as a very nice note reading, "I would like to offer my deep appreciation for your hard work and devotion to this motion picture. It certainly would not have been as successful with you. Sincerely . . ."

Was I terribly disappointed at being edited out of the film? Would Custer rather have been on the *Titanic*? I remember driving home from the theater that night in shock and looking over at my wife and realizing she was my wife. She sensed that I was very upset and tried to comfort me. "Oh, it's not so bad," she said soothingly, "you can always grow a beard or change your name. Do you speak Portuguese?"

Truthfully, it was not for personal reasons that I was so upset, but rather for the damage that had been done to the integrity of the film. It would have been selfish of me to place my own career above the success of the film, and I would never do that. I'll bet you can't name two actors who would do such a thing. All right, then I'll bet you can't name two thousand. I think the reviews of the film justified my feelings. Oh, sure, it received ten Academy Award nominations and won seven Oscars, including Best Picture, and was among the top box-office hits of the year. But remember, that was without me!

My friends and business associates tried to be supportive. Several friends of mine celebrated my performance in the movie by throwing a small dinner party in my honor and neglecting to invite me. Others tried to find humor in the situation, telling me that *Larab* was the best movie I'd never been in. I disagreed with them; I've always believed that *Gone With the Wind* was the best picture I never made.

Unfortunately, my publicity agent had booked me on "The Tonight Show" starring Johnny Carson two nights after the opening of the movie, and it was much too late to cancel. I met

Carson for the first time when he came into the makeup room about a half-hour before airtime. "There's absolutely no reason to be nervous about this show," he explained. "The great thing about it is that it's all spontaneous. If you make a fool out of yourself, the audience thinks you're being hip. So, just be yourself and you'll be a big hit."

A few minutes later I walked out into the corridor and bumped right into Big Ed McMahon. But I got right up and introduced myself, telling him, "It's a real pleasure to meet you."

"Eeeee-yooooo," Ed replied with a friendly smile, then laughed heartily.

I was Johnny's second guest that night, right after Dr. Martin Luther King, Jr., who discussed advances in vitamin therapy. Dr. King was a tough act to follow. At first I was a little shy, but then I remembered something I'd been very curious about. "At the end of the show," I asked Johnny, "Ed always says that the 'Tonight Show' is live on tape. Does that mean that right now we're live or not?"

Johnny considered that, finally deciding, "We're live, unless you're watching us. If you're watching us, we're not live."

"So am I live?" I wondered.

"Yes and no," Johnny explained. "Depends on when. Right, Ed?"

"Eeeee-yooooo," Ed said thoughtfully, then laughed heartily.

Johnny and I chatted a few minutes more about the usual talk show subjects, the latest scientific advances, the growing illiteracy rate in America, the drought in West Africa, male lesbians with unmanageable hair trying to become country singers, and finally *Lawrence of Arabia*. "I understand you've brought us a clip from your new movie," he said. "Let's take a look at it and you can tell us what we're seeing."

This was the moment I'd been dreading. Rather than looking at the monitor, where clips were usually shown, I reached into my pocket and pulled out several feet of exposed film that had been cut out of the movie. As I held it over my head for the audience to see, I explained, "This is a key scene in which Peter O'Toole as T. E. Lawrence is leading me into his tent."

Someone from the audience shouted, "Could you hold it up a little higher, please?"

Johnny leaned across his desk and pointed to some dark marks on the film. "And what are these things right here?"

"Footprints, Johnny," I explained. "That's where people in the cutting room were stepping on it."

"I see," he said, shaking his head in wonderment. "Well, I've always been fascinated by the technical side of filmmaking."

"Eeeee-yoooo," Ed agreed, then laughed heartily.

As I rewound my clip, the audience gave me a nice round of applause. "That was terrific," Johnny said, "just terrific. Hey, can you stay with us for a few more minutes, or do you have to run?"

I didn't know how to respond. I fumbled for an answer. Johnny had three types of guests on his show: young performers who did their act and were not invited to sit on the couch, celebrity guests who finished their interview and moved to the far end of the couch while the next guest was brought on, and the stars who were so busy that they didn't have time to sit on the far end of the couch for fifteen minutes while Johnny paid attention to someone else. Big stars generally had to rush off immediately after their interview. So, what to do? I really wanted to stay, I wanted to sit next to Big Ed and kibitz with Johnny and his next guest. On the other hand, I wondered what the audience would think of me if I stayed. Perhaps: If he's such a big star, how come he has nothing to do for the next fifteen minutes? Bob Hope always has something to do. "I'd like to stay, Johnny," I finally said with a sigh, "but I've got an emergency excuse I've got to take care of."

"Hey, it was great having you. Come back and see us again soon, huh? And we'll all go and not see you in *Lawrence of Arabia*."

"Love to." I turned and shook hands with Ed. "Nice meeting you."

"Eeeee-yooooo," Ed agreed.

For many years the existence of these "lost scenes" from *Lawrence* was overlooked in courses taught about the film. It was only a few years ago, when film historians began "restoring" classic motion pictures such as *Spartacus, Napoleon, The Wizard of Oz,* and *Superman and the Mole People* that I was approached about these scenes. Apparently the clips in my possession were the only known copies of these "lost scenes" in existence, and I was offered a considerable amount of money to provide copies of them so that they might be reedited into the film. It was a difficult decision to make, but finally I decided against it. I decided to let the film stand as David Lean had released it, let it remain a monument to his genius, to his talent and his passion. I felt the film for which he had won the Academy Award as Best Director should not be changed, rather it should serve to honor his memory.

However, if you act quickly, a copy of these scenes can be your very own. For a limited time only, a select number of signed and numbered copies of these scenes is being made available for the amazingly low price for this incredible piece of motion-picture history of only $129.95 plus shipping and handling. This offer will not be repeated in this book, and these clips will never be available in local video stores. One copy to a family, please. For more information, please contact the publisher in your local area. This offer is not valid in New Jersey.

In this way I can protect David Lean's legacy.

I wanted to get back to work as quickly as possible after *Larab* was released. Hollywood has a very short memory: it's the only place in the world where they give refresher courses about the meaning of traffic-signal colors. People in the movie business live by the code, What have you done for me . . . for me . . . recently? No. Last week? No. I instructed my agent to find me a picture getting ready to start shooting. He sent me the "treatment" of the first Hollywood vehicle to be directed by legendary Italian director Federico Fellini. It was called *La Bessa Me Mucho*, or, as it is roughly translated, *Much Bessa Me*. This was an autobiographical film about the tortured process Fellini had gone through in order to film his own life story. They wanted me to play the role of the Killer of Dreams, which in real life was probably Fellini's father or his accountant.

In the language of Hollywood, when a script is submitted to an actor after other actors have been offered the part and turned it down, the script is described as having "fingerprints all over it." For example, producer Blake Edwards had offered me the lead role in his gripping detective movie *The Pink Panther*, the story of an obsessed detective's relentless pursuit of a master jewel thief. Unfortunately, the script was ruined by attempts at humor that slowed down the action. I met with Edwards several times and agreed to play his Inspector Clouseau only if those jokes were taken out of the script. When he refused, I turned down the part. So when Peter Sellers got the script, he found "Leslie Nielsen's fingerprints all over it."

There is no formal script for a Fellini film, rather a long "statement of purpose" from the master, outlining the way the action may or may not proceed "depending," as he wrote, "on my fortunes the night before." This statement was about twenty-five pages long, and as soon as I looked at it, I knew the part had been offered to several other actors before me. It didn't just have Cary Grant's fingerprints on it, it also had the remnants of his tuna fish sandwich. From Grant it had obviously gone to Paul Newman, who left little pieces of popcorn stuck to some of the pages with olive oil. After Newman, Steve McQueen had left his whiskey-glass stains on several pages, Walter Matthau had noted his selections for the sixth race at Santa Anita on it, Warren Beatty had written several phone numbers on it, Orson Welles had left a lovely béarnaise sauce with just a hint of basil on it, Yul Brynner had left several stubby little hairs, and Walter Brennan had left one false tooth embedded in a page. When my agent called to find out how I liked this document, I told him the truth: "This is the dirtiest thing I've ever read."

"Great," Weisman said, "it'll make a fortune."

Although I had some minor reservations about the part as it was described, I thrilled at the opportunity to work with Fellini. Besides, the role offered me exactly what I was looking for at that time: a job. I accepted the part.

I met Federico Fellini the morning we were scheduled to begin filming my scenes. It was a meeting I'd been looking forward to for a long, long time. I'd seen every motion picture he'd ever made, and I was convinced that Federico Fellini was either one of the greatest filmmakers who has ever lived, a true genius, or that he was totally bonkers. A real nut job. I wanted to find some way of relating to him in a meaningful way, some language to communicate with him on a level he might understand, the words to let him know that I understood him and that I was not just another actor looking for a paycheck. When we were introduced he greeted me rather formally, but politely, and said in English that he was pleased to work with me. I responded by looking right at him and singsonging, "Fellini, Fellini, Bo-Bellini, banana-fana-foe-alini, fee-fi-foe mailini, Fellini."

It worked! Federico Fellini looked at me as if *I* were strange. I was thrilled. I'd gotten through to him. Fellini thought I was strange!

Among the many aspects I'd appreciated about Fellini's films was his use of symbolism set against a canvas of stark realism. His films are peopled with bizarre characters: a prostitute who has sex with men for money, a chicken farmer who willingly sells his stock to be brutally slaughtered, a nurse who spends hours every day taking blood from living, breathing children, a garbage man who earns his living by picking up the waste of society. So naturally I was curious to see how his characters would employ symbolism in this film.

Before we began shooting my scenes, Fellini gathered the actors around him, like a shepherd gathering his flock, to explain his intention. "I believe in the truth of reality," he said, "but there is more than one truth. A man and a woman together; is it sex or is it love? A beautiful drawing; is it art or is it a comic book? A roasted turkey; is it Thanksgiving or cannibalism? The dream sequence we will shoot now; is it really a dream or is it simply a scene in a movie? These are the perceptions of reality with which we must contend. You will do just as I command when I command. Someday, if you become a famous Italian director, you make your own dream come true. But today, my dream."

Fellini then described his dream for us: it takes place in the stark white operating room of a great metropolitan hospital. The walls of the room are slanted at severe angles, both horizontally and vertically. Hanging on these walls are very formal portraits from the seventeenth century. An operating table is in the center of this room. A beautiful woman is lying naked on the operating table. A man wearing a clown's bright red nose and a cardboard witch's hat enters the room and takes off all his clothes, then climbs onto the table and begins making love to the woman.

The faces in the portraits come alive and begin laughing derisively. In the background, the lightly tinkling bells of an ice cream vendor are heard. In one corner of the room, an aged rabbi is crying in despair. Suddenly, I enter, dressed in a gray flannel suit, carrying a sharpened penis in my hand. I go over to the couple as they writhe in ecstasy, grab the man's shoulder, and pull him off the woman; then I start cutting her with my sharpened penis. Blood spurts from her wounds. Everyone is stunned by a blinding white light. The entire screen is bleached white, and as the brightness fades, everyone reappears dressed in white, wearing angels' wings. The only color in the entire scene is a stream of bright red blood dripping from the wounded woman.

As he finished describing his dream, Fellini's head dropped to his chest in emotional exhaustion. Emily Connors, who was playing the woman, leaned over and whispered to me, "How come all I dream is that I registered for a college class and forgot to go, and they're giving the final exam and I can't find the classroom?"

"I wonder what he had to eat the night before," I whispered right back.

Fellini finally asked if any of us had questions before we began filming. "Yes, I have one," I said. "Could you explain the symbolism of the sharpened penis?"

"Ah, you noticed that," he replied. "Good. The penis is a phallic symbol."

"Uh-huh!" I responded. "Just as I suspected. Representing what?" Fellini hesitated, then admitted, "The Washington Monument."

The acclaimed Neil Simonian actor Joseph Spinelli was cast as the Lover. Several of the film industry's most respected stunt laughers were playing the Faces in the Frames. And Rabbi Attia of the Reformed congregation St. Andrew by the Sea was making his screen debut as the Rabbi in Despair. Just before we began, Fellini reminded us, "It must be real. Make it real." Then he ordered, "Lights," and the hot lights were turned on; "Cameras," and the twin Bolex Regents began rolling; and finally, he pointed his wooden crutch toward the set and commanded, "Begin, please."

Connors was lying naked on the operating table. Spinelli entered and happened to notice her. He moved toward her, shedding clothes faster than Oliver North got rid of the evidence. He climbed onto the operating table. "Make love to her!" Fellini screamed. "Make it real. I demand reality." Incredibly, Spinelli actually began making love to Connors as the cameras rolled.

In the background the stunt laughers began laughing derisively. "More hysteria," Fellini ordered, "I need real laughter, from the mind."

In the corner, Rabbi Attia began crying. "More despair," urged Fellini, "I need more despair. Cry for humanity. Cry for man's brutality." Clearly he was not getting the despair he wanted. "Cry like I'm going to hire a rabbi with more despair." Finally, Rabbi Attia produced real despair.

The scene became a cacophony of emotion: sex and love, laughter, despair. It had taken on a reality of its own, it had become Fellini's circus of life. It looked real, it felt real. I had become the Dream Killer. On cue, I entered and looked around. I took five steps and reached the operating table, hitting my marks as if they weren't even there. I grabbed Spinelli's shoulder and brutally tore him off Connors and threw him to the ground. In that moment, I had become the scorned lover intent on destroying this dream. It was all so real. I held the sharpened penis above my head, my hand started moving down. Fellini screamed, "Cut! Cut!"

His voice shocked me back to real reality. "No!" I yelled, whirling on him. "I won't. You're crazy. Do you understand, you're crazy!" I looked at my hand and now the offending phallic symbol there, still poised, ready to cut. It seared into my hand and I dashed it to the ground, then stormed angrily off the set. For a moment I'd become part of his mad dream. Fortunately, I'd escaped before it was too late; I didn't care if I had ruined the shot.

"Bravo!" I heard Fellini shout from the darkness behind the camera. "Bravo!"

When I calmed down, I returned to the set and went to speak to him. "I'm sorry for ruining the scene," I apologized.

"No matter," he said.

"You're not upset?"

"I have different dream every day. Maybe tomorrow I dream it this way. Dreams are the most wonderful value. They come in full color, they star people you like, they give best imitation of reality, and they cost nothing. But film? Film is very expensive. It's much cheaper to redream than to reshoot."

As long as I live, I will never forget the third day of filming. We were just getting started when Fellini suddenly halted the scene and called us together to tell us the tragic news: President John F. Kennedy had been assassinated in Dallas, Texas. We were stunned, shocked, but after discussing it, we voted to continue working. We felt the president would have wanted it that way. And keeping busy, keeping our minds occupied, seemed to help. It was rough on everybody, but particularly on the stunt laughers, who really struggled. Everyone moved as if they were in soft Jell-O. This was a tremendous tragedy for the entire motion-picture industry.

No one will ever forget where they were when they heard the news. Being on the set of a Fellini movie, I couldn't decide if it was real or surreal.

Soon after the shock of those few weeks had lifted and we'd returned to our normal lives,

Among the few souvenirs I've kept is the slate, or clapper, from the only film I made with Fred Fellini, La Bessa Me Mucho (Much Bessa Me).

speculation began that Lee Harvey Oswald had not acted alone, that in fact he was part of a complex conspiracy to murder the president. Through the years just about everyone has at one time or another been accused of being part of this conspiracy, from the CIA and the Mafia to officers of the Triborough Bridge and Tunnel Authority. Personally, I paid little attention to these "conspiracy theories" until I was offered the role of Texas Court of Appeals Judge John "Sage" Brush in Ollie Stone's controversial film *JFK*.

As part of my research for that role I read almost anything that had been written about the assassination. One day, as I read and reread Warren Beatty's testimony before the Warren Commission, suddenly it all became clear. All the pieces fit together, except for a little one with sort of rounded edges that might have come from another puzzle. I realized that I knew who had killed John F. Kennedy, and I'd known it all along. I called Stone at his farm and told him I had to see him right away.

"What are you trying to tell me?"

"I think I know who killed you-know-who. I'll meet you in your cornfield."

"No, not there," he said nervously, "cornfields have ears."

As I drove to his house late that night, I used back roads whenever possible. When I had to use the Santa Monica Freeway, I slipped casually into the middle of a funeral procession. That provided good cover, although eight cars followed me into Stone's long driveway.

Stone and I met in the middle of his swimming pool. "It just happened," I explained. "I was reading all this material about the assassination, and then I put one and one together. And guess what I came up with?"

"Eleven?" he asked suspiciously. His eyes narrowed in thought. "You think a football team did it?"

"Uh, not exactly," I admitted. "What I meant was, all of a sudden everything became clear to me. With all the books and magazine stories that have been written, there's only one theory that has been completely overlooked."

"Evil spirits?" Stone suggested.

"No, there's only one person who had the motive, the access, and the alibi to pull this off."

He paddled closer and said very quietly, "Go ahead."

I looked around to be certain no one was lurking nearby. Somewhere in the dark night, a dog howled. I said bluntly, "Marilyn Monroe."

Stone started paddling toward the side of the pool. "She happened to be dead at the time."

"Sure," I agreed, "the perfect alibi. No one would ever suspect her. A lot of people are supposed to be dead. Elvis. William Casey. But what if she wasn't? When people are dead, you don't see them. Since people think she's dead, when they see her, they don't believe she is who she really is, so they could be missing her anywhere in the country. It's the perfect cover. Did anyone report seeing her in Dallas that day?"

"No", he admitted.

"I rest my case."

Stone drifted on the rippling surface of his pool. I could see I'd caught his interest. "Why?" he challenged me.

"It's obvious. She loved the guy. There was no way he could get a divorce. So she set up her death first. Then with him supposedly dead, they could be together and no one would be the wiser. They could go live on an island somewhere where no one would recognize them."

"I don't know," Stone said. "What about the story that he'd dumped her when she found out about his relationship with the Mob?"

"Okay, that's her second motive. She hated the guy. But I don't think that was true, I think that was a red herring."

Stone took a deep breath. In the distance I could hear the crickets singing their song, an a cappella version of "Peggy

Sue." "The whole thing sounds kind of fishy to me. Where's the proof?"

"It's obvious. You know as well as I do that the only people in this country who can keep a secret are Woodward and Bernstein and the dead. If any of the other theories was true, somebody would have talked to the *Enquirer* by now. But nobody's sold a word. Therefore, it had to be someone already dead. And who had a better motive?"

He shook his head. "I don't know. How'd she set it up?"

"That was the easy part. She had plenty of money, she'd collected all her life insurance benefits."

It made such obvious sense to me that I was surprised no one else had put these pieces together before me. It was simply the old story of love gone south, in this case all the way to Dallas, Texas. Stone didn't know what to do with my theory. He'd invested a lot of time and energy in his own assassination theory: if you blame absolutely everybody, you can make a lot of money.

Stone asked me to keep quiet about my suspicions, and until this page I've never revealed them to anyone else. Can I prove it? No. Do I believe it? The answer is certainly questionable. Just remember one thing: you read it here first.

Bessa Me Mucho was probably Fellini's most misunderstood picture, perhaps because the creative energy we shared seemed to dissipate after the assassination. I think we all simply wanted to finish the work and take some time off to reexamine our lives. Fellini was very gracious; he told me once that he'd never seen an actor with the kind of talent I have. I knew I'd earned his respect the day we finished shooting my scenes—I'll never forget his parting words: "Nielsen, Nielsen, Bo-Bealsen, banana-fana-for-ealsen, fee-fi-foe mameilsen, Nielsen."

As with so many other people, the assassination of John F. Kennedy marked the end of one chapter of my life. I'd come to Hollywood and established myself as an actor. Finally, it was time to begin an exciting new chapter—a chapter I call Chapter 6.

6

THE BEST TIME OF MY LIFE — 5:45 P.M.

I 'd been looking forward to this chapter since the very beginning of my life. President Kennedy's assassination reminded everyone that life is fragile, and I felt closer to my wife than at any other time in our entire marriage. The knowledge that I had someone who really cared about me as a person rather than simply as a handsome movie star made me feel secure. I remember asking her one day, "Suppose I lost everything, every penny, and I couldn't get a job. Would you still love me?"

She answered immediately, "Of course I'd still love you. And I'd miss you very, very much."

For the first time in my life I felt a tremendous desire to settle down, to buy a house, put down roots, raise my own weeds if I wanted to, and I began looking for that dream house.

Fortunately, we could afford to buy something very nice. I'd earned a lot of money in the movie business, and Cronson, my financial adviser, had invested it well. He'd protected a substantial amount of capital by investing it in a solid tax shelter, one of the largest mosquito-breeding farms in southern New Jersey. Apparently we were breeding some of the healthiest mosquitoes on the East Coast. Good for fishing and things like that. He'd also bought several thousand shares of Hearse Motor Corporation when company executives had announced plans to produce a full line of passenger vehicles. He felt strongly that Hearse's high consumer-satisfaction rating, their proven ability to produce a luxury car with a large amount of rear storage space, and their catchy slogan, "Hearse—Going in Style," almost guaranteed their success. Although we'd lost some money on that investment the first year, he reassured me that that was due primarily to start-up costs and that the stock would recover when the sports Hearse went on sale.

Courtney and I worked with the former child actress Barbaree Earl, the legendary real estate counselor to the stars, who showed us numerous houses and was able to recite the history of each of them. Looking at houses was like peering into Hollywood's past. We saw the small, but comfortable house where Ronald Reagan and Jane Wyman had lived during their marriage. We saw the house Mae West built with eight bedrooms and no kitchen. Barbaree showed us the small bungalow in which Gary Cooper and Clara Bow had consummated their affair. We saw the fabled Tin estate, which she said had been built by Rin Tin for his bride, a real bitch whose expensive tastes forced him to work like a dog. That was her real estate story for that day. The house was lovely, but very small. It consisted of one large windowless room, and the fact that we had to crawl in and crawl out made it somewhat inconvenient. Barbaree said we could steal it for $675,000. Conversely, we saw the Young mansion, built by Mighty Joe as a wedding gift to Loretta after his early successes. I could tell even before we went inside that the place was too big for us—the knob on the front door was eleven feet high. Barbaree called it a bargain at $2,225,000. I told her that the only thing that was a bargain at $2,225,000 was $3,000,000. Eventually Courtney and I found a house that we both liked, a beautiful ten-room ranch on a lake, surrounded by majestic trees, with a perfect view of the sun setting over the crystal-clear water. "It's all wrong," Barbaree said as she dismissed it, "the location is terrible."

"Terrible?" I couldn't accept that. "Look at it, it's perfect."

"No, it's not," she corrected me, "it's on the wrong side of the fold."

A fat trout broke the surface of the lake, sending gentle ripples to the shoreline. Birds circled in wait, screeching at the billowy clouds floating across the August sky. "The wrong side of the fold?" Courtney repeated. "I don't understand. What does that mean?"

"It's a real estate term meaning just about your entire career, that's all," Barbaree replied. "See, this house is so far out of town that it'll be on the back side of the fold of every important map of the movie stars' homes in existence. It probably won't even make the auxiliary bus tour."

"Is that really important?" I asked, perhaps naively.

"Only if you want to keep working. You know the expression 'Get on the map'? Well, this is the map they're talking about. Studio executives pay close attention to those things. They'll look at the map and wonder why you're living all the way over there on the other side of the fold. That'll make 'em a little nervous about you, and maybe they won't offer you an important part, and then, before you know it, there goes the career. Maybe this is a nice place, but it's on the wrong side of the Santa Ana fold."

That afternoon Barbaree drove us across the map into Beverly Hills. Actually, it wasn't Beverly Hills proper, rather a small area on the outskirts of Beverly Hills known as Beverly Landfill. And there, nestled in a grove of dead trees, overlooking a swamp, was an old run-down house that looked as if it had been abandoned by the Addams family. All the windows were broken, the door was off its hinges, grass was growing through cracks in the concrete, and there was a large hole in the roof, a hole that Barbaree insisted on referring to as "the skylight."

"That's not a skylight," I pointed out, "that's a big hole in the roof."

"Pessimist," she hissed, then said politely, "Now, this is the kind of place that you really want to buy."

Courtney started crying. "It's awful," she said.

"It's a wreck," I agreed. "Why would anybody want to buy this place?"

"Because it's got the right address," Barbaree explained. "It's very simple. You're not buying a house—anybody can buy a house—you're buying an image. An address. Believe me, this address is a bargain at a million two, an absolute bargain."

I had an idea. "Couldn't we just move this address to a cheaper neighborhood?"

So that I would never forget where I came from, I purchased this old cottage from Ft. Norman (left) and had it moved to Los Angeles (below).

Barbaree chuckled. "You see, this is what's wrong. You think you're buying this house for yourselves. You're thinking only about your own pleasure. It's your duty as a movie star to buy this house, to live at this address. For a movie star a house isn't a home, it's a statement, it's eight pages in *Architectural Digest*, it's a statement to all your fans: 'This house is who I think I am!' You're not buying it for yourself, you're buying it for all the people who could never possibly afford to buy a house like this, all those people whose fantasies you're fulfilling, all those people who can sleep at night secure in the knowledge that their idols are living out their dreams. Are you going to tell them that being a movie star isn't really as wonderful as they think it is? Are you going to destroy the entire Hollywood myth by not buying this house? Because if you are, I don't want any part of it."

"But look at this place," I insisted. "It's old, it's run-down. What are all those people going to think when they see it?"

She looked at me quizzically. "See it? Oh, they're never going to see it. The very first thing you'll have to do is put up a big fence in front so they can't see it. I can tell you from experience, the less they see of this house, the more impressed they're going to be."

I wavered. "How soon can we get a fence put in?"

Barbaree smiled triumphantly. "I'll call Sammy Davis, Jr., and find out."

There are three stages to any home construction or renovation project: planning, building, and divorce. Courtney and I learned more about each other during the renovation of our exclusive Beverly Landfill address than we had in all the time since we'd known each other. Until that time I'd just never realized her tastes were so extravagant. For example, when I asked her where she wanted the washer and dryer to go, she told me, "Oh, they can live downstairs." And one day she went to a garage sale in Bel Air to pick up a few things: that didn't work out; she bought two garages.

But we had our biggest fights over the swimming pool. Swimming pools have long been among the movie colony's most important status symbols. There is a story that after Sam Goldwyn had built what was then the largest private swimming pool in the Western Hemisphere, Walter Winchell told him that Freud would have described the pool as "the material manifestation of an insecure ego."

"Yeah?" Goldwyn supposedly replied. "And how big is Freud's pool?"

Initially, status was derived from the size of the pool. Mine's bigger than yours. Then it became the material used to construct the pool, which ranged from imported Italian mosaic tiles to mirrors. Mirrors were made illegal, incidentally, when Mae West almost drowned because she couldn't tear herself away from her pool bottom. Then the shape of the pool became important, and those shapes included Jayne Mansfield's heart-shaped pool, Artie

Shaw's elongated clarinet, Randolph Scott's cowboy hat, and W. C. Fields's liquor bottle. Fields surprised everyone, I was told, by filling his pool with water. Recently, the most important thing about a pool is that it look like anything except a pool. When Bob's Actors president Jack Larson bought a Bel Air estate, he had a natural pond on the property drained and filled. Then he installed a swimming pool that looked exactly like a natural pond. And when TV producer Aaron Spelling built his mammoth home, his pool and poolhouse were designed to resemble the hydroelectric plant overlooking the Niagara River—only bigger.

Courtney and I just couldn't agree on the type of pool we wanted. Eventually we sought the advice of a respected "pool therapist," who helped us work through our fears that we would build a pool of which we would be ashamed. "Remember," he explained, "it's not the size or the shape of the pool that matters, It's the status of the people who swim in it Real friends will swim in any pool you build.

"A pool is nothing more than a reflection of the way you think about yourself. Do you see yourself as a plastic, above-ground individual, or a more substantial, well-grounded person?"

We finally decided on a heart-shaped pool and met with legendary pool adviser Robert Fielding to determine precisely what we would build. Fielding told us that there were many variations of the heart-shaped theme: the Danny Kaye, which was just a large heart; the Gable-Lombard, two smaller pools forming a broken heart; the Lawyer's Heart, which was a smaller model; and finally, he said, "the Agent's Heart."

"What's that?" I asked.

"Actually, it's no pool at all, but you're permitted to tell people you have one." I asked him about the size of the pool and he replied, "That depends. How big is your checkbook?"

That was a problem. My checkbook probably wasn't much bigger than three inches by five inches. I could barely dip my toe into that.

During the renovations Courtney and I seemed to find something to fight about every day. One night I came home and she was sulking in the bathtub and . . .

"That's soaking," she corrected, "I was soaking. But that's the problem with you. Every single thing I do or say is wrong and . . ."

"Excuse me," I told her, "this is my book and you were sulking. You're wrong about that."

"See," she said happily, "I'm finally right about something."

One of the most important lessons I learned during this renovation was that the size of a house is inversely proportional to the amount of time you spend in it. The larger it is, the more expensive it is, the longer you have to work to pay for it, the less time you get to spend there. So I owe a great debt of gratitude, as well as several mortgage payments, to this house.

Although I've never read any of the biographies or magazine articles written about me, most of them consider the next few years the most productive period of my career. As Pulitzer Prize–winning critic Robert Allen wrote in the biography *Actor: The Leslie Nielsen Story*, which I've never read twice just to be certain I hadn't read it the first time, "Then followed the halcyon period of Nielsen's illustrious career, during which he appeared in a remarkable range of leading and supporting roles in several of the most important motion pictures ever produced by American filmmakers. Nielsen's presence in these films brought attention to some of them that might otherwise have been overlooked by all but the most serious filmactics."

I guess the beginning of this period could be dated to the brief appearance I made as a favor to Al Hitchcock, who had run into serious difficulty with his daring thriller *The Birds*. After completion of principal photography of this film, which was the story of a sharp-beaked revolt by thousands of little tiny birdies, Hitch realized his film wasn't working because his birds lacked motivation for their attacks on the town of San Pedro, California. After Hitch and I viewed the rough assembly, the first version of the film, we decided to add the prologue featuring my character, an insane ornithologist ridiculed by the people of San Pedro as "The Birdbrain," who tortured canaries with electric canary prods, then forced them to listen to Dominugo Mundungo's recording of "Nel Blue Del Pinto de Blue"/"Your Love Has Given Me Wings," before turning them loose on the town.

From there I went right into *Doctor Zhivago*. In one of those odd twists of show business fate, the legendary Zero Mostel had been signed to play the role of Teyve Budinsky, Dr. Zhivago's malpractice attorney, but he dropped out when director David Lean decided to eliminate all the musical numbers from the film. Lean then offered me the pivotal role of the idealistic lawyer who successfully defends Zhivago against government charges that while performing emergency brain surgery during Franco's Prussian War, instead of putting in a steel plate he had mistakenly installed a Limoges plate with a floral pattern.

I've always believed that Lean offered this part to me as a gesture of apology for editing me out of that movie. People often ask me why an actor will accept certain roles while turning down others, and there are as many answers to that question as there are roles. My reason for taking this part was that my contractor had found termites in the roof beams and had to install an entirely new roof on the house, at a cost of $72,000. Of such mundane matters is movie history made.

To prepare for the role as a malpractice attorney, I spent several days working in the real estate investment division of one of California's most successful negligence firms.

Much of *Doctor Zhivago* was filmed in Spain with the permission and full cooperation of Spanish dictator Generalissimo Francisco Franco. Late one afternoon, as we were filming my blistering interrogation of "government minister" Charles Laughton, the cameras suddenly ground to a halt and everything stopped. The Spanish technicians on the set seemed to recoil in fear as a thirty-car convoy arrived. Drivers jumped out of each of those cars and opened the rear doors, and from three cars, three Francos emerged. Later it was explained to me that Franco always traveled with several impersonators to foil assassination attempts. I'm embarrassed to admit that I didn't recognize him at first. With all the braid on their uniforms, I thought the three of them might have been actors from Richard Lester's sequel to *The Mouse That Roared,* which was filming in Barcelona. Fortunately, the three Francos recognized me and introduced themselves, each of them shaking my hand and advising, "Call me Franco."

"And call me a cab," I responded. Unfortunately, the Francos had never seen vaudeville. I invited them into my trailer for a cuppa.

People tend to believe that dictators are very different from anyone else, but the three Francos seemed to be an ordinary guy, who shared many of the same hopes and dreams as the rest of us. The Francos seemed very interested in events taking place in the United States. They particularly wanted to know how Joe DiMaggio was doing. Just before they had to go back to work, I said to them, "You've won a civil war and have led a great nation for decades. You've become an important world leader who is acknowledged to be one of the most complex and charismatic men in European history. You've been named Dictator of the Year an incredible six times, once supposedly dictating a record two hundred and thirty-four letters in an hour. Is there anything else you've ever dreamed of doing?"

The three Francos nudged one another, then blushed and admitted, "Well, is true, me think I mucho like to direct!"

I would probably have taken some time off after the completion of *Doctor Zhivago*, but my wife had decided to add a detached carport with a bedroom for her mother, so I agreed to create the role of Archer in Billy Wilder's classic tragicomic social commentary *Archer's Transformation*. Billy often claimed that this was the best picture he ever made, although at the time I don't think people appreciated its brilliance. It was considered somewhat experimental, combining the magic of animation with hard-hitting live action. Billy wrote the script with his longtime collaborator, I. A. L. "Aisle" Diamond. *Archer's Transformation* was a typical Hollywood metaphorical fable loosely combining the characters created by humorist Don Marquis, the legendary cockroaches Archy and Mehitabel, with Kafka's cockroach from *Metamorphosis*.

This marked the first opportunity I'd had to work with Walter Matthau, who played broken-down screenwriter Jack Dinglebee. Dinglebee had traded his once great career for broads and booze and could barely pay the rent on his one-room sublet underlooking Beverly Hills. One night, after Dinglebee had fallen into a drunken stupor, an ambitious young cockroach named Archer climbed onto his old Royal Standard and wrote twenty-five fabulous pages of a screenplay by leaping from key to key. It's never explained how Archer managed to put in clean sheets of paper, but sometimes the viewer just had to suspend belief.

Dinglebee is stunned when he finds these pages that he can't remember writing. This continues for several weeks, through three screenplays, until one night Dinglebee is awakened by Archer's cries and saves him from the cat. At that point Archer tells him the whole story. In this first part of the film I was the animated Archer's voice.

Dinglebee and Archer become friends and collaborators, earning a fortune. Dinglebee offers Archer anything he wants to keep writing, but all Archer wants is a safe, warm home for himself and his wife, Metha—who is pregnant with their 1,243,435th child—and those kids still living behind the refrigerator.

Through Archer's selfless guidance Dinglebee gradually recovers his pride and his talent. He stops drinking completely. In what I believe is one of the most poignant scenes ever filmed, the two of them reveal their innermost feelings and fears. For Dinglebee, life is a complex subject involving his relationship with his rigid father, tremendous self-doubt, and an unhealthy attachment to women's high heels. For Archer, life is much simpler. "Basically," he explained, "what it comes down to is, don't get squashed."

The second half of the film, certainly the more complex half, begins when Archer is accidentally exposed to fumes emitted by an array of cheeses that had been left in Jack's refrigerator for several years, then wakes up to discover that he has been turned into a human being. This is the point in the script at which the animation ended and I played the role. As time passes, I began to change emotionally as I had physically: I began savoring the material rewards my writing ability had earned for me. I abandon my family, leaving them just a few scraps of rotten lettuce, I lie to women, cheat on my tax returns, and finally demand a percentage of the gross receipts.

Ironically, now that I've become human, I'm turning into a real monster. I start to build a house, and it is obvious that the transformation is complete when a wasps' nest is found in the foundation and I hire an exterminator to kill them. I have become what Jack once was.

In the climactic scene, an Italian producer played flamboyantly by Jack Palance discovers me in bed with his mistress and shoots me. I stagger through the streets back to Jack's home, dying, and being transformed back into a cockroach. As Jack cradles me in his hand, with my last words I say, "Maybe"—cough, cough—"maybe you shouldn't have ever left that Velveeta in your refrigerator for three years."

"I'm glad I did," Walter responds, a river of tears flowing from his eyes, "and I'll never forget you, never. I'll take care of your kids, I'll find every damn one of them a college with really bad sanitary conditions, and I promise you this—as long as I live, I'll never again pick up a can of Raid."

Matthau and I shared a lot of laughs while making this movie. At that point in his life Walter was a heavy gambler; I mean, he'd bet on absolutely anything. Personally, there were a few times when I thought it might be getting a little out of hand. So at dinner one night I offered him a challenge. "Walter," I said, "I'll bet you couldn't even go one night without placing a bet."

"For how much?" he demanded.

"See. See?"

"And you've gotta give me good odds, too."

I was thrilled when the Academy nominated him as Best Actor for his performance. Sadly, though, as we parted, I made the mistake of saying to him, "I got a thousand that says you speak to me before I speak to you."

"You're on," he said, and we've never spoken again. And in some strange way, that's how we've managed to stay such close friends.

Although I'd originally intended to spend several weeks at home once *Archer's Transformation* wrapped, my wife had

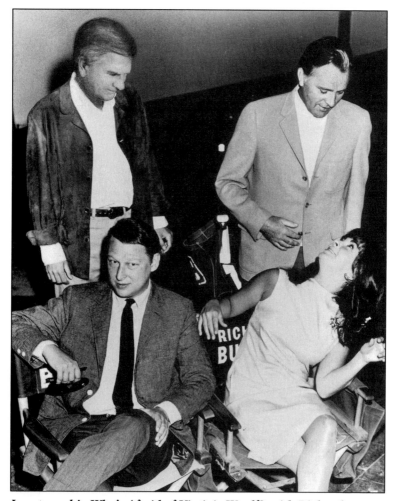

I costarred in Who's Afraid of Virginia Woolf? *with Richard Burton and Liz Taylor, directed by Mike Nichols. I played the cowardly liar, the only person really afraid of Virginia.*

decided to add a media room next to the salon. That meant taking out a wall, so I joined Elizabeth Taylor and Richard Burton in Mike Nichols's debut as a film director, *Who's Afraid of Virginia Woolf?* I played the cowardly liar Arnold Nurf, the only person in the film who actually was afraid of Virginia Woolf. It wasn't a particularly difficult role. Basically all I had to do was respond to Burton's sadistic taunts: "Virginia's waiting under your bed tonight" or "Watch out, Virginia's hiding in your closet," or "Arnie, would you go into the cellar and see what's making that strange noise?" Elizabeth, meanwhile, taunted me by singing the familiar children's rhyme "Virginia Woolf took a gun and shot her lover just for fun. / And from that day forth this tale she told, 'Don't blame me, blame Lee Harvey Oswald.'"

Nichols was a brilliant stage director, but since this was his first movie, he relied on us to help get him through some of the more difficult moments. In several interviews he has graciously credited me with teaching him the technique he still uses, as well as some of the basic directing terms: "Camera," "Lunch, thirty minutes," "Take off that blouse, sweetheart, and let's see your talent," and "Call my agent." It's nice of him to give me credit, but I never taught him any of those things.

It seemed odd that after all Elizabeth and I had been through apart, this was the first time we'd ever worked together, and the media revived all the old stories about our "affair." Elizabeth, Richard, and I laughed at those stories and . . . well, Elizabeth and I laughed at them. Elizabeth was the ultimate movie star. Until I worked with her I don't think I ever really appreciated the power of a true movie queen. Elizabeth could not do anything wrong. When she coughed in the middle of a scene, the sound man apologized. No matter what she did, someone was willing to make an excuse for her. There were, for example, some days when she was just a bit tardy arriving on the set. One day she showed up almost six hours late for her call. Six hours! We all had to sit and wait for her. I thought that was terribly unfair to those of us who had been there promptly only two hours late, so as she put on her makeup I confronted our producer, J. Dylan Richman. "How can you put up with this?" I demanded.

"With what?" he asked innocently.

"With what?" I replied sarcastically. "With Elizabeth being six hours late for her call today, that's with what."

"Oh, that. You don't understand. See, she wasn't six hours late today, she was actually eighteen hours early for tomorrow."

That's when I understood what it really meant to be a movie star.

Burton was great to work with. On the set he was completely professional, always on time and prepared, never complaining, always willing to share his scenes. The only problem was his drinking. Although I'd heard all the stories about his celebrated drinking problem, until I worked with him I didn't really believe those stories were true. I remember arriving on the set early one morning and finding Richard there, reading a tattered copy of Dylan Thomas's *Under Milk Wood*, finishing a fifth of Jack Daniel's. "It's a little early for that, isn't it, Richard?" I said softly.

"Not at all," he replied, raising his glass, "you can read Dylan Thomas anytime."

"That's not what I meant." I pointed to his glass. "That. Why do you drink so much?"

He sighed deeply, putting down the glass. His head dropped onto his chest and he told me, "My friend, I drink to forget."

I decided to press him. "To forget what?"

He looked up at me and smiled. "I forget." Then he threw his arms triumphantly into the air, looked into the heavens, and screamed, "IT'S WORKING!"

I was physically and emotionally exhausted by the time I'd finished *Woolf*. And frightened. Even now, every time I open my closet I'm a little afraid of what I'm going to find in there. I was anxious to get home; my bags were packed and I had my bus ticket. But just as I got ready to leave, my wife called, crying hysterically. Our landscaper, Mr. MacTavish, had discovered lime in our topsoil, which meant that he had to rip out the entire lawn, both the upper and lower gardens, even the tennis court. As Mr. MacTavish himself explained on the phone, "Ooo, Mr. Leslie, 'tis a sod, sod day."

I began to wonder if we had grounds for divorce. This was getting to be too much. Courtney and I had a big fight, but the result was that I went right back to work. Woisman had sent me a pile of scripts to read, among them Robert Bolt's screenplay for *A Man for All Seasons*. One of the few serious mistakes I've made in my career was that I didn't take the time to read this script. Only later did I learn that it was the stirring story of Sir Thomas More, who was beheaded by King Henry VIII for refusing to recognize the king's right to divorce. I'm embarrassed to admit that I turned it down when I read the title because I just sort of assumed it was the story of Princess SummerFallWinterSpring's husband, a man for all seasons, and I was sensitive to any story that exploited the proud Indians of the Television tribe.

Instead, I agreed to costar with Steve McQueen and Annette Funicello in Samuel Z. Arkoff's production of *The Sand Pebbles*. McQueen and I were just about the hottest young actors in the business, and this pairing created quite a lot of publicity. Annette really wasn't Arkoff's first choice, but when Katharine

Hepburn decided to pass on the role of the prudish school-teacher trapped in China who is rescued by McQueen and me, Arkoff had the part rewritten for a younger woman. Annette was just coming off her blockbuster hits, *Beach Blanket Bingo* and *How to Stuff a Wild Bikini*, and Arkoff believed she could make the transition to serious beach dramas.

From the first moment I met Steve McQueen it was obvious that he felt very competitive with me. You never really know what's going on inside an actor's head, sometimes it's nothing, but McQueen seemed to have a grudge against me. Actually, that helped our performances. I was cast as the captain of the old Chinese boat *The Sand Pebble*, on which we make our escape up the lazy Yangtze River, while he played a stroker on my crew. The conflict between us began the moment he came onboard my boat, looked around, and said, "Boy, this is some old junk."

"Maybe it's not the *Queen Elizabeth*," I bristled, "but that was a little harsh."

The conflict between us continued long after the cameras stopped. McQueen was the most outrageous scene-stealer I've worked with in my entire life. Scene-stealing is a fine art, the object being to attract the attention of the audience even when you're not the central character in the scene, and there are as many different ways to steal a scene as there are actors. These methods range from the subtle—Bette Davis would demurely avert her eyes when another actor was speaking to her—to the obvious—Marlon Brando gained so much weight there simply wasn't enough room on the screen for another actor. There was also the ridiculous; in *Grandma's Wacky Affair* Al Pacino had a long, dramatic monologue. Right in the middle of that monologue John Candy suddenly looked over Pacino's shoulder, opened his eyes as wide as possible, pointed, and screamed,

"Oh, my God! Look at that!" Pacino turned around, and naturally, there was nothing there. But Candy had stolen the scene from him.

McQueen should have worn a mask and carried a gun when he acted. He would do anything to dominate a scene. He was the kind of man who had intentionally been born ruggedly handsome and intensely charismatic just so he could attract the attention of the audience. But that wasn't enough for him. Then he deliberately studied acting at the Neighborhood Playhouse and Actors Studio so he would know what he was doing. But even that wasn't enough for him. Just to be on the safe side, he went into my trailer and found my marked-up copy of the

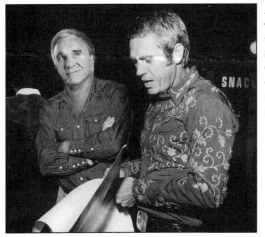

I never got along with Steve McQueen, my costar in The Sand Pebbles. *He was the kind of actor who'd use his looks, talent, and charisma to steal scenes.*

script, then literally stole my scenes. I still consider that the most blatant act of scene-stealing in motion-picture history.

I don't know why he was so jealous of me. Besides my good looks and my widely applauded talent and my winning personality, what else could have bothered him? Perhaps it was my legendary generosity. Maybe it was my renowned mastery of the cards. Could it have been the fact that small birds and butterflies somehow felt secure landing on my shoulders? I suspect it might even have been my widely praised humility. Whatever it was, while we were making the movie, he did everything possible to try to show me up. Every morning he'd come roaring onto the set straddling his turbocharged 1,250cc Harley-Davidson, raise his front wheel off the ground—a so-called wheelie—and do a complete 360-degree turn on his rear tire, then skid more than one hundred feet, stopping abruptly inches away from Annette, who smiled appreciatively. Now just imagine how humiliated I'd feel a few minutes later when I pedaled up on my bicycle and did a training wheelie.

I took just about as much abuse as I could without striking back. I turned my other cheek, then my other cheek, then my first cheek again, then the other cheek, until I got too dizzy. Finally, I ran out of cheeks. I decided that the time had come to teach Mr. McQueen a little something about "hogs," as I like to call motorcycles. So while he was busy one afternoon, probably stealing someone else's scenes, I climbed up on that ol' Harley, kicked on that big engine, put my hands on the brake, and shifted into gear. Oh, that engine roared! I revved it into second gear, then third gear, then fourth gear. That roar grew into a frantic whine, louder than a million dental drills, the rear wheel began spinning faster than a cowboy's heart when he kissed his first cow, a spout of dirt and pebbles burst into the air twenty feet high, that whine of sheer power reached a crescendo—and I slowly released the brake.

My injuries were not nearly as serious as the newspapers reported, and I missed less than a week of shooting. And the scars were not permanent. But just to add insult to injuries, when I returned to the set, McQueen, who wore the colors, the motorcycle jacket and patch of his gang, the Devil's Avengers

MC, awarded me my own colors—the Our Gang MC, which included a patch featuring Spanky McFarland.

I knew that one of two things would happen if McQueen and I duked it out: either I would get hurt, or I would get hurt bad. I warned him to stay away from me, though, reminding him, "My stunt double can beat up your stunt double." But it didn't seem to do any good. Finally I confronted him, demanding, "What is it with you? What's your problem with me?"

"Don't you get it?" he sneered. "Little kids look up to you."

"They have to. I'm much taller than they are."

"Besides that, your mother always liked you best."

I hesitated. "But you didn't even know my mother."

"See!" he yelled. "See, that's the problem with you. You always have a smart answer for everything."

That's where I proved him wrong. "Oh, yeah?" I said. "Well, your mother wears combat sandals."

McQueen and I never really became friends, but we were able to channel the tension that existed between us into our performances, and that helped us create complex characters in conflict with each other as well as the enemy. *Sand Pebbles* turned out to be both a critical and commercial success.

But personally, perhaps the most important thing that took place during the production of *Sand Pebbles* was that I "cheated" on my wife for the first time. Cheating seems like such an ugly word for such a nice thing. To me, "cheating" means something really serious, like moving one more space than you've rolled to avoid going to jail in Monopoly, or "accidentally" knocking over the table when you're losing at Scrabble. But sharing a few seconds of intimacy with another needful human being? How can they call that cheating when you didn't even have to roll the dice?

It happens. In the movie business it happens more often than you think; unless, of course, you think it happens all the time, every day, on every movie set, in which case it probably happens less often than you think it does.

One of the questions I'm asked occasionally during the lecture series I give at film schools is exactly what a typical day on a movie set is like. While making a movie sounds glamorous and exciting, in reality it's actually very boring. Most of our time is spent waiting: waiting for the cameras to be set up for the next shot, waiting for the proper lighting because the sun went behind a cloud, waiting for the roar of an airplane to fade away because the microphones are picking it up, waiting for Elizabeth Taylor, waiting for the *Robert E. Lee*, waiting for Godot, and finally, after all that waiting, we shoot for a few minutes, then begin waiting again while the crew prepares for the next shot.

While that next scene is being set up, there is really nothing for the actors to do. Generally, we just sit around getting to know each other, then getting to know each other a little better. We talk about every conceivable subject, but inevitably there comes a time when we have absolutely nothing left to talk about. And at that point, rather than risk having the other person think we're either not very interesting or not very intelligent, we have sex.

While most conversation during sex consists basically of "Oh, wow, baby, you're the best," actually having sex provides a range of new topics to discuss. Am I really the best? How good is Warren Beatty? Can we do it again so we have even more to talk about?

Ironically, this is the primary reason many actors end up having affairs with young actresses rather than more mature actresses. Young actresses have had fewer experiences and are often less well educated; therefore, actors run out of things to talk about with them much sooner than with an older woman and are forced to resort to sex to keep the conversation alive.

The real truth is that I didn't intend to have an affair, I didn't even want to have an affair, but I had to do it to protect my wife's reputation. I had the affair with a beautiful young starlet named Daisy Rose, with whom I had one scene in the picture. Daisy and I spent a few minutes together and quickly ran out of topics to discuss. I had the affair with her because I didn't want her to think I was dumb—not for my sake, I didn't care what she thought about me—but because I didn't want her thinking my wife would have married a dummy. We had so little to say to each other that I was forced to save Courtney's reputation several times a day for weeks.

It would be absurd and untrue for me to claim that I didn't enjoy our affair. Daisy was a veteran starlet, and I knew that I had finally become a star because she let me do whatever I wanted to do. I don't honestly know if it was her beauty or the excitement of the situation, but this was certainly the most erotic experience I'd ever had. For the first time in my life I actually smoked after sex. Little tiny puffs of smoke came out of my ears. Or, at least it seemed that way. I was careful never to lie to Daisy; I told her right after we'd made love for the first time that a long-term relationship was impossible. "Oh, I don't care about that," she replied sweetly. "I was just hoping for something longer than fifteen seconds."

It's impossible to keep anything secret on a movie set because so many people work so closely together for so long, but I tried. My guess is that people began to suspect something was going on between us when the costume designer found several long blond hairs on my captain's costume. It was either that or the squadron of skywriters who drew a heart with the words *Leslie and Daisy* inside it. I immediately turned on the wind machines to blow away the evidence, but it was too late.

When I told Daisy that our love affair had become public, she became hysterical. I tried everything to calm her down. "Daisy," I pleaded, "please stop laughing." But it did no good. For a lot of people these affairs that take place on the set are trivial, even meaningless, but I feared Daisy was different. I was afraid this was going to have a lasting effect on her life. So I'll never forget how broken up she was when it finally ended, when she had finished her work and had to leave. The last time I saw her was in the hotel lobby as she was checking out, her luggage in her hand. She turned and saw me across the lobby, looking as empty as Twiggy's bra, and she came to me and kissed me lightly on the cheek and said those magic words: "Would you please tell Steve I'll be right there?"

No one in the motion-picture industry will ever admit that they are out of work. Rather, they are "between pictures." Some actors are even "between picture." In fact, inscribed on the tombstone of the famous silent-film star George Boyle is the epitaph "Just Between Pictures." I was one of the fortunate actors. When I finished *The Sand Pebbles*, I really was between pictures. Actually, I was so fortunate that I was more than "between pictures." I was "between projects." So I was anxious to get home and enjoy a long vacation. I intended to sit by the pool and relax. But incredibly, just as I was getting ready to board the stagecoach, Courtney called. "Terrible news," she began.

"The house," I said instantly, a touch of panic in my voice.

"It's okay," she reassured me, "it's fine." I took a deep breath and relaxed. "They found it right at the bottom of the gully where the river dropped it."

It wasn't really a river, she explained, just a simple flood. As we discovered, leaves had accumulated in my neighbor's roof gutters, trapping a tremendous amount of water. Finally, like a dam bursting, a great tidal surge had overflowed, sweeping my house off its foundation. It was going to be expensive to repair, so for the first time in my life I found myself working for a new foundation.

I had a lot of scripts from which to choose, and while I took my time making that choice, I accepted an invitation to lecture at the new and quite prestigious American Film Institute in Washington, D.C. At the AFI young filmmakers were really taught how to make a film, beginning with making their own emulsions and all the other sticky stuff you mix together. I gave a brief talk about the history of motion pictures, from the very beginning when moving pictures consisted of people looking at a lot of still pictures very fast, to recent technological innovations like Smellovision.

After I concluded my speech a pleasant young man asked to speak with me for a few moments. I remember him quite well. He had a winning smile and was very intense; his name was Brian De Palma. He told me he had been working on a script that he thought would be perfect for me. It was a horror story, he explained, the story of a man who went to sleep each night only to become entranced by his neighbor's music, and while in that trance he was compelled to stalk a beautiful woman living nearby. That sounded vaguely familiar to me, and it took me only a few minutes to remember why. "Um, Brian," I said, "isn't that exactly the same plot as Alfred Hitchcock's *The Sleepwalker?*"

He smiled at my naïveté. "No, it's completely different. I've studied every frame of every picture Hitchcock ever made, just so I would never copy any of them. I know

Hitchcock, and there are no similarities. For example, *The Sleepwalker* takes place in Great Neck. My picture takes place in Little Neck. And in *The Sleepwalker* it's Liberace's music that causes the trance; in my movie it's Beatles music. So, except for the plot and characters, these two pictures have nothing in common."

I tried to be delicate with his feelings. "But isn't that like . . . borrowing?"

"Not at all. In the cinema we refer to it as 'homage,' meaning respect. What I'm doing is 'paying homage' to the master of suspense."

"Well," I said jokingly, "I guess it's cheaper than royalties." I declined to read De Palma's script, explaining to him that since I'd once played that type of role, I didn't want to repeat my performance. Although that picture never got made, I watched proudly as De Palma's career grew. He is recognized as one of the movie industry's most creative and daring directors, and the master of the "homogenized" film.

In addition to the numerous film offers piling up, I was also offered the leading role in a Broadway play and a television series. Theatrical producer Caroline Hirsch wanted me to play the role of boxer Jack Jefferson, the first black heavyweight champion of the world, in Howard Sackler's new play, *The Great White Hope*. I loved the play, but as soon as I started reading it, I knew I wasn't right for the part. Jack Jefferson was described as 6'5" tall, and I'm only 6'3". With regrets, I told him it would be too much of a stretch for me to do it.

But the irony of the situation wasn't lost on me. I'd had to leave the theater to get a leading role in the theater. That realization made me wonder: If only I'd left the theater sooner, could I have become a great Broadway star?

Through the years I've been offered roles in several television series, but the very first serious offer came from legendary producer Norman Lear, the creative genius who conceived of adapting hit British TV shows for the American audience. The show he wanted me for was the story of a foul-mouthed middle-class man who hates absolutely everyone who is different from him. It was a situation comedy.

"So he's just a bigot, right?" I asked Lear when we discussed the show. "I've got to tell you, that doesn't sound very American to me."

"Oh, it's very American," Lear protested. "See, this is the kind of guy who doesn't discriminate against anybody. He hates everyone equally, regardless of race, creed, or color. It's a riot."

"It certainly might be." I knew Lear was smart, but this just didn't sound like the type of show that would appeal to the American television audience. I decided to help him. "Let me ask you this, Norman. Are you sure there are no cowboys in this show? You know, he could hate varmints."

"No, no cowboys."

"Well, then how about making him a detective? Detective shows are very popular. He could, like, hate criminals."

"I don't think so. He's not a detective either."

"All right. Does he at least sing or dance? Maybe impersonations? He could do . . . Hitler impersonations."

"I'm beginning to think you don't really understand the concept."

"Excuse me, Norman," I replied, perhaps a bit curtly, "but I know television. I started in television, so please. I'm just trying to help you. Maybe you should make him a doctor, like Marcus Welby or Ben Casey. He could hate viruses."

"I don't think so."

I had to be blunt with him. "Norman, do you watch television?" I explained to him that under the then-existing television rules, heroes were permitted to hate criminals, rustlers, diseases, Communists, people on other networks, and impersonators who did poor impersonations of Cary Grant saying "Judy, Judy, Judy," and that this did not include next-door neighbors—unless the hero lived on a ranch in Moscow.

Perhaps I made a mistake, perhaps my life and my career would have been different had I accepted Lear's offer to play Archie Bunker in "All in the Family." But nothing like it had ever been successful in the United States. As I've learned since then, the only thing about the American public that is absolutely predictable is that there is absolutely nothing predictable about the American public. Before I had time to really consider the role, though, Warren Beatty called and offered me one of the most important roles of my career.

The world was changing rapidly in those days. America was divided over issues such as the drug culture, the free-sex movement, and the war in Vietnam. I was firmly against drug use, I didn't know why anyone would want to pay for sex, and I was somewhat confused about the war. I could understand the arguments of the pro-war people; if you're going to have a war, you want the pros to be fighting it; there's nothing worse than an amateur war. And I could understand the arguments of the anti-war people.

Although I was often asked my opinion, I refrained from taking a stand. Only once in my career had I become politically involved, and that hadn't worked out very well at all. I had just finished a lovely dinner with Tab and Kim Hunter when a matronly woman approached me and, after apologizing for interrupting our meal, asked, "Mr. Nielsen, do you honestly believe in free speech?"

"Absolutely," I told her, "I firmly believe that free speech is the bulwark of democracy. Without free speech the exchange of ideas is halted, all forms of individual expression are doomed, and tyrants rule."

"I'm so glad to hear you say that," she gushed, "because my garden club would like you to make a free speech next Tuesday night." She had me there, so she got me on Tuesday.

With so many significant events taking place in the world around me, I felt that it was important for me to do something relevant. With the success of the talking horse, Mr. Ed, on television, Warners seriously considered bringing Francis the Talking Mule out of retirement to costar with me in *Francis Goes to Vietnam*. MGM wanted me to join Bob Hope and Bing Crosby in the first civil rights musical, *On the Road to Birmingham*. But it was my old friend Warren Beatty who found a way to make meaningful entertainment.

I was getting ready to start hitching home when he stopped me. "Don't move," he said, "I've been looking for something we could work on together for a long time, and I've finally found it. This is one of the great American folk tales. It's the true story of vicious bank robbers and killers. It's a beautiful love story."

And that was my introduction to *Bonnie and Clyde*, the motion picture for which I was honored with my second Academy Award nomination. I've got to admit that initially I was confused by Warren's description of the film, but with people in America ready to fight for peace, with Norman Lear making a comedy about a bigot, I guess I shouldn't have been surprised by a love story about killers.

The beautiful Miss Faye Dunaway was set to play Bonnie Parker, a gun moll with a heart of ice, while Warren intended to play Clyde Barrow, the man who melted it. The script was based on the exploits of Bonnie and Clyde, who romped through the Midwest and the Dust Bowl in the 1930s robbing banks before being killed in a police ambush. "This is going to be a landmark film, Leslie," Warren said in his most serious voice. "It's going to change movies forever. And we need you."

Change movies forever? "That sounds great, Warren."

"It will be, trust me on this. I've got a whole new vision. Ready? In this film, the bad guys are going to wear white hats!"

I paused to let him continue. He didn't. "That's it?"

"Yeah, that's it, but listen to this. Not just white hats. White fedoras. They're going to be the most stylish bank robbers in motion-picture history."

"What about me? What have you got in mind for me?"

"I want you to play the lawman who tracks them down and kills them."

That sounded like a good part, but with Warren you can never be sure. "So that means I get to play the good guy, right?" He didn't respond immediately. "Right?" I repeated.

"These things are complicated," he finally replied. "I guess it depends how you look at it. When you finally track down Bonnie and Clyde, you and your posse shoot them about a thousand times. I mean, it'll just look fabulous. They'll have more holes in them than the entire Warren Commission Report."

"A thousand times, Warren? Don't you think that's overkill?"

"Not at all. That's entertainment." Even then Warren was far ahead of everyone else in the film industry. It had taken me years to graduate from simply "making movies" to becoming

In Bonnie and Clyde *I played the sheriff who ambushed Beatty and Dunaway. Oddly, remembered as one of the bloodiest movies ever filmed, no blood at all was shown on the screen.*

involved in "projects." Warren was already beyond "projects"; he was making "visions." And *Bonnie and Clyde* was entirely his vision, a good old-fashioned gangster movie with great clothes.

We met to discuss his vision further at the New York City showroom of fashion designer Yves Saint Laurent. Saint Laurent's new models were about to be revealed, and Warren wanted to look them over before they hit the market. During that first phone call Warren had insisted that *Bonnie and Clyde* was a film with a message. Besides "If you rob banks, the cops'll turn you into a screen door," I didn't know what that message was, and I wanted to hear him explain it.

Saint Laurent's new collection had a Middle Eastern theme, so as a particularly sleek new model was unveiled, Warren explained his vision to me. "I don't want the studio to know about this because they'll get very nervous. Like Goldwyn once said, 'when I want to send a message, I tell my wife a secret.' Believe me, the only thing the studios want people thinking about in the movies is what kind of topping to put on their popcorn. Now please don't tell anybody, but *Bonnie and Clyde* is actually a strong anti-war statement. The studio thinks that just because the main characters are gangsters and the plot is about robbing banks, this is a gangster film. Well, it isn't, not any more than *Gone With the Wind* was about the weather."

I thought about this. "Huh?" I decided.

Warren paused to admire the body design of a new model, then continued, "It's really very simple. What happens if you eat too much chocolate? You get sick of chocolate, right? Right. Same thing with violence. The more violence in this film, the more popular the film'll be, the more nauseated the audience will be. The key is to make the violence incredibly realistic, lots of blood, guts flying all over the place, the real thing. I'm going to show in graphic detail how horrible violence is until people can't even look at it anymore." He grew so intense that he gripped my elbow in a viselike hold, looked at me fervently, and declared, "This is going to be a movie about peace."

I was still confused. "Chocolate?" I asked. The only violent act I could think of involving chocolate was assault with a frozen Hershey bar.

Warren explained his vision to me. *Bonnie and Clyde* was going to be the most violent anti-war film ever made, with the possible exception of John Wayne's *The Green Berets* and *Sands of Iwo Jima*. People would want to see it because of what Warren described as "designer violence," but the violence would be so realistic that the audience would realize how terrible it is, and turn against the war.

"The climactic scene in which Bonnie and Clyde get blown away with several thousand bullets is clearly a metaphor for the entire Vietnam War," he added.

"Metaphor?" I said, laughing. "That's at least a metafive. Maybe even a metasix."

I accepted the role of the obsessed lawman who tracks Bonnie and Clyde through mid-America and sets up the fatal ambush for several reasons. I thought I understood Warren's vision that this would make a strong anti-war statement, I believed that the film would be commercially successful as long as it contained enough violence to turn the audience against violence, and most of all, it sounded like more fun than anything I'd done since my brothers and I had played Mounties and Indians.

Movies had become such a big business, and for most actors parts had become so difficult to get, that many of us had lost sight of the reasons we'd originally decided to become actors. And that is that being an actor was much better than having a real job. Being an actor allowed fully mature human beings to play children's games and still claim we were working. So here was an opportunity for me to carry six-guns, drive beautiful old cars as fast as I wanted to, stage an elaborate ambush to bushwhack the bad guys, hang around with beautiful women, and get paid a lot of money to do it. And I was going to turn that down?

Making *Bonnie and Clyde* was almost as much fun as I'd hoped it would be. Warren produced the film, and although he'd wanted François Truffaut or Jean-Luc Godard to direct it, he'd finally hired the legendary Arthur Penn. The rest of the cast—Gene Hackman, Mike Pollard, Estelle Parsons, Gene Wilder making his film debut—were all wonderful. Most of the production went extremely smoothly, and it wasn't until we were filming the ambush scene in which Bonnie and Clyde are killed that we encountered any problems.

That was a very difficult, very elaborate scene to film. Warren wanted it to be the most violent gunfight in movie history. He even brought in some veteran stunt victims to teach him and Dunaway the proper way to respond to being shot about a thousand times. Even the stunt victims had never done a scene quite this violent. It was so different from anything ever done that one of them asked Warren, "Are these wounds fatal?"

Penn spent four days preparing to put the scene on film. He insisted on using four cameras, which would be shooting from various angles; he rehearsed the cast numerous times to make sure that the timing would be perfect; he supervised the explosives experts while they loaded the hundreds of charges wired to the car. It took the weapons master three full days just to load the blank cartridges into the array of weapons. We weren't simply going to shoot this scene, we were going to blast it to smithereens. "Listen up," Penn boomed through the small megaphone he often carried. "You all know what we have to do. Please, I don't want anyone firing his weapon until I give the word. Wait until you hear me; then let loose with everything you've got. It took us four days to get ready for this, so let's get it right the first time."

In the scene, Bonnie and Clyde stop on a country lane to assist an acquaintance whose car has broken down. Meanwhile, all the lawmen in the world are hiding in the bushes on the side of the road waiting for them. I was hunched down behind a big tree, waiting for Penn's command to burst out of the treeline and begin firing. When I looked down the dirt road I could see a cloud of dust rising in the distance as Beatty and Dunaway drove toward us. I waited . . . I waited . . . Sometimes during the production of a motion picture certain events transpire that cannot be anticipated. So, contrary to many of the nasty stories that later circulated, what happened next was not entirely my fault. Apparently I'd hunkered down on top of an important army ants' fortress. Before I realized it, a very tiny trumpet had signaled charge, and an entire battalion had attacked. The infantry scooted into my clothing, into my pants, and they started biting. Without thinking, I ran out of the trees and started shaking, and I probably did, in fact, scream, "Shoot!"

Maybe I should have screamed "Shit!" But I didn't like to curse. Unfortunately, as soon as the other actors saw me charge out of the trees and scream "Shoot!," they did. More than one hundred and fifty handguns opened fire. The machine gun began chattering. Behind me I could hear the unmistakable *whomp-whomp* of mortars being fired. From somewhere in the distance I heard the whine of incoming heavy artillery. Seconds later, an antique fighter biplane appeared and dived on the car in which Beatty and Dunaway were riding, which was still about a half mile from the camera mark. The violence was tremendously impressive, even if none of it was being filmed.

When the smoke lifted, Penn was livid, absolutely livid. "What happened?" he was screaming. "What happened? What happened? Who told you to fire? That's gonna cost us four days. That's hundreds of thousands of dollars."

As casually as I could, I said, "Oh, so you noticed, huh?"

"Noticed? I Noticed? Yes, I noticed. Are you crazy? Do you want to direct this picture?"

"That's two questions," I pointed out. "Let me take them one at a time. No, I'm no crazier than I've ever been. And the truth is, I haven't thought much about directing, although it's certainly something I'll consider in the future."

He squinched his eyes closed and said as calmly as possible, "Please, tell me what happened. What happened?"

"It was the strangest thing," I confessed a bit sheepishly. "You know how this is supposed to be an antiwar film?"

"Yeah? So?"

"Well, I suppose you might say I just found the ants."

Bonnie and Clyde became a trendsetting motion picture. Fashion designers produced several collections based on the classic gangster chic of the costumes worn by Beatty and Dunaway. The death scene, in which Beatty and Dunaway jerked violently in all directions, proved so popular that a dance craze called the Jerk swept the country. And we received ten Academy Award nominations. In addition to both Beatty and Dunaway being nominated as Best Actor and Actress, Hackman, Pollard, and I were all nominated as Best Supporting Actor, the first time in history that three actors from one picture had been nominated in the same category.

I was feeling wonderful when I finished *Bonnie and Clyde*. Finally, I was going home. I had my pick of great parts. My investments seemed to be doing very well. I was so well established that casting directors were posting notices for "a Leslie Nielsen type." I'd even received one of the greatest honors that can be bestowed upon an actor: I'd had a sandwich named after me at the Stage Deli. So I had it all—a woman I loved, a successful career that brought me fame and satisfaction, and the security that money could bring. I was feeling so confident that when my Dream came back, when the Acting Police showed up at my door, I told them, "You guys are in the wrong dream. I think you want Clint Eastwood's dream."

In 1969, I received one of filmdom's great tributes when New York's famed Stage Deli named a sandwich after me.

I felt as if I were standing on top of the world. So perhaps I should have heeded the famous words of wisdom of Sir Edmund Hillary, the first man to climb Mt. Everest, who said as he stood atop the summit, "It's all downhill from here."

The first of the many surprises that were to change my life came from my wife. Perhaps I'd been fooling myself for a long time—maybe things hadn't been quite as wonderful as I'd imagined they were. But Courtney had always left such nice messages for me on our answering machine. It took me only a few days after I'd gotten home to read the handwriting on the wall: "Dear Leslie," she'd written in lipstick, which had smudged, "I've sold the house and run away with the contractor. We're going to build a new life together. Please don't be mad at me. (Continued on next wall.)"

I couldn't believe the filth I found on those walls. Apparently she'd run out of lipstick and written with mud. But no matter what materials she'd used, the meaning was still the same—she was gone for good. Or, for not so good, depending on your point of view. In her letter she told me to see her lawyer. I didn't want to; I knew her lawyer, and she was already married.

I packed my bags and moved into a bungalow at the fashionable Château Marmont Hotel. I spent night after night staring at the flowers on the wall, and gradually I could feel myself becoming a wallflower. I knew I had to get out of that room, go back to work, establish a new life, and find the happiness that had deserted me faster than television sets had left electronics stores during the riots.

My life began to get better the day I received a prized invitation to attend a party at one of America's most respected houses, Hugh Hefner's Playboy Mansion. For days I tingled with excitement, but finally I ran out of quarters for my "magic fingers" bed. At the Playboy Mansion anything was possible. I might cavort with gorgeous playmates in the famed grotto, dine with Julia Child, discuss politics with Hank Kissinger, or go one-on-one with Wilt Chamberlain.

In those days, Hef's Playboy Mansion was *the* place to be, and it was possible to meet some of the most fascinating and important people in the world there. Besides the playmates, I mean. As I walked through that front door for the first time, I took a quick look around, and within seconds I'd spotted Woody Allen, Joe Namath, Ed and Maureeno Sullivan. In a corner John Huston was laughing, the legendary cinematographer Berry Stainbeck was with Tuesday Weld, the acclaimed actress Louise Tranford was whispering in the ear of Academy Award–winning cinematographer Joseph Lipari, Muhammad Ali was throwing play-punches at Joe Louis, a young and intense Yasir Arafat was engaged in a serious discussion with his older brother Nosir. I was even pretty sure I caught a glimpse of the famous Her Majesty Queen Elizabeth as she ducked into the ladies' room to straighten her crown.

I wanted to thank Hefner for inviting me to this party, so I began wandering around the mansion looking for him. I got a little lost, and when I opened a door off a small corridor, I apparently interrupted a small group of people huddled around a coffee table, because in unison they looked up at me as if I'd caught them doing something wrong. One of them, a distinguished-looking man with thinning white hair, stood to greet me. "Hi," he said, extending his hand, "name's Cliff. Why don't you drop over sometime."

I thought it was very kind of him to invite a stranger to his home, but the other people in the room disagreed. They actually started booing him; some of them even groaned. Personally, I thought it was very cruel of them to boo a person's name. Cliff isn't such a terrible name. He could have been Wilford.

The people in that room made me feel very uncomfortable and I couldn't wait to get out of there, so I made up a silly excuse about having to catch a train. One of the other men in the room asked immediately, "Really? How much of a head start does it have?"

I was glad to be out of there. Somehow I found myself in the grotto, the famous pool that ran below much of the mansion. There were so many beautiful women lying around on the rocks that I just didn't know where to start. As I was looking around for Hef, an absolutely beautiful woman wearing a sash reading MISS OCTOBER came up to me and asked in a seductive voice, "Would you like to take a dip in the pool?"

"Absolutely," I said without hesitation.

"Good," she said, then turned around and yelled to an overweight man wearing red plaid pants and a bright yellow bow tie, "Hey, stupid, this guy'll go in with you." And then she laughed.

I was beginning to feel very uneasy about this whole place. It was as if everyone there was sharing a secret that I didn't know. I was thinking about leaving when I finally spotted my host, the legendary Hugh Hefner, carrying a pipe and dressed, as always, in his bedclothes, a sheet, and pillowcase. I went over to speak to him. "Hey, Hef," I began, "what's up?"

Hefner looked at me and smiled broadly, then pointed to the ceiling with his index finger. "That's up, Leslie," he said confidently. "I'm surprised you didn't know that."

And then he laughed and laughed and laughed. His laughter was infectious. I couldn't help it, I started laughing, too. At that moment, although I didn't realize it, my world was about to be changed forever.

7

WAITER, MY CAREER'S IN THE SOUP

I t started so innocently. I told one really dopey joke and got a little laugh. Then I told another really silly joke and people laughed a bit louder. Then another and another, and before I knew what had happened, I was turning every line into a bad joke. As comedians say, I was doing dope.

It seemed so simple, so safe. So innocent. It was just an amusement. Nobody got hurt. When I did it, it made me feel good inside, so warm, even loved. All my insecurities just drifted away, my inhibitions disappeared. At first, just like everyone else, I believed I could do a good line whenever I felt like it, then stop whenever I needed to. I'd heard all the horror stories,

216

I'd heard what had happened to other people, but that was other people. It couldn't happen to me. I was too strong, too tough, I would never become addicted to dopey jokes. No, not me.

And that is how I discovered the next real naked truth.

People in show business had been doing dope as long as anyone can remember. The old-time stand-up comedians used to do it down in Greenwich Village, in those smoke-filled comedy clubs. Dope was real big on the vaudeville circuits. Big stars like Smith & Wesson built their whole acts around it. Smith would walk across the stage carrying a briefcase, and when asked by Wesson where he was going, he'd reply, "I'm taking my case to court." Moments later he'd return, this time carrying his briefcase and a ladder, explaining, "Now I'm taking my case to a higher court."

Probably one of the greatest dope lines in cinema history came from the Marx Brothers film *A Night in Court*, in which Groucho responded to Judge Margaret Dumont's demand for "Order in the court" by requesting, "Swiss cheese on rye, hold the mayo, please."

Being a dope was mind-blowing, mind-expanding. The word itself probably was derived from the Old English *dopey*, meaning to do or say something ridiculous or foolish. Ridiculous or foolish? Perhaps, but once I'd heard that sound of laughter ringing in my ears, it became harder and harder to stop.

Learning how to "do dope" was easy, as I discovered that night at Hef's. I was standing in a small group of people, among them Sir Winston Churchill, the actor T. P. Panther, who seemed particularly animated that night, Andy Warhol, and Mr. and Mrs. Paul Fishsticks, when I noticed Queen Elizabeth flirting with director Milos Forman, who'd recently emigrated to America from Czechoslovakia. Suddenly, Queen put her arm in

Forman's and practically dragged him away. "Look at that," I commented, almost without thinking about it. "It isn't often that you see a Queen picking up a czech." Everybody laughed happily. I felt like I belonged. For the first time in weeks the pain of loneliness in my heart was gone. I liked it.

What was amazing to me was the discovery that so many people were doing it. Normal people, average Americans, the type of people I would never have suspected. Two nights later, for example, I strolled into what appeared to be a typical greasy diner. The counterman wiped off a place for me and asked, "What'll you have?"

I didn't care. "Just give me whatever's on the menu," I said. A few minutes later he served me a squashed fly. It was only then I'd realized I'd accidentally wandered into one of the doper bars that were springing up across America.

Once I knew what to look for, I discovered that there was an entire parallel culture, the dope joke culture, that had been existing around me for a long time without my being aware of it. It seemed as if everyone was trying to "get groaned" as they say.

Before I realized it, I was doing a couple of lines every day. I couldn't help myself. I'd be perfectly straight and then someone would say something to me and . . . and I couldn't resist. They didn't even have to be good lines. For example, one night I was having dinner at Chasen's and the waitress asked me if I wanted some converted rice with my steak. How could anyone resist that challenge? "It depends," I told her, "what was it originally?" The waitress groaned; I loved getting groaned.

Doing dope was intoxicating. People were laughing at me. It just got easier and easier. I still didn't see anything wrong with it. As long as it didn't affect my work, I figured, what difference did it make? I tried to convince myself that I was just a recreational doper, that I wasn't hooked. I truly believed I could stop anytime I wanted to.

Unfortunately, by the time it began affecting my work, it was too late. I remember the night director George Roy Hill called to ask me if I'd be interested in playing opposite Paul Newman in the film *Butch Cassidy and the Sundance Kid*. We discussed the film in broad terms for a while, and then George told me he was also considering Bob Redford for the part. "Why Redford?" I asked. "He's a lightweight."

"Maybe," George admitted, "but I like his presence."

I couldn't resist. "Oh? Why, what'd he give you?"

Hill ignored that line, maybe he didn't even get it, but as we finished this conversation a few minutes later, he asked, "Why don't you give me a ring tomorrow?"

"But George," I pretended to protest, "we hardly know each other. Wouldn't a small bracelet be enough?"

He couldn't ignore that. After a long silence, he finally asked, "Leslie, have you been smoking some pot?"

I laughed at that. "Are you kidding? You know how tough it is to get that aluminum lit?"

That was probably the first good role I lost because of my habit. It certainly wasn't the last one. But at the time I still didn't believe it was possible. I knew there were a lot of producers who wanted to hire me. I was box office; my movies made money. As the handsome TV star Armand Dove reminded me one night, "In this town, money talks."

When I started doing dopey lines my career went downhill faster than a sledder on Mt. Everest. Da-dum.

"Oh?" I said in mock surprise. "Why? Are the Japanese manufacturing it now?"

He was right, of course. As long I showed up at work on time prepared to do my scenes, the studios would overlook my habit. One night, for example, Kirk Douglas and I sneaked onto the set of Josh Logan's musical *Paint Your Wagon*. And we did—we painted it in Day-Glo colors. But because we could make money for the studio, it was dismissed as a harmless prank.

Gradually, I got deeper and deeper into it. Everything began sounding like a straight line to me. I guess the first time my habit actually interfered with my work was on the set of young director Steven Spielberg's first theatrical movie, the cult favorite about a husband and his pregnant wife moving into a haunted house, *The Miller Place*, in which I costarred with Tippi Hedren.

In one of the first scenes we shot, Tippi and I were being shown the old house by real estate agent Myrna Loy, who was trying to play down the fact that a family of seven had been murdered there, and the killer had never been found. "It's a sweet old house," she said earnestly, "full of history."

Naturally, or perhaps unnaturally, as it turned out, Tippi was drawn to it. "It's so . . . pretty," she said.

My line was, "If you don't mind sharing it with ghosts."

"Oh, silly," Tippi responded, "there's no such thing as ghosts. When we fix it up, it'll be beautiful. All it needs is some love."

"Maybe" I agreed, "but considering its history, they want a lot for it."

Everything was going well until Tippi said her line. "What's a lot?"

For the first time, I couldn't stop myself. "What do you think it is?" I said, "It's a piece of land with dirt on it."

Just about everybody laughed pleasantly at that. We reshot the scene, and that second time I read the line exactly as it had been written. I was the only one who knew what had happened: that the words seemed to have come out of my mouth without any thought, that I hadn't been able to stop myself from doing a line of "dope." I didn't know where the words had come from, and I had done very well in high school anatomy. And I got scared, really scared.

It affected my performance. From that moment on I was afraid to really get into my character. I was afraid to take a chance. I knew I had a problem and I knew I had to do something about it, but at that time society hadn't realized how widespread the problem was, and facilities to treat it didn't exist. People in the business were beginning to notice that something was wrong with me.

I turned to the experts for help. In *Easy Rider*, for example, I was cast as an expert motorcycle mechanic, and Jack Nicholson drove into my place and asked, "Think maybe you can soup this up?"

I tried so hard to resist. "Are you sure you want me to 'soup it up'?"

Jack thought I was improvising, and went with me to see how far we could take it. "Sure do," he said, "go ahead and soup it up."

I gulped, fighting the urge with every muscle in my head. "I mean, you really want me to actually soup it up?"

"Yeah, man, I really, really want you to soup it up."

I now know that you can get more mileage from clam chowder than from chicken gumbo. I ruined two engines before I gained control of myself. That night I went to see Nicholson to talk about my problem, and I found him discussing the scenes we were to shoot the next day with director

Dennis Hopper. "I've got a problem," I admitted for the first time, and it felt good to say it out loud. "And I need help. I was thinking maybe you guys might know what I can do."

"We'll be glad to try, Leslie," Dennis said.

I took a deep breath. "How do you beat a habit?"

"Ah, man, that's not tough," Jack said, smiling easily. "Basically, you just hang it on a clothesline and smack it with a broom."

"He's right," Dennis agreed, "but just make sure the nun takes it off first."

"Please, guys," I said, "I'm serious."

"Nice to meet you, Serious," Nicholson replied. "I'm Jack. This is my pal Dennis."

I pleaded with them, "How do I go straight?"

Dennis sighed. "Best way is to stay away from corners."

"Don't you understand? I'm hooked. I'm hooked."

Jack shook his head. "Boy, that sounds fishy to me."

They were all around me. Somehow I managed to get through that picture. But things quickly got worse. The Academy Awards ceremony took place during a dark time in my life: Night. In emcee Bob Hope's monologue he mentioned that Nicholson had played a lawyer in *Easy Rider,* that Sidney J. Furie had just finished directing *The Lawyer,* and that Robert Wagner had been a lawyer in *Hard Evidence,* then asked rhetorically, "Where do all these lawyers come from?"

I was no longer in control. Before I knew what I was doing, I shouted out, "Sioux City!"

A few members of the audience laughed nervously, but most people were stunned by my outburst. I hunched down in my seat, turning redder than a badly sunburned Joseph Stalin.

George Kennedy won the Oscar as Best Supporting Actor for his work in *Cool Hand Luke,* but I got all the attention. After the ceremony I was mobbed by newspaper reporters and photographers. I couldn't breathe. "Please, guys, gimme some room," I begged them, "I'm impressed."

Producers were beginning to get very nervous about hiring me. I suspect that Peter Fonda had asked his sister, Jane Fonda, to help me, because she offered me an important role in Alan Pakula's film *Klute.* In that film Jane played a call girl and I was supposed to play a man with a very large phone bill. Pakula had obviously heard the rumors that I was getting difficult to work with because he asked me to audition for the role. It was the first time in years that I'd had to audition for a part, but it was such a sweet role that I agreed to do it. Jane and I did a key scene from the film, the classic scene in which she seduces me.

When the scene began, she was lying seductively on a divan, her robe partially opened, falling away from her body. We could hear people arguing through the thin walls of our seedy motel room, so Jane asked, "Would you please turn on the radio?"

The radio was on a small table. I just stared at it. I tried to resist the urge to do a dopey line, I tried so hard, but I just couldn't. I went over to the radio and started rubbing its dials suggestively, then said in a whisper, "You know, for a radio, you're pretty damn cute."

The part went to Donald Sutherland. The pile of scripts on the floor began shrinking. Occasionally, though, I'd still get an offer. Warners asked me to audition for the role of a tough, street-smart San Francisco cop named Harry Callahan in a movie entitled *Dirty Harry.* I really wanted this part, I needed it, so I prepared for the audition by not bathing for a week. Dirty Harry? I was going to be Filthy Harry!

The audition scene was pretty simple: I held a .38 Magnum on a wounded killer, whose own gun was lying just a few feet away. As he debated trying to go for his gun, I was supposed to sneer at him, "Go ahead. Make my day!"

The audition went very well right up until that point. I held my .38 on him, he looked at his gun, and I curled my lip and snarled, "Go ahead. Make my bed!" And I couldn't resist adding, "And don't forget the hospital corners."

The part went to Clint Eastwood.

My agent stopped receiving calls about my availability. It looked as if my career was over when I got a break; producer Irwin Allen offered me a small role in his film *The Poseidon Adventure*. Unfortunately, it turned out to be a disaster.

With the popular success of Stanley Kramer's *Ship of Fools*, every studio began developing stories set aboard luxury ocean liners. Few people know this, but *The Poseidon Adventure* was originally slated to be a complex character study of lives inexorably entwined during a fateful sea voyage. It was going to be a soap opera at sea, or as people called it, "a soap suds opera." I was cast as the captain of the U.S.S. *Poseidon*; I enjoyed telling people that in this role I was traveling steerage. Fox had spent $6,000,000 constructing an entire "ship" that actually floated on a huge pool in their backlot. With the exception of the pyramids built for *Cleopatra*, this was the most expensive set ever built. The prop ship actually responded to the wheel, so I could move it from side to side. The first few days of shooting went very well, and perhaps I got too secure. On the fifth day of filming I was on the bridge, spinning the wheel back and forth, around and around; the ship started rocking from side to side, back and forth and around and around, the ship rocked a little more, back and forth, around . . .

224

Everyone makes mistakes from time to time in their life. This was my fault and I admit it. I accidentally turned over the entire ship, okay? I did it, I admit it. I still don't understand why this was such a big deal. Was it really my fault that their ship turned over so easily? Fortunately, no one was hurt, but much of the set was underwater. And that was how I saved the picture. After Irwin Allen made some of what I choose to call silly suggestions about my ancestors, I told him, "I don't care. This picture was a big disaster from the very beginning anyway."

And that's when he turned the film into a disaster picture, making it the story of people trying to escape from a ship suddenly turned upside down. The picture was a huge success, but I received no credit for my contribution. All I got was the blame for turning over the set.

After that incident it became much more difficult for me to get parts. My publicity people tried to hide from the press the fact that studios wouldn't hire me, claiming that I simply refused to do any more exploitation pictures and that I was "searching for projects with artistic integrity." When reporter Jim Jerome from *People* called to ask me about that, I explained, "I'm lying on my couch right now, and I'm not moving until I find a picture that utilizes my talents. Actually, I'm hoping that they proceed with *Dr. Zhivago II: Murder in Moscow*.

"Is that true?" Jerome asked me.

I guess I ruined the whole interview when I replied, "Aren't you listening? I just told you I was lying."

Occasionally, I did get a serious offer. The future-legendary Francis Ford Coppola thought I would be perfect for the role of adviser to the Mafia Corleone Family in his film *The Godfather*. I got very excited about that, but Coppola tried to keep me focused. "I have to ask you this," he said almost apologetically.

"I've heard some stories about you, that you're . . . you know, you've been doing dope. Any truth to that?"

"You know, Francis," I replied angrily, "I'm lying on my couch right now and I can tell you . . ." Clearly, I was still in the denial stage of my addiction.

"Good," Coppola said. "But just to be sure, the bonding company wants you to take a yourein test so that they can insure you and you can be in the picture."

I had to take that test. I had no choice. The test was simple. I was brought into a small, windowless room with a table in the center and a large mirror hanging on one wall. I sat down at that table opposite a man I'd never met before, a Dr. something. "Please finish this sentence for me," he began in a cold voice. "You're in a bar when a man walks in with a duck on his head. The bartender tells the man, 'I'm sorry, but we don't serve ducks in here.' To which the man replies?"

He looked at me and pushed his glasses up his nose. I started sweating. I tried to think of all the possible answers. I wanted to tell him, "Nothing. The man said nothing, he just left." But I couldn't. I couldn't resist the dope. "He said, 'That's okay, I don't eat 'em!'"

The doctor made a notation. "Question two," he continued impassively. "You're in a restaurant when the man sitting next to you taps you on the shoulder and asks, 'What's that fly doing in my soup?' To which you reply?"

I wanted so badly to resist that I started crying. The despair poured out of me. But I was addicted. "The backstroke!" I screamed, and then I completely lost control. "Is that what you wanted to hear? Is that what you wanted me to say? I hope you're happy now, I hope you're satisfied!" I bowed my head into my hands and cried and cried.

He waited until I calmed down, then continued, "You're in the pope's bowling alley . . ." I failed the yourein test, but I called Coppola to beg for a chance. "All I'm asking for is a chance," I pleaded. "I've got a great record. That should count for something."

"And what's that?" Francis wanted to know.

I couldn't stop myself. *"Elvis's Greatest Hits,"* I screamed. "The boxed three-record set on Decca."

Coppola was forced to settle for Robert Duvall.

I couldn't deny it any longer—I needed help. I could barely get through a simple conversation without doing a line or two. I couldn't get a job. I pounded the pavement until my hands were bruised and bloodied, but nothing helped. Then I heard about an organization for people just like me. I called them and cried, "Help!"

They recognized my cry for help and invited me to attend their next meeting. This was one of the original twelve-step programs that has subsequently become so popular. Its purpose was to bring together people with

I tried to go straight line, but I just couldn't break my habit. My career was ruined. No one would hire me, no matter how hard I pleaded for a part.

similar difficulties to discuss them openly, in front of people who would understand and offer support. This particular program was called Mensa, and it was a place where people went to solve their problems.

I'll never forget the first meeting I attended. It was held in a classroom at a local public school. If anyone recognized me, no one acknowledged it. There were about thirty-five people there, both men and women. One of the men stood in front of us and said in a firm voice, "Hi. My name is John and I have a problem."

Most of the other people responded in unison, "Hi, John."

"This is my problem. If a train leaves Indianapolis going east at one o'clock and travels at a speed of forty-eight miles per hour, and a second train leaves Cincinnati going west on the same track at one-fifteen and travels at a speed of thirty-eight miles per hour . . ." As I listened to him describe his problem, I suddenly remembered I'd heard it before. ". . . and they collide one-point-three miles east of the Ohio-Indiana border . . ."

I leaped out of my chair and shouted the answer: "They don't bury survivors!"

John coughed nervously. Several other people shifted uncomfortably in their seats. Then John continued, ignoring me: "At what velocity will the people in the first train travel through the air, how far will they land from the point of collision, what injuries will they suffer, and what percentage of the award will the personal-injury lawyers get to keep for themselves?"

And I thought I had a problem.

But that was the beginning for me. I went back again and again until finally I could stand in front of those people and admit, "My name is Leslie, and I've got a problem."

Something wonderful happened when I spoke. Nothing. No matter how good my dope was, nobody laughed. For a while that made me nervous, anxious, but as soon as I got used to not being laughed at, I grew stronger. I liked it, I liked it a lot. At first I could get through only a few sentences without doing a dopey line, but gradually those sentences became an entire paragraph, and that paragraph became a complete statement, which became a monologue, and eventually I could get through a whole speech without doing a single line. Was I cured? No. I learned in Mensa that no one ever solves all their problems, but at least I found some answers.

The great difficulty I faced was that while I was struggling to get myself under control, dope behavior was becoming widespread throughout American society. The guru of dopes, Prof. Irwin Corey, reminded people, "You can get more with a kind word, and a gun, than you can with just a kind word." The dopey show "Laugh-In" was at the top of the television ratings. Even the Catholic Church was becoming publicly alarmed at what it termed "Mass hysteria."

It was all around me. I fought as hard as I could to resist it. I went to Mensa meetings almost every night. I stayed away from dope clubs, the kind of clubs that advertised "Eat Here, Get Gas" and had no gas pumps outside. When I called producers to ask for an audition and they promised, "I'll call your agent tomorrow," I was actually able to resist replying, "But he prefers to be called immediately." Maybe I wasn't winning the battle, but I was waging a good fight until . . . until I succumbed to something far more potent than a line of dope: the terrible scourge of wisecrack.

Wisecracks were so much easier to do than dope lines. Wisecracking didn't even require any thinking. I could use the same crack over and over, as cracks were adaptable to so many different situations. "Why not, boobie?" "Sock it to me." "Far (explicative optional) out." "Let's not and say we did." "No shit, Sherlock." "Nice play, Shakespeare." "Smooth as Ex-Lax." "Sorry about that, chief." "Yessss . . . and loving it." "Ah, the old (fill in the blank) trick." "But noooo . . ." "Now that's an offer you can't refuse." Even good became "bad."

Within days of doing my first wisecrack I was hooked. I couldn't hear a single sentence without responding with a crack. I bumped into Henry Fonda one Sunday morning at Nate 'n Al's and he told me, "I just finished playing Clarence Darrow at the Pasadena Playhouse."

"Far out," I cracked. "Who won?"

I was wisecracking all over the place. I couldn't take anything seriously. I reached the point at which I was actually frightened to go out of my house for fear of what I might do if someone asked me to give them a hand. I couldn't travel; I knew exactly what I would say when my travel agent asked me if I wanted to fly United. When my phone rang, I wouldn't answer it, causing a friend to ask me one day, "Aren't you going to answer the phone?"

To which I replied, "I didn't even hear the question."

The fact that I'd stopped receiving offers didn't bother me. With the money I had in the bank, and my investments, I didn't think I'd ever have to work again. And I continued to believe this until I got that fateful phone call from my business manager. As soon as I heard his first two words, I suspected something was terribly wrong. "*Buenas días,*" he said.

"Where are you calling from?" I asked.

"Outta sight, man, way outta sight. Would you believe . . . Cape of Good Hope? Hey, go with the flow, know what I mean? Look, I've got some good news for you and some bad news. Which would you like to hear first?"

I heard strange noises in the background. It sounded very much like chickens and war drums. I was alarmed. "You'd better give me the bad news." He did: One, there had been a bumper crop of mosquitoes in the Northeast, so my breeding farm had gone out of business; two, almost no one considered a Hearse a "fun car"; and three, he'd made a slight mistake when I purchased the music publishing rights to the national anthem from the Key family: "I guess I forgot to include the word *exclusive.*"

I took a very deep breath, closed my eyes, and asked, "And the good news?"

"The good news is that you weren't completely wiped out . . ."

I let out that deep breath, and then he continued. ". . . Otherwise I never would have been able to afford living down here."

So began that time of my life that I refer to as my forgotten period   I was broke, I couldn't get a job, and yet, as long as I could wisecrack, I still didn't care. Of course, some of the things I did during that period of my life can never be forgotten. One night, for example, when I was scraping bottom, I hooked up with Don Johnson and Alice Cooper, and we tried to knock over a bank. It wouldn't budge, so we settled for knocking over some garbage pails.

Then with other friends, we decided to form an "environmental orchestra" to play at weddings and bar mitzvahs. We limited ourselves to natural instruments. We had an excellent soda-bottle section, a fine two-blocks-of-wood player, a small water-in-glass combo, two very good knuckle crackers, and although it took me quite some time to find an instrument I could master, I turned out to be somewhat of a virtuoso on the naturally occurring wind instrument. I was the bass flatulist.

Unfortunately, the band wasn't as popular as we'd hoped. We couldn't get any national TV exposure and, except for the Cohen bar mitzvah, which turned ugly when we played the *1812* Overture, we had no bookings.

I don't remember when I hit bottom. But I knew I was there when the only offers I got were to share a square on "Hollywood Squares" with Chevy Chase, or to make an appearance on "To Tell the Truth" as one of the impostors.

I was broke. I thought I'd lost everything, but I hadn't. Being broke enabled me to rediscover my virginity. It was during this time that I learned the truth about those so-called "cheap" women—they're very expensive.

My agent tried to cheer me up, reminding me that I had qualified officially to be in the running for the Comeback of the Year Award. All I had to do was come back.

Money was no problem. Not having any money was the problem. I was getting desperate when I came up with what seemed like a foolproof idea. So I knew I could do it. As president and employees of What's-His-Name Productions, Inc., I fired myself after telling me, "You're too old for this business. Hollywood is looking for younger men." Then I sued the company for age discrimination. I claimed that the only reason I was fired was that I was the company's oldest employee and was earning the highest salary. My strategy was simple: if I won the case, my insurance company would have to pay off.

Unfortunately, with no employees, nobody answered the mail, so I didn't know I was being sued. What's-His-Name Productions, Inc., went out of business before I could cash in.

I was so deep at the bottom of the barrel that when I looked up, I could see pickles floating over my head. In my dreams I'd call my old visitors, the Acting Police, and they'd tell me they were busy at Robert Culp's house. I knew the only chance I had to salvage my career was to stop doing wisecracks. I needed help, real help, and fortunately I found it. I owe my life to the Gerald Ford Clinic for Dope Addiction.

I checked myself into Gerald Ford for three months. They were very nice to me, even after that check bounced. There were many familiar faces there trying to kick their habits, but I'm not going to invade their privacy by naming them unless this book doesn't sell and we need the publicity. The Ford Clinic is in Palm Springs, and while I was there, I had a lot of time for reflection, so in addition to learning how to control my wisecracking, I got a great tan.

When I finished the program at Gerald Ford, I felt strong and healthy and serious—and ready to start rebuilding my career. I didn't kid myself, although admittedly on occasion I did tickle myself under my arms. I knew it was going to be difficult. I was at that awkward stage of my career at which I had become "Didn't you used to be Leslie Nielsen?" When I heard that young director George Lucas was looking for a "Leslie Nielsen type" to play the lead in his science-fiction-adventure-comedy-love story *Star Wars,* I managed to get an audition. It didn't go well. Not only didn't I get the part—but rather than simply telling me, "Don't call us, we'll call you," Lucas had someone follow me home and rip out my telephone.

And worse, they told me I was no longer a "Leslie Nielsen type." I demanded to know what type they thought I was.

"B-positive," they told me.

"I usually am," I explained, "but under these circumstances it's difficult."

I needed to restore my confidence in my ability, so I accepted a job at a dinner theater in New Jersey. That didn't work either. I kept getting customers' orders mixed up. I guess I began to accept the fact that my career was in serious trouble when I called my agent at his office and he told me angrily, "I thought I told you never to call me here."

And then, just when I was so washed-up I was growing five-o'clock barnacles, my luck finally changed. Earlier in my career I had been offered several TV commercials, but I'd turned them down, believing they compromised the serious image I was trying to project. I felt that commercials were simply cheap exploitation, and that using my name to sell products I didn't use was the lowest form of selling out.

Well, wasn't I a silly! There is a great deal to be learned from the "wisdom of poverty." I came to understand that commercials were a legitimate art form, a form that required true creative genius to present an important message to an uninformed public in less than one minute, in an entertaining and educational way. Commercials make a vital contribution to the future of American commerce, hence to the very future of this great nation, and I believe they rank with the creation of the musical theater as uniquely American contributions to world culture. So I felt it was a great honor to be invited to perform in the commercial medium, to make what I call "mini-epics."

Ironically, for one who in my younger and foolish days had railed against commercials, the first commercial in which I appeared was for commercials. It was a public-service message reminding the hard-working moms and dads of this land that without commercials they wouldn't know what to buy, and therefore it was the wise shopper who watched as many commercials as possible before venturing into mall-land. It was a strong message, and in it I came across as honest and sincere, proving I could still act. Perhaps because it was too strong for young children, it was shown only late at night, when there would be less competition from other commercials.

It was a beginning for me, a small one, but definitely a beginning. While many corporations felt my recent stay at Gerald Ford eliminated me as a spokesperson for their products, others felt it helped me project just the right "seriously zany" image. Forest Lawn Cemetery, for example, had decided to utilize their vacant land by opening a small amusement park on the grounds, and in their commercials they wanted some-one, as they put it, "warm, yet grave." "Visiting the final resting place of a loved one no longer needs to be depressing," I promised on this spot, "not at Forest Lawn's new action-packed Ghostpark. It's guaranteed thrills and chills for the whole fami-ly—and while you're there, make sure you visit America's most realistic Haunted House. Who knows who you'll meet there. And please—don't go into the basement!"

After that, to respond to the blatantly political ads promoting clean air, I did a series called "See What You're Breathing," which told the other side of the story for the auto-emissions industry.

The only commercial I did that I felt might compromise my integrity was a controversial spot for the Tobacco Producers Association. It took place after a funeral, where several bereaved people were standing around a coffin discussing the deceased. One of the mourners said regretfully, "If only he hadn't smoked three packs a day . . ."

I began my comeback by doing TV commercials. Although few people remember, I was the spokesperson for the first Japanese imported car, the Toyauto, which later became better known as Toyota.

At which point the mourners froze in place and I stepped in front of them, explaining, "America's tobacco producers are worried about your health. Tobacco packs contain potentially harmful paper and cellophane, in addition to the glue on the back of that little stamp. So please, stop smoking those packs and live to enjoy the cigarettes inside. This messenger has been brought to you by your friendly tobacco producers, who remind you that a Free Smoking environment is up to you!"

While the commercials enabled me to pay the rent, they were not artistically fulfilling. I was desperate to get back into motion pictures, but so many of the studio executives with whom I'd worked had been replaced by much younger people who thought Shinola was an Italian movie studio. I had to get their attention, and Weisman felt the best way to do that was through television. If there was one thing these young movie executives knew, it was TV. He did his best to find me work on the tube, but at first it was very difficult. One day, for example, he called me and announced, "It's 'Mission: Impossible.' "

"Terrif," I said. "What do I play? The megalomaniacal ruler of a small nongeographically specific nation whose name ends in *a*? A master criminal with dirty pictures of the president?"

"Uh, no. I mean, that's how tough it is to find you work."

My comeback began one payday at a time. On the new "Twilight Zone" I played a clumsy inventor who discovered how to make things invisible, then accidentally dropped his only batch of the solution on the formula. I did a very early episode of "Cheers," in which I played a member of Alcoholics Anonymous who just sat at the bar and cried. Gradually, I began proving that I'd beaten my dope habit, and I started getting offers.

I did several of those so-called "disease of the week" movies made especially for TV, among them the Emmy-nominated drama "Star Kids," the tragic story of the children of famous entertainers who are born without any talents; and "Splinters," a fictionalized account of the economic disaster that destroyed a resort community when the boardwalks were allowed to rot, sort of a modern-day version of Ibsen's *An Enemy of the People*.

Some of the movies were silly, I can't deny that. For example, I did "The Little Billy Roberts Story," which was based on the bizarre true story of a six-year-old from Midland, Texas, who got his hand stuck in a cookie jar, then suffered potentially serious head injuries when he tried to scratch a mosquito bite on his ear. Truthfully, making these movies wasn't very satisfying, but it was work, and an actor without work makes an unhappy waiter.

I just needed the opportunity to prove I could still act on the big screen. And it was the legendary producer Dino de Laurentiis who gave me that chance. Several years earlier Clint Eastwood had made the transition from television cowboy to movie star in a series of westerns made in Italy by director Sergio Leone. These "spaghetti westerns," which were so low budget they couldn't even afford to give Eastwood's character a name, were successful both critically and financially. De Laurentiis believed he could follow the same formula, although he decided to make his westerns in Israel. I starred in the first two of the six "falafel westerns" he eventually produced, *The Sheikh of Laramie* and *The Man from Kibbutz Dodge*.

Dino did everything possible to save money on these productions. Instead of ten-gallon hats, for example, we wore what he called 7.5-gallon hats. Instead of six-shooters, we carried four-shooters. Rather than using branding irons, the cattle rustlers used steam irons, so we had the only cattle in movie history from the Proctor-Silex Ranch. The town was so small that instead of the saloon being named Diamond Lil's, it was called Zircon Lil's. It was ridiculous. It really was a one-horse town; that's all Dino would pay for, one horse. So instead of horses we used camels. Overall, that worked fine—except when we filmed the chase scenes, in which the posse mounted the camels from the rear. The rear mount is a staple of every western; to make a quick getaway, the cowpoke runs up behind his horse, puts both hands on the horse's hindquarters, then vaults into the saddle. It looks great. But we discovered almost immediately that a rear mount is much more difficult to do on a camel. You really have to get a lot of height on the vault. This is probably where the expression *getting over the hump* comes from. It may also be where the term *cowpoke* comes from. We lost several stuntmen this way.

While we were making these films, I got to know Dino quite well. I used to do a very funny imitation of him. I'd wave an imaginary cigar through the air and exclaim, "Iffa I wanna makea art, I buya painta brusha. If I wanna makea money, I make the movie picture. There'sa only two kinda movie, there'sa movie that makea money and there'sa movie that losa money. There'sa no such thing asa gooda movie that losa my money."

Dino used to claim that that was "Da nakeda trutha," but I didn't agree with him. That was more like the partially clad truth, meaning that some very worthwhile films have lost money. For example, the first *Batman* film starring Michael Keaton was certainly a well-made film, but after three years in release it had grossed only $275,000,000, so according to Warners it was still showing a loss of more than $25,000,000. Yet because it was such a fine film, Warners valiantly decided to make a sequel, knowing full well that if it was only as successful as the first film, the studio would be in danger of going out of business.

Dino overheard me doing my imitation one afternoon and was so impressed with my talent that he thought I was wasting it on his low-budget films, so he graciously released me from my contract. And he gave me a nice bonus. As he explained, "I'ma noa gonna breaka your kneecaps."

Word spreads quickly in the motion-picture industry, and that word was *box office*. These falafel westerns made a lot of money, and once again I was considered bankable, meaning the audience would pay to see me in a movie. Offers didn't pour in, but they did start dripping in. As the next step in my comeback, I accepted an offer from director John Carpenter to star in a quirky film he was making for Fox. Low-budget horror films, the so-called fright films or slasher films, had become exceedingly popular, and the studio believed that a well-made slasher film would do very well. Carpenter had crafted a brilliant script aimed directly at women. Focus groups had identified an area that terrified women and had not yet been the subject of a movie or book—something men knew almost nothing about. As the promos for this film warned, "This was the man that women feared most. He ruined their lives, destroyed their relationships, kept them prisoners in their own homes. He brutally cut them off from the rest of the world. Leslie Nielsen is . . . the Hairdresser from Hell in *Bad Haircut*."

I'd originally intended to pattern my performance after the character created by Warren in *Shampoo,* but Carpenter wanted it quite differently. He wanted me to play it much more broadly, more like Jack in *The Shining*. "Remember," Carpenter told me, "you've spent your whole life working in women's salons, listening to their sniveling, whining problems, dealing with their whims. They've driven you totally nuts. This is your chance to get even."

"So you want me to chew the scenery," I said, using the acting term to describe particularly broad acting.

"To the very last bite."

LESLIE NIELSEN

That eventually caused a problem on the set. I assumed Carpenter was speaking figuratively. But to prove I was insane, he actually wanted me to eat some of the props. So I can honestly claim that making this picture made me sick to my stomach.

But to my surprise, my character struck a responsive chord in American women. I don't think that anyone realized before this movie was made how much anger women secretly harbored toward their hairstylists. Directly because of this picture several books were published examining the relationship between women and their hairdressers, focusing on a woman's emotional dependence on her stylist and her feeling of helplessness about the entire process. This led to Germaine Greer's controversial essay "The Samsonia Factor" in *Vanity Fair*, which blamed everything on men, pointing out that women had their hair styled and colored to please men, and therefore a bad haircut caused them to lose their self-esteem, feel unattractive, and suffer serious trauma. The whole thing came to a head with a nationally covered trial in Fort Lauderdale, Florida, in which a woman name Susan Koenig sued her hairdresser for "intentional mental cruelty" for ruining her wedding day by giving her an unflattering haircut—and was awarded $65,000.

This incredible publicity served to remind me just how powerful the moving image can be in creating public awareness and reasoned debate about issues vital to our well-being. Personally, *Bad Haircut* put me back on top. By grossing $80,000,000 worldwide, it proved without doubt that audiences would support my work.

Women either loved or hated my character. During my promotional tour, I actually had women throw their hotel room keys at me. And if they missed, they threw ashtrays, lipstick containers, whatever they could get their hands on. Fortunately, most women throw like women.

It was while I was still basking in the glow of success from this film that I married Michelle Pfeiffer, who had had a small part in the film as a nail decorator. This was several films before her career really took off, and at that point she was just another incredibly beautiful young actress with great karma. I don't know what it was about me that she found so irresistible; perhaps it was my sophistication, my worldliness, but she just wouldn't leave me alone.

Oh, I liked her very much. She was as sweet as milk chocolate. At night, we would sit together by the fire reading out loud the poetry of Rod McKuen or excerpts from *Jonathan Livingston Seagull,* while listening to the wisdom of Leonard Cohen on the stereo, but the harsh truth is that I was never really in love with her. I just felt that something was missing between us, that there had to be something more. She knew it, but she didn't care. "It doesn't matter if you never love me as I love you," she declared "Just to walk in the coolness of your shadow is all I ask."

Why did we get married? I guess I just couldn't bear to hurt her. It's very difficult when someone as young and innocent and beautiful as Michelle continues to profess such deep feelings of love and promises to dedicate her life to you and begs just for the privilege of being your love slave. Could I honestly tell her that she was wrong, that someday she

My former wife Michelle Pfeiffer is one of America's greatest actresses. Ask her about our marriage, and she'll act as if it never happened.

would meet another man like me? That someday she would love someone as completely as she loved me? That someday she would find a man who pleased her as much as I did, who could penetrate to the very core of her soul? Maybe another man could've told her that, but I couldn't. I just couldn't lie to her.

We were married at the legendary Candlelight Wedding Chapel in Las Vegas, Nevada, after driving all night from Los Angeles. Pfffff, as I called her (pronounced "ffff"), was wearing a lovely Chanel number. I think the number was $3,499.99. Although some people claimed later that I never took this marriage seriously, in fact I took it just as seriously as I've taken every one of my third marriages. And I really did hope that someday I would fall in love with her, that I would be able to overlook that beautiful exterior, look deeper than her lovely interior, to find the real person.

People who know about this part of my life ask me what it was like being married to Michelle Pfeiffer. I tell them the truth; it was exactly as I imagined it would be. It was just like a fantasy. But I think I knew from the beginning that it would never work. I just couldn't deal with her jealousy. I'd take out the garbage and she'd demand to know whom I was seeing. I'd watch "Wheel of Fortune" on television and she'd claim Vanna White was flirting with me. In addition to that, she had several habits that drove me absolutely crazy. She insisted on walking around the house totally naked while I was trying to read, which can often be distracting. And she refused to let me hire a housekeeper because she insisted on being the only person cleaning up after me.

I began to worry that she was becoming too attached to me. I knew it for sure when I awoke in the middle of the night and found her trying to glue herself to me so we'd never part. It was obvious that our marriage had to end, but I wanted to end it without destroying her for every other man she might ever meet as long as she lived. So when I read that Brian De Palma was doing a new remake of the 1932 gangster film *Scarface,* I sneaked out of the house on the pretext that I was having heart palpitations and called Brian to beg him to find a part for her.

Several days later I found Michelle crying in our bedroom. That was very strange; I was used to hearing her laugh in our bedroom. She told me that De Palma had offered her the lead in his new movie opposite Al Pacino. "That's fabulous, Pfffff," I sprayed. "It's everything you ever dreamed of."

She gracefully wiped the spray from her lips. "I can't do it," she said. "I can't give you up just to become a star. What good is superstardom and more money than I ever imagined possible if I can't have you?"

I had to admit she had a point there. It took me a little while to come up with a good answer. "Look, Pfffff, I care about you deeply, but there's just something missing . . ."

"I didn't take that bracelet," she protested, wiping her cheek. "I found it in the bottom of my pocketbook. You've got to believe me . . ."

"Of course I do, sweetheart. But you see, I come from a broken home."

Her eyes glistened again. "I never knew that. You mean your mother and father split up when you were young?"

"Oh, no. I mean we lived in an old house. Nothing worked. And so, I learned that sometimes we have to get along without those things that seem to mean so much to us. Indoor plumbing, for example."

"But you're so much more important to me than indoor plumbing," she said sweetly.

I pushed a wisp of hair from in front of her eye. "Sure, now, in the summer. But in the winter, when you have to go outside and sit . . ." I stopped, and said firmly, "I want you to accept this part. I want you to make me proud."

"How can I?" she emoted. "How can I leave you alone? I can't, I mustn't."

"You know there is so much about you that is so wonderful. I've never known anyone who cared about other people more than you do. Suppose we stay married. That would be the easiest thing to do. But what about all those other women I'd never be able to go out with? Those women whose dreary lives I'd never be able to enrich? Who will have to go through their entire lives without knowing for a single second the pleasure you've known for months? Do you really want to be responsible for that? Have you ever thought about them?"

She started crying once again. "I've been so selfish."

I put my arm around her shoulder. "No, sweetheart, you're just human."

And so I convinced her to accept the part in De Palma's film. Naturally our separation was painful. That superglue really works well. But her performance marked the real beginning of her career and proved to be best for all the other women in the world. Eventually we had the marriage annulled, meaning legally it never happened. In fact, whenever Michelle is asked about it, that's what she says, that it never really happened.

Legally, she's absolutely correct. But someday I hope that she'll learn how to forgive me and forget me.

I missed Michelle after we parted; it was twilight and she was driving up Beverly Glen while I was driving down Sunset. I didn't see her and had to swerve at the last moment, but that was the end of our relationship. I knew that the best thing for me to do was to get back to work as quickly as possible. I was choosing between several fascinating projects when Weisman reported that I'd received an exciting offer. "It's a big secret," he told me. "I can't tell you anything about the picture. I can't tell you who the director is or what part you'll play. I think it's perfect for you."

That could mean only one thing: Woody Allen wanted me to star in his next project. That, or my agent was a moron. It turned out to be the Allen picture. "Mmmmm Mmmmm's Summer Project," as Orion Pictures billed it, was scheduled to be filmed somewhere starring other actors and actresses. As with other Woody Allen movies, the entire cast and crew were sworn to secrecy. It was certainly one of the most difficult productions in which I've ever appeared. Because of Woody's extremely well publicized aversion to publicity, he wouldn't tell us where we were filming or when or precisely what parts we were playing, or even what the picture was about. In fact the project was so secretive that even Woody didn't show up to direct, unless I was in the wrong place.

To ensure that the actors didn't reveal too much, no one was given a complete script. All we received were sheets of paper that looked to be blank until we exposed them to heat and then read them in a mirror. Each actor was given only his or her lines. That made our job even more difficult because we were never quite sure when we were supposed to say them, to whom we were supposed to say them, or even in what order they were supposed to be said. When I asked about this, I was told, "Mr. Mmmm is a firm believer in the creative process."

When we actually started filming, it turned out to be one of the most bizarre, unusual, fascinating, weird stories I'd ever heard. While we were filming the high-diving scene on the

Empire State Building observatory platform, Tony Roberts, who'd appeared in many other Allen films, told me confidentially, "This is all autobiographical, you know. Everything Woody does comes from his own experiences."

That was difficult to believe. "What about the elephant and the chess match?"

Roberts nodded. "That really happened to him, only it wasn't an elephant and a chess game."

I smiled. "I didn't think so."

"It was a hunchback and the game was water polo. He changed it because he's very sensitive about handicapped people."

The film was finally released under the title *The Bitterness of Comedy,* and when I saw it, I was stunned at how successful he'd been in preventing anyone from discovering what the film was about. And I think the audience was just as stunned as I was.

Personally, it was a privilege to work with a comic genius like Woody Allen, even if I never actually met him. Although I'd always admired his classic comedies like *Take the Money and Run* and *Interiors,* it was clear after seeing this film that he'd taken humor to a new level, a place where writers like Neil Simon, Herb Gardner, and Mordecai Richler have not yet dared to tread. In this film he pioneered a new form of humor, comedy without any laughs. As *The New York Review of Books* wrote in its rave review, "Sartre would have died."

The only real complaint I have about the entire experience was that Orion took Allen's demands for secrecy much too seriously. I remain convinced that it would have been good business to advertise the film, revealing details about it such as where it was playing and what time it started. I have no doubt the film would have been more successful if people had known it was in the movie theaters.

My personal problems were over. My difficulties with dope and wisecracks were just bad memories. My comeback was complete. Once again, the pile of scripts on my floor was growing, and this time I didn't even have to water them to make the pages swell so the pile would get bigger. I had so much confidence in myself that for the first time I felt the urge to develop my own project, a movie I could work on and be proud of the finished product. Something with deeper meaning. A film I could really call my own.

The era of my superstardom had dawned.

8

THE FINAL CHAPTER

W hile instructing doctoral candidates in Theory of Mad
Scientist Films at the famed UCLA Film School and
24-Hour Developing Center, I met three very bright
young men with raw talent, tremendous enthusiasm, and that
vitally important intangible, family trust funds. Their names
were Jim Abrahams, David Zucker, and Jerry Zucker. As I later
discovered, David Zucker and Jerry Zucker were brothers, meaning they shared the same biological parents. David got them on
Mondays, Wednesdays, and Fridays; Jerry had them the other
days. I sort of took them under my wing, trying to help them
develop their talent and channel it in a positive direction.

When I grasped the opportunity to make motion pictures that I would find personally rewarding, I asked them to join me. One afternoon we were at UCLA's Film Testing Laboratory watching scientists running crash tests to determine the impact of a reel of film hitting a wall at fifteen frames per second, and I told them about the kind of film I wanted to do: "I've always loved the classic adventure films, those films about common people who find themselves in uncommon jeopardy, where life and death hang by a single thread. For instance, how long has it been since anyone has made a film about passengers on an out-of-control airplane, who have to depend on a reluctant hero with serious character defects to save their lives?"

One of the Zuckers estimated, "About eight months."

"Exactly," I agreed. "But remember, everything in the film industry goes in cycles, and I think it's time to revive this formula. Try to imagine this—four hundred and fifty terrified passengers on an airplane that has lost its wings: among them a sick child, a singing nun, a scientist with a vial containing the cure for cancer, and a corporate executive about to close the biggest deal of his life. The entire flight crew is unconscious, except for the navigator, who's just stupid, and the only chance to prevent the plane from smashing into a snow-capped mountain, where, if everyone doesn't die from the crash, they'll freeze to death or starve unless they cannibalize the other people, is to risk an almost impossible air-to-air transfer of a pilot who hasn't flown one of these big birds in more than two decades."

Abrahams snapped his fingers and said, "A comedy!"

"Sorry, son," I said, calming him down, "but there's nothing funny about that situation. There are many things in this world to make fun of: mines, obsessive love, Geraldo Rivera,

249

"Jeopardy" interviews, women drivers, pro-football quarterbacks who wear brassieres, even politicians, but not airplane flights.

"And let me tell you why," I continued, sharing something I'd learned in my years in the cinema industry. "You see, nobody thinks it's funny when Mr. Death comes a-knocking on the door, unless, of course, he's wearing plaid bell-bottoms and a Nehru jacket. But I digress. I see this as a hard-hitting action-packed adventure film, an old-fashioned kind of movie that keeps the audience sitting on the edge of their seats with their hands over their eyes. I want this movie to be so exciting that nobody can stand to watch it. So, what do you guys say? Are you with me?"

The result was the classic of the genre—*Airplane!* I starred as "the doctor." We had an all-star cast. Costarring with me was the great Lloyd Bridges. I'd never met Bridges, but I'd admired his work for many, many years, particularly his portrayal of undersea adventurer Mike Nelson in the popular TV show "Sea Hunt." Although I suspected that after all these years he was tired of talking about that old series, when we were introduced, I told him, "I just want you to know how much I admired your work on 'Sea Hunt.'"

"Thank you," Lloyd said, and a chain of little bubbles popped out of his mouth.

I thought he was kidding. "And . . . it's nice to be working with you," I said.

He smiled, and more bubbles rose. As I soon learned, Lloyd had never really gotten over playing the role of Mike Nelson.

In addition to Lloyd Bridges, the movie costarred the wonderful Robert Stack, the tremendous Peter Graves, the unusually talented Robert Hays, the lovely and brilliant Julie Hagerty, and Ethel Merman as the screen siren. I knew the movie would be successful because it would have the full support of my fans, but I never dared hope it would become the top-grossing film of the year. So when it didn't, I wasn't the slightest bit disappointed. It did incredibly well, though, and in addition to its commercial success, I was honored by my peers in the Academy of Motion Picture Arts and Sciences with my first nomination as Best Actor.

Although I was thrilled and gratified, I knew I had no realistic chance to win. The Best Actor category included the strongest group of nominees in Oscar history. My competition consisted of Bob Redford, for his stunning portrayal of an embittered and unemployed Ozzie Nelson in *Ordinary People,* Bobby De Niro for his stunning portrayal of a cowardly farmer who finds his courage just in time to save his family in *Raging Bull,* Jack Nicholson for his stunning portrayal of a man who dared to go out with women and then refused to marry them in *Terms of Endearment,* and Dusty Hoffman for his stunning portrayal of a father who learns to love his own child in *Kramer vs. Kramer*

The odds were very much against me. De Niro was the 3–1 favorite, Nicholson and Redford were at 8–1, Hoffman was at 12–1, and I was at "Bet the house."

Since I did not expect to win, I decided not to campaign for the award. In the past, Academy members have been known to vote with their hearts rather than their heads—the so-called "last operation wins" factor (plastic surgery not included). But unlike my competition, I refused to resort to cheap exploitation of my personal problems to evoke sympathy from the voters. De Niro, for example, ran a rather gruesome photograph of himself holding the remains of his little puppy after it had been run over by a sixteen-wheeler. Redford, in an advertisement thanking the Academy for its support, wrote that, since he was a college dropout, he was offering to assist in paying the first year's college tuition for the oldest child of anyone voting for him. Hoffman ran a letter from his doctor warning that he had only a few months to live unless "something meaningful happens to help you overcome your deep depression. Some sort of recognition. An award of some kind perhaps." And Nicholson simply offered to sleep with any women who voted for him.

Elizabeth Taylor ran an ad describing her latest operation, but this was just tradition, as she hadn't been nominated for anything.

I refused to lower my personal standards. I would win or lose on the quality of my performance, and I stated that firmly in the series of advertisements I took in the various trade publications: "Although there is a tendency on the part of some individuals to exploit their personal problems, I will refrain from that. While my recent stay at the famed Gerald Ford Clinic, where I overcame my dependency on dopey jokes and wisecracks, and my subsequent nomination as Best Actor, might serve as a shining example to the millions of Americans waging their own silent battles, I urge you not to vote for me if your only reason for doing so is to enable me to stand up as the representative of all that is good in the Academy and urge the billions of people watching worldwide to seek help when it is necessary, to act toward others in good faith, to love their children and respect their parents, to pray to the God of their choice or not pray to the non-God of their choice, and always remember the words of John 'Duke' Wayne: 'A few hours spent regularly in the movies adds up to a fortune in memories.' "

Even though I remained confident I wouldn't win, I wrote a brief speech thanking those people who had made my comeback possible. It was loosely based on President Eisenhower's farewell address in which he warned Americans against allowing the military-industrial complex to gain control of the country. Unfortunately, when I left my house for the ceremony, I forgot to bring my speech with me, which led to one of my most memorable triumphs.

As I sat through all the minor awards, I continually reminded myself to smile when they announced that I had again lost. At least I would have the honor of losing a much more important award than in the past. Audrey Hepburn and David Niven were presenting the Oscar for Best Actor. As Audrey announced each of the nominees, a brief clip from their performance was shown. Then David opened the envelope. He fumbled with it for a few seconds, using a technique known in the theater as "pretending to be nervous to get a laugh from an audience that doesn't think it's funny but knows it's supposed to be so they laugh so the people watching at home think it's real." Finally, David got it open and pulled out the card. "Oh, my," he said, "this is a great surprise." He handed the card to Audrey, who read it, then looked at David and arched her eyebrows in surprise, then announced, "The winner is . . . it's Leslie Nielsen."

Well, you could have knocked me over with a wrecking ball. I was stunned, shocked, thrilled. I didn't know how to react when I heard my name. I suspect I felt much like Christopher Columbus must have felt when he discovered the New World while searching for the Spice Islands—I had no idea where I was. At most, I thought I had a chance to win Mr. Congeniality and the $5,000 scholarship. But the Big O himself? Never. I admit it, I was incredibly lucky; the bulk of the vote had been split so evenly among the other four nominees that I had managed to squeak in by a few votes. A wave of emotion swept me onto my feet and up to the stage. I kissed David Niven and shook Audrey Hepburn's hand, then reached into my jacket pocket for my speech. It was at that moment that I discovered I'd left it home. I looked out at the audience, waiting expectantly for my reaction. I stared into the camera, knowing untold millions more were watching around the world, and then I told them the truth, "I'm speechless."

They applauded so loudly that no one heard me add, "I left my speech home." I was much too nervous to remember what I'd written, so I simply held up my Oscar as high as I could and said, "I'd like to thank everybody in the world. I hope I haven't forgotten anyone." Then I walked off the stage into Oscar history.

I was stunned when I beat Redford, Nicholson, De Niro and Hoffman and was named Best Actor for Airplane!

The next morning the *Hollywood Reporter* called it "one of the most emotional and heartfelt speeches in Oscar history. And the shortest. Nielsen was so overcome with emotion that he was rendered speechless." My speech was widely praised for its sincerity, its clarity, and its brevity. In the Unites States Senate, Sen. George Mitchell (D-Maine) read it into the *Congressional Record* in its entirety, then suggested legislators learn the fundamental lesson that so much can be said in so little time. Ironically, it took him longer to read that into the record than it had taken me to deliver my speech.

My shocking victory caused quite a bit of controversy. Academy president Jack Valenti called it "the biggest upset since Lassie won the Kentucky Derby." I think Bobby De Niro was overreacting when he called it "a night that will live in infancy." I think Redford was the most reasonable, telling reporters, "*Sic transit gloria,*" which naturally made me wonder what moving a sick girl named Gloria had to do with my winning the Academy Award.

My life changed immediately and drastically. Early the next morning Sylvester Stallone called and offered me the role of an over-the-hill former champion in *Rocky V: Repeating His Comeback Again*. Almost as soon as I hung up, George Lucas was on the line offering me the lead in *Star Wars IV: Extremely High Noon*. I hung up and Cubby Broccoli phoned to ask me to play an older, more mature James Bond in *Bond Retires*. The doorbell rang continuously for hours, and then we discovered that De Niro had jammed a pin in it. CAA's Michael Ovitz, the most powerful agent in Hollywood, honored me by inviting me to sit at his table at the exclusive restaurant Morton's, although he did ask me to finish by eight o'clock so the table would be available when he arrived. Weisman informed me that I'd finally made Tinseltown's A-list. I got invited to all the best parties. One night, for example, I went to a lavish spread at producer Joe Silverblatt's, and among the guests were the self-esteemed Kirk Douglas, Pulitzer Prize-winning journalist Geraldo Rivera, even Joan Collins. Things happened that night that . . . well, I'd intended to include them in this book, just to give the reader an example of . . . that sort of thing, but both Kirk and Geraldo asked me not to. "There are just some things you don't put in writing," Kirk reminded me.

"He's right," Geraldo said supportively, "and don't forget not to mention Joan Collins either. You do and you'll leave yourself wide open to critics, who'll say, 'Joan Collins? Hasn't everybody?' "

But perhaps the nicest invitation of all came from my old friend Ronald Reagan, who asked me to join him and Nancy for an intimate dinner for three hundred at the White House.

Dinner at the White House. It was a night I shall never forget. Ambassador Dobrynin from the Soviet Union was there.

Henry Kissinger was there, James Stewart was there, and I had to go and accidentally drop a fish down the front of Mrs. Reagan's dress. After dinner, Ronnie and I sat in the Lyndon Johnson Bathroom and talked about the good old days. "Golly," he said, "we sure had fun making *Bedtime for Bonzo,* didn't we? Wowee, we sure made a monkey out of that little kid."

"Uh, Mr. President," I corrected him, "that, uh . . . that actually was a monkey."

He considered that for a few seconds, then frowned. "You know, I thought he had a lot of hair. Damned good poker player, though."

Many people consider my performance in *Airplane!* the greatest role of my career. People often stop me on the street to tell me how much they enjoyed it. One woman I'll never forget stopped me on the street, looked at me, pointed at me, and said, "I know who you are. You're Lloyd Bridges, aren't you?"

I smiled, then replied politely, "No, I'm not, but I am an actor. My name is Nielsen, Leslie Nielsen."

She gasped and said, "Oh, I'm so embarrassed. Of course, Leslie Nielsen, of course." Then she looked at me almost timidly and added, "But . . . but . . . but you play Lloyd Bridges?"

I knew I would win my first Oscar as Best Actor only once in my life, so I intended to take full advantage of it. I believed quite strongly in the old phrase "Strike while the iron is hot"— unless, obviously, you're a union member working in an iron manufacturing plant, in which case the iron is always hot, and if you were always on strike, you'd never get any work done.

As the Academy Award–winning Best Actor I have to admit I felt a little like the proverbial five-hundred-pound gorilla. I had an incredible craving for bananas. But I also realized that this award gave me real power in the film industry and presented me with the opportunity to do something I'd always dreamed of doing, but had never dared tell anyone: it gave me the chance to direct.

Most of the important Hollywood filmmakers were anxious to work with me on my next project, and Weisman and I met with many of the top producers—Francis Ford Coppola, Peter Guber and Jon Peters, Mark Tarlov, Dave Winfield and Jose Canseco (who'd produced several big hits), even Tom Stimson and Jerry Bruckman—to discuss any projects that might be right for me.

As always, I wanted to do something meaningful, something that would change lives. Starting with mine. When I'd started in the film business, producers would create projects from short stories, magazine articles, books, even original ideas. That proved to be a terribly inefficient way to run a business, as there was no way of accurately predicting which films would be profitable. In recent years, producers have been able to eliminate much of the speculation that went into making those decisions by conducting extensive audience surveys, as well as utilizing focus groups and in-depth interviews to determine exactly what elements combine to make a picture attractive to an audience: what stars, what type of story, which period. It's sort of like a Produce-a-Movie-by-Numbers kit, and it's the primary reason that most movies made today are financially successful. "What we've discovered," Tom Stimson told me as he propped his rhinestone-covered cowboy boots up on his desk, narrowly missing his Tiffany ashtray, "is that audiences like stories about fish out of water."

"I see," I said, "outdoor pictures."

Jerry laughed out loud. "I think I can explain what Tom means. See, what we've discovered is that our audience likes pictures about Indians off their reservation."

"Oh, oh, now I see. You mean, cowboy pictures."

"Excuse me, Jer," Tom said, "maybe I better take this one. See, what Jer means is that the audience is fascinated by stories focusing on deer out of season and . . ."

Jerry interrupted. "That's not precisely right. What we really mean to say is that people want to see movies about mothers who have never had any children."

"That's not what I meant at all, Jer," Tom said pointedly. "What I said was that people will always go to see movies about carpenters without cars."

"I don't think that's what you meant at all, Tom," Jerry said emphatically. "What you meant to—"

"Okay, okay," I said, raising my hands, "let's just hold it. It seems to me that what you guys are telling me is that people want to see movies about characters who are thrown into a culture far different from their own and who must come to understand that culture and adapt to its mores in order to survive."

"Isn't that what I just said?" Tom wondered aloud.

"After you heard me say it," Jerry corrected him.

The project they had in mind for me wedded two completely different worlds. It was the story of a man of intellect, a man deeply devoted to the peaceful resolution of conflict, who eventually had to resort to physical violence to avenge a terrible crime while saving his own life. Their working title was *Ninja Gandhi*.

As soon as I heard them explain the plot, I knew it had real commercial potential. "It's obviously an interesting concept," I said coolly, "but whatever picture I do next, I want to direct as well as star in it."

Tom didn't even hesitate. "I don't see that as a problem. Jer?"

"Hell, no," Jerry agreed emphatically, "the real true fact is that with all this sophisticated equipment, as long as you have the right cinematographer, anybody can direct."

"He's right," Tom continued. "Like Arsenio Hall could direct if he wanted to."

"Absolutely," Jerry said. "I'll bet Mother Teresa could even direct."

"Sure, of course," Tom said firmly. "Even Dan Quayle could . . . well, certainly Mother Teresa."

Jerry leaned back in his calves-embryo-leather lounger with its shimmering mother-of-pearl arms, slicked back his hair, and asked, "One question, though. You ever done any directing before?"

"Well," I admitted, "actually, no."

"That's okay," Jerry said. "You know, that's just the way Steven Spielberg started.

"Just one thing, though," Jerry finished. "It's not like the deal or anything depends on this, and I hate to ask, but what the hell. Nothing ventured, nothing ventured. You think maybe one night Tom and I could sit with you at Ovitz's table at Morton's?"

"Just for the appetizer, we mean," Tom said hopefully. "It's an important statement in this town."

I agreed to do what I could to make it happen.

We decided to go against type in casting *Ninja Gandhi*, primarily because we had an extremely difficult time finding a Nobel Peace Prize–winning former Indian prime minister who was also a member of SAG. We even had an open call, a so-called cattle call, for which several hundred actors showed up. It was only natural that we eventually decided to offer the role to Arnold Schwarzenegger. Tom pointed out that he brought something unique to the role—he was one of the very few actors who tanned easily and who spoke Hindustani with an authentic Neanderthalian accent.

I think every actor secretly harbors a desire to direct a motion picture. While acting can be extremely rewarding, as well as making it easier to meet girls, directing seems to offer so much more creative satisfaction. The picture truly becomes your own vision. And besides, as the great American entrepreneur Henry Ford once said, "It's good to be boss."

Having worked with so many talented directors in my career, I knew that there were as many different philosophical approaches to directing as there were directors, ranging from the Hitchcockian "Actors are like putty, the only thing they're good for is plugging up leaks" to Martin Scorsese's lazy-fare method of "You show up, you act good, you go home to Brooklyn." I fell somewhere in the middle, but fortunately I didn't suffer any serious injuries.

The primary thing I'd learned while observing directors through the years was the importance of preparation. When a good director walks onto the set in the morning, he knows precisely what he intends to accomplish that day and exactly how he intends to do it. Some directors actually "storyboard" every shot they want to make, literally drawing the entire movie before they start filming. I had neither the time nor the budget to do that, so to prepare for *Ninja Gandhi* I spent several weeks attending yoga classes and studying the art of meditation. It worked out very well. By the time we were ready to begin shooting my mind was a complete blank.

I became somewhat of an expert on the martial arts. At thirty feet I could identify every portrait ever done of Dodge City's marshal Matt Dillon, even the quite unusual and highly praised western series of Peter Max fingerpaintings.

We had a good script, we had a terrific crew, and we had the unusually talented Arnold Schwarzenegger. It was certainly the best movie I ever directed. Working with Arnie was one of the great pleasures of my life, although admittedly at times it got very complicated. Because of the specialized nature of the martial arts scenes, we were forced to use an experienced martial artist to perform all the fight scenes for Schwarzenegger. And because our bonding company felt Arnold was too valuable a corporation to risk, we also had to use several doubles to do all the stunt work for him. Naturally, this was in addition to the body double we used in the nude scenes, the Gandhi double who did all the religious scenes in the Hindu temple, the professional dancing double we used for the dance number at the date festival, the jazz double who played the sax in the smoky nightclub scenes, the hand model we used in all hand close-ups, the special-effects double who stood in for him in the climactic scene that required him to rapidly age one thousand years, and the Schwarzenegger impersonator whose voice was dubbed in for Arnie's during post-production. Overall, I honestly believe that this was Arnold Schwarzenegger's finest performance.

I had wanted to direct in the worst way, and fortunately this motion picture gave me the opportunity to do just that. Arnie was very easy to work with: I'd simply point to the spot where I wanted him to stand and command, "Arnie, go there. Speak word." Arnie would nod and go to that spot and get his word right every time.

Directing myself was far more complicated, perhaps because as an actor I wasn't my first choice for director for the part. My performance wasn't as strong as I wanted myself to be as the director. Even now I'm not certain if it was my lackluster performance that hurt my work as a director, or my somewhat insecure directing that hurt my work as an actor. Perhaps if I'd been a stronger director, my acting would have been better and my direction would have improved.

Looking back, the most difficult part of the process was editing the film. After working as long and as hard as I had on *Ninja Gandhi;* every frame was like gold to me, and cutting out a scene was like cutting out my own liver with a nail clipper. But even I knew that at five hours and twenty-two minutes the film played too long. Cutting out the first eighty-two minutes was relatively simple. We simply deleted that entire "How to make a Polar Bear Meat Loaf" scene. But after that it got tough, very tough. Could the story afford to lose Aunt Blossom and Uncle Ernie lighting the candles? Or did I want to cut out the fight on the roof of the Empire State Building? Sometimes there were no quick answers, and I'd have to do what I'd learned in my meditation studies—close my eyes and cut.

The editing was made even more difficult by those things that had to be left in due to contractual obligations. The opening credits, for example, ran more than eleven minutes, and there was nothing I could do to shorten them. In the old days, films were made by producers and financed by studios. Today each film is an independent corporation, and the financing to make the film comes from a wide variety of sources, each of which has to be acknowledged in the credits. And almost everyone who works on a film demands a "full card," meaning that their name appears on-screen by itself for a certain number of seconds. So the opening credits for *Ninja Gandhi* read: "Screen Star Partners and The Omnibus Entertainment Corporation, in association with Cinema Enterprises, A Five Star Group Ltd., present a Tom Stimson and Jerry Bruckman/Paramount Pictures production of a film by Leslie Nielsen. Released by Major Domo Inc. and distributed by American Good Film Distributors: The Stimson-Bruckman Partners and What's-His-Name Productions presentation of the Leslie Nielsen film, *Ninja Gandhi*. Created and developed by Tom Stimson and Jerry Bruckman from a story by Richard A. Woodley. Based on a concept by Alex Langsam of an idea by Ira Berkow and James Kaplan and an afterthought by Michael Seeherman, suggested by a mutter of Stephen King Inc. A film by Leslie Nielsen, starring (in alphabetical order) Arnold Schwarzenegger. Costarring Leslie Nielsen, Anna Marie Klunk, Mickey Freeman, and Rabbi Nathan Edelman as himself. Introducing (in no particular order) Courtney Chandel, Catherine Carlen, Mighty Joe Young, Jr., Jordan Burnett, Buck Fisher. Produced by Tom Stimson and Jerry Bruckman in association with the Enigma Group and Big Bucks Entertainment. Executive producer, Joseph Cariccola, Jr. Executive Executive producer, Wendy Friedman. King of producers, Juan Carlos III. Coexecutive producers, George Kaufman and Richard Leibnir. Director of producers, Geri Simon. Executive producer of directors, Tom Klutznick. Coexecutive director of producers, Richard Soll. Executive director of producers' credits, Ronal Luciano. Producers' referee, Andrew Fox. Coexecutive producer director of directing producers, Louis DiGiaimo, Jr. Producers' promise to credit in exchange for sexual favors, Linda O'Boy. Utility producer, Bobby Zarem. Split end, Mark Bavarro. *Ninja Gandhi.* Soon to be a videocassette."

Despite what I would charitably describe as "tepid" reviews, a lot of people raved about this film. Part of the reason for the somewhat negative reviews, I believe, is that the critics simply missed the subtext, which was that people of all races, religions, and political parties can get along harmoniously as long as they are properly armed. The critics chose instead to focus on what they called "gratuitous violence," claiming that the six hand-to-hand combat scenes, the four handgun battles, the major machine-gun exchange, the very brief mortar fight, the naval bombardment, the F-16A strafing mission and dog-fight, and the carpet bombing by the B-52 squadron, in addition to the mass mugging, were simply too much.

Personally, I felt these action scenes were necessary if we were going to tell this story honestly, the way it needed to be told. Sometimes the truth is just special effects. I also believe that the critics, in their haste to find fault, completely overlooked the obvious moral significance of this film. But perhaps that's why they're known as "critics" rather than "good guys."

Admittedly the picture wasn't perfect. Several of the scenes were slightly out of focus, but the reality is that in our society, in order to attract the attention of the audience, you must produce a product that will interest them. The most important thing is what you do with that attention after you've got it. Certainly there was a lot of violence in *Ninja Gandhi,* but it was included specifically to make an important point: violence will attract a really big audience. The real question is: What does that say about our society? I also feel it is necessary to point out that after the city of Boston had been transformed into a rather large vacant lot, my character, Crazy Matt, looks over the landscape of that once-thriving city with regret and asks, "Was it worth it? I mean, really, really worth it? I mean, like, was it like worth it to the tenth power worth it?"

And that was the question the audience left the theater pondering.

Unfortunately, *Ninja Gandhi* did cost several people their jobs. Perhaps, due to the negative reviews, the studio didn't expect the picture to go into profits, causing someone in the accounting department to pay less attention to its bookkeeping. But *Ninja Gandhi* became the studio's first picture in more than a decade to show a profit in its first year of release. The studio was shocked at the laxity of its accountants, and several of them were fired. A high-ranking studio official who refused to be quoted by name told *Variety,* "This sort of thing happens from time to time, and there really isn't too much we can do about it. But if it happens too often, we'll be out of business. We make films, not money."

The fact that the film went into profits, costing the studio considerable money, virtually eliminated any possibility that the planned sequel, *The Ninja Gandhi Meets Freddy Krueger While Home Alone,* would ever be made.

My Best Actor Oscar and the subsequent popularity of *Ninja* had made me a powerful man in the film industry. I had become "bankable." "Packages" could be built around me. I was a "key element." I was being offered as much as $3,500,000 a picture, getting up into the so-called Nicholsonland. Women I hadn't met called me up and asked me for dates. "Inside Edition" searched through my garbage. I was permitted to sit at Mike Ovitz's table during Morton's early seating. My invitation to Swifty Lazar's Oscar party arrived six months before the Academy Awards. "Lifestyles of the Rich and Famous" offered to send me on an all-expense trip to San Diego. The prestigious Lagos Film Festival wanted to hold a gala retrospective of my oeuvre. I owned all the accoutrements of success. And yet, truthfully, I wasn't happy. And I couldn't figure out why.

I realized that something was missing from my life. I mean, besides a Ferrari Testosterone. Although I had so much, I felt completely lost. Adrift. Material things just didn't matter to me anymore. I could afford whatever I wanted, but I needed imma-terial things. What was missing was some meaning to my life, something deep inside that allowed me to thoroughly enjoy everything on the surface outside. And so I began my search

Endorsements are a big part of the movie business today. Movies have become "marketing vehicles." Ninja Gandhi *led to a series of popular comics, while* The Naked Gun *bullets have become collectibles. Each one is autographed and numbered, making them too valuable to shoot.*

for spiritual fulfillment, a search for the inner peace that can come only from inside yourself—the kind of peace, I knew, that some men had spent their entire lives searching for.

I began by spending a whole weekend at an EST seminar. At EST, the Erhard Seminar Training, I ran into a lot of people I knew from the motion-picture industry, from actors to agents, who were searching for their inner being as well as material for a screenplay, people who also felt completely lost. Initially, I'd believed this program had been named after Amelia Earhart, the famed aviatrix who was so completely lost that people have been searching for her for decades. But, in fact, it was named for its founder, Werner Erhard.

It was a fascinating experience. Part of the discipline of the weekend was that we were not permitted to leave the room to go to the bathroom. A lot of people objected to that, but I didn't mind. I didn't know exactly where I was going to find the contentment for which I was searching, but I felt certain it wasn't going to be in the men's room. The real emphasis of the weekend was placed on getting in touch with our emotions and learning how to express them openly. Learning how to share our feelings with other people. Well, I don't think that went over very big with this particular group. A lot of these people had become very rich by figuring out how not to share with other people. In fact, as I walked out of the seminar Sunday night, I overheard an agent discussing what we'd learned with a theatrical attorney. "Look," he said, "I don't object to sharing my feelings with you in principle, I just want it to be equitable. Tell you what, I'll give you a straight five percent of my domestic feelings, but no back end."

The attorney laughed derisively. "You call that sharing? That's not sharing. Here, this is how you share your feelings—'I think you're a putz.' That's sharing. And I wouldn't even consider settling for less than fifty percent of all feelings, domestic and foreign, and that includes electronic rights."

"Forget it, just forget it. There's four studio execs who've already indicated they're interested in my sharing my feelings."

After EST, I decided to try channeling. Channels are people whose body and voice are used by the spirits of long-dead people to communicate their thoughts and knowledge to living people. Perhaps there were some people who found this valuable, but I kept getting the wrong channel. For example, one channel, a very nice older gentleman named Martin Walsh, was supposed to be channeling Cindar, a third-century Boorish religious leader who was especially knowledgeable about herbal weight loss, but who somehow got his psychic wires crossed and instead channeled Hall of Fame pitcher Christy Mathewson. Needless to say, that was disappointing. When someone in the audience asked Mathewson the secret to a happy life, he replied, "Never hang a curveball to Babe Ruth." Good advice, perhaps, but not exactly what I was searching for, so I changed channels. My new medium claimed to be channeling the legendary gangster Al Capone. Maybe she was because, characteristically, Capone refused to talk.

A lot of people in the film industry claimed that they'd found inner contentment through transcendental meditation. So I went to a TM center in Santa Monica to learn how to do it. I didn't really expect to find inner contentment in Santa Monica, I was happy just to find a parking spot, but I was willing to try. The correct way to meditate, I was taught, was to repeat my mantra, a sound with no specific meaning, a nonsense sound, over and over and over silently in my mind. This would supposedly put me in a trancelike state, known as a karloff, allowing my mind to relax completely.

Although I was asked not to tell anyone my official mantra, which was given to me by my personal trainer at the TM center, I'm going to reveal it here rather than have it made public by the National Star. My mantra, my nonsense sound, is CAA CAA. I did just as I had been taught; I sat down in a comfortable, quiet place and silently repeated my mantra over and over and over, CAA CAA, CAA CAA, CAA CAA. And incredibly, I drifted into a state of deep relaxation. As I'd been taught, I let my mind go wherever it wanted to go, and when I became conscious of the fact that I wasn't repeating my mantra, I simply began repeating it. The process worked well, except for one afternoon when my mind wanted to go for a pizza and I wanted to continue meditating. While I was in that trance, I was indeed happy and content, I felt completely relaxed and at peace. It was only when I woke up that this feeling disappeared. So I realized that I'd found inner contentment, but only when I was in a trance. What I really needed, I knew, was outer contentment.

I continued my quest for self-discovery. This search was made much easier by the fact that I live in California. Los Angeles is the only city in the world where mile markers inform you how far you are from help: "Tranquillity—4 Miles." "Assertion—Next Exit." On this journey I discovered the one thing that all self-help programs had in common: the more you wanted to help yourself, the more you paid someone else.

I tried so many different things. The actress Penelope Farber taught me about the incredible powers of crystals, for example. Holding a crystal supposedly made you feel better, increased your energy, and helped you focus. I went to Tiffany's and bought a set of Waterford crystal glasses. Sure enough, the salesperson felt better immediately. But I soon discovered that it wasn't the crystal that made me feel better, rather what I put inside it. The crystal wasn't even strong enough to heal the hangover.

I was willing to try anything to rid myself of the feeling that I didn't deserve my great success. I took a course in actualizations. I read and reread M. Scott Peck's The Road Less Traveled. For me, I discovered, it wasn't much of a road, it was more of an overgrown path in the woods, and I kept stepping in the poison ivy of life. And the mosquitoes were terrible. I rented all the Anthony Robbins videos. I tried sandbox therapy, in which we were taught how to play nicely with other people in a sandbox. The object was to remind participants that true joy and happiness in life have nothing to do with material possessions and status symbols. This really was fun, although it was very expensive. In order to get the guys to come play at my house, I had to buy a Ralph Lauren sandbox, fill it with Mario Buatta's imported sand, and provide each playmate with his own set of Martha

Stewart's sterling-silver sandbox tools. About the only self-help technique I refused to try was rebirthing, in which you go through the entire experience of birth all over again, this time with love and support. I just knew I'd never fit in there again.

I even tried the highly experimental Gilligan's therapy, in which you watch twenty-four continuous hours of "Gilligan's Island." This supposedly served to remind everyone that no matter how bad you thought your everyday life was, it could be worse.

When chanting became popular in Hollywood, I decided to try it. Chanting was similar to TM. I'd get up every morning and sit cross-legged in front of a little statue of the late William Morris and repeat a harmonious chant in a singsong. In this case my chant was "Iwannathreepicturedeal, Iwannathreepicturedeal." This chant actually caused a pleasant resonance in my body, similar to that which I'd felt by putting a quarter in the machine next to my bed when I stayed at the Château Marmont.

I was running out of things to try, so I decided to try running. I enrolled in a course in Elementary Jogging at USC. That course proved to be very important to me because I learned that I just couldn't run away from my problems. I didn't have the stamina and it was just too hard going uphill.

And that was when I discovered yodeling; for me, that has made all the difference. Yodeling had become a lost art form; true yodeling is not at all similar to Western-style yodeling popularized by Gene Autry in his cowboy films. Rather, it's an ancient and revered form of communication between distant mountain villages. Each yo of a yodel had a very different and distinct meaning, and this language enabled isolated villages to yodel for help when it was needed. Classical yodeling, the type I've studied, is meant to represent the ups and downs of everyday life, which is symbolized in modern society by the yo-yo. A perfect yodel is believed to emanate from the exact center of the human body, which is why people over six feet, four inches tall with very long legs generally have difficulty yodeling.

Obviously yodeling isn't for everyone. The committed yodeler begins each day by standing comfortably in front of a small statue of the honored Yodel Master, Yoda the Jedi, and yodeling for approximately fifteen minutes, attempting to find that point at which the body is in tune with the mind. Among yodelers, this is known as a "spiritual tune-up."

Although I claim no credit for the yodeling craze that subsequently swept the entertainment industry, I will concede that my ground-breaking video, *In Search of the Perfect Yodel*, played an important role in this phenomenon. I'd often heard it said that there is no accounting for taste, but I'm pleased to be able to report that my new accountant proved that to be incorrect. At the beginning of each month I received a complete statement showing the number of videos sold and our profits.

While yodeling enabled me to put my mind and body in harmony, it did not provide the answer for which I'd been searching. But what it did do was help me understand the real, unabashed, no-kidding-this-time, naked truth. And that is, that no matter how far or long we search for serenity, the only place it can be found is inside ourselves. And that's the naked truth. I learned so much from my long quest, but certainly the most important thing I came to understand is that it is not *what* you are that matters, but rather *who* you are. Or, for people in the entertainment industry, whom you're *supposed* to be.

Sometimes, those of us in the film colony get so caught up in the glamour and the adulation and the financial rewards that we forget who we really are, and at those times, times when I was so confused or anxious or egotistical that I forgot who I really was, I was fortunate enough to be able to go outside and read my license plate: and I knew that I was Lsle Nlsn!

Naturally, individuals with two cars were able to learn twice as much about themselves.

It was at a yodel-in that I met another local yodel, as we called ourselves, the beautiful legend Barbra Streisand, and that led to my next great film role. I suspect the thing that first attracted me to Barbra was the ethereal beauty of her yodeling voice. It's not an exaggeration to say that she had the yodel of a mountain goat. And she was much prettier.

We hit it off immediately. Actually, we didn't hit it off, we sort of tripped it off; apparently she never saw my foot sticking out on the aisle. At that time she was just beginning preproduction of the movie *Nuts*. This was the story of a call girl with a heart of goldcard who was considered insane because she's killed one of her clients before he'd paid, while she insisted she'd killed him because she was sane. Obviously, that's why she was *nuts*!

Probably the most important thing to know about Barbra Streisand is that she is a workaholic; she had absolutely no patience for anything that wastes even a second of her time. As she confided in me one evening, that was the reason she took the second *a* out of *Barbara*. She felt it was extraneous, and she estimates she's saved as much as a year of her life in autograph signings. Barbra was also a perfectionist, which is why she so desperately wanted me to costar with her, Dickie Dreyfuss, Karl Malden, Eli Wallach, Jimmy Whitmore, Maur Stapleton, and Dommie DeLuise in the movie.

I played the role of Al Green, a "client" of hers from Chicago whom she kills by stabbing him in the neck with a sharp sliver of broken mirror. I think the good Dr. Freud might have an opinion about that.

Working with Barbra was pleasant, although she insisted on being photographed only from the so-called "good side" of her face: the front. I'd often heard it said of certain stars that they "owned the cameras," meaning they photographed extremely well. But this was the first time I'd worked with an actor who really did own the cameras: she'd bought and paid for them and would take them home with her every night.

My death scene began when I asked Barbra if she'd join me in a "nice, sexy bubble bath," adding, "I like to bathe my girls."

To which she replied curtly, "I'm not a girl."

Well, imagine my surprise. I knew she had a reputation in Hollywood for being tough, and I'd heard she was insecure about her looks, but I hadn't realized it had gone that far. So very gently I pointed out to her, "You're not a boy."

That's when she killed me.

I felt that this was probably the best time I'd been murdered in my career. The actual shot was filmed artfully by director Marty Ritt. Barbra and I wrestled onto the floor, and she picked up a sliver of broken mirror and stabbed me. I let out a bloodcurdling scream, "Arrrrggggghhhhoops," and rolled over, eyes open, tongue lolling. I was extremely proud of my loll; many young actors make the mistake of exaggerating their tongue loll and end up looking more like a pig on a platter than a murder victim. I also allowed one finger to tremble rapidly, then gradually slow down and slow down further and finally stop in midair. Since the release of this film several actors have copied this movement, but I claim credit for introducing it to the silver screen. Some people claim that Charlton Heston first introduced it, but that is not so. Heston was the first to draw his right index finger from just below his left ear across the left lower portion of the front of his jaw—all this done with a look of deep thoughtfulness.

For my work in this scene, the American Society of Coroners awarded me their coveted Golden Mackerel as Corpse of the Year. In other years the prestigious "Mac" has been won by such people as Kevin Costner for his death in *The Big Chill*, Chief Dan George for *Little Big Man*, Warren Beatty for *Bonnie and Clyde*, Terry Kiser for his unstirring portrayal of Bernie in *Weekend at Bernie's*, and the entire cast of the original *Night of the Living Dead*.

Working with Barbra Streisand was truly a memorable experience. But contrary to those reports that our torrid love scene continued about an hour later in her dressing building, we remained "just good friends." I mean, "really just good friends." Was there anything between us? Of course, Barbra wanted it that way. Once it was a large table. Another time it was a couch. A bowling ball. So we never got too close.

But we did enjoy each other's company, and sometimes she would come into my dressing closet and ask me to join her in singing a duet of "People." On one of those afternoons I asked her why she'd insisted that I play this role. "I had to kill somebody," she explained. "I've seen every movie you've ever made, and I just knew that you were the man I most wanted to kill."

"Thank you very much," I said, meaning it. "I've always admired your work, too."

She continued: "For this picture to work, it was necessary that the audience dislike my character in the beginning, and I was certain that if I killed you, they would hate me."

"That's so sweet of you, Barb. I just want you to know that I consider it a real honor to receive a paycheck from you."

"And," she agreed sweetly, "killing you has been one of the great pleasures of my life." Then we sang a final chorus of "Memories" and she was gone.

Perhaps the best thing that happened to me while we were making *Nuts* was that I met the woman destined to become my fourth wife—Joyce Collyer. At that time Joyce was still a struggling actress who had a small part in the movie as a serial jaywalker. For someone so young and so well built, it was amazing how much we had in common. As we got to know each other, I discovered that she loved so many of the same things I did: food, music, transportation, entertainment, laughter. After we became close I discovered that there was hardly a man in Hollywood who didn't know her and love her, but she promised me that that part of her life was in the past.

Since we've been together, I've had the great pleasure of watching her grow as an actress as well as a human being, and that doesn't even include the augmentation. Joyce is a woman of great talent who has worked hard to make a career for herself, and today she is considered one of the rising young stars of the 1-900 telephone numbers.

After the completion of *Nuts* I wanted to do something that I'd never done before, but Joyce wouldn't go for it. So instead I met with the Zucker brothers, Jim Abrahams, and Pat Proft, one of America's most respected crime writers, who were just beginning preproduction of a gritty police drama. They wanted me to create the role of their gritty hero, Los Angeles Police Department lieutenant Frank Drebin. Although police dramas, cops and robbers, have long been a staple of the movie industry, the Zuckers and Abrahams firmly believed that the essential police story had yet to be filmed. It was their intention to make a film noir, *The Naked Gun*, the most realistic police drama ever done.

When they explained this concept to me, I literally jumped at the chance to play gritty Frank Drebin. Unfortunately, when

I landed, I twisted my ankle slightly and was on crutches for several days. But I was very excited; my father had been a law enforcement officer, and since the beginning of my career I'd wanted to make a serious police drama. Finally I was being given that opportunity.

At the time *The Naked Gun* was being written, so-called buddy films, movies emphasizing the relationship between two men as they fought a common enemy, were extremely popular. The Zuckers, Abrahams, and Proft conceived of *The Naked Gun* as more of a "booby film," in which Drebin was his own best friend. Sort of a one-man-relationship film.

The character of Drebin was written quite broadly, and it was up to me to give life to him. One night, as I lay in bed trying to picture this dedicated officer, I heard a familiar knocking on my brain. And then I remembered my career-long associates, the Acting Police. They were stern and professional, yet

No policeman ever pounded a beat like Frank Drebin, the tough cop I play in The Naked Gun. *He wasn't satisfied being just a flatfoot, so he worked very hard and became a b-flatfoot. It was a great beat.*

276

not without humor and charm. That, I decided, would be the character of Lt. Frank Drebin.

As I'd learned to do at the Actors Studio so many years earlier, I began preparing for this role by observing my real-life counterparts. Arrangements were made for me to spend several days with officers of the LAPD. This was my chance to see real life up close, and I leaped at it. This time I landed without incident. It didn't take me long to appreciate how extremely difficult police work really is, although the uniforms are fabulous. I will never forget that bitter, blistery night when two brave, freezing officers dragged an obvious killer into the station house. The killer made the mistake of boasting contemptuously, "Youse guys'll never pin anything on me."

That man lived to regret those words. The police managed to pin all sorts of things on him: ribbons, old newspapers, pieces of toilet paper. And when they ran out of pins, they taped things to him. It got a little out of hand; eventually eight officers were brought up on charges of police hilarity.

That incident helped me find the key to Frank Drebin's character. Like Pete Falk's brilliant creation, legendary TV detective Columbo, Frank Drebin would use the weapon of humor against those people who did evil things. Using his rapier-sharp wit, he would cut them down to size. Just as Columbo did, Frank Drebin would intentionally make criminals overconfident, then swoop down on them like a politician on a campaign donation. Drebin might look like the kind of cop who couldn't shoot his way out of a paper bag, but shoot his way out he would—although several innocent bystanders were accidentally wounded because he had a paper bag over his head.

Frank Drebin was the kind of cop who broke all the rules, in addition to an occasional rare vase!

And that's the way I played him. Many people—in fact, everybody in the entire world—made the mistake of trying to underestimate Frank Drebin. But Drebin was not the kind of cop who could be underestimated, no matter how low people estimated. Because under that droll exterior, and under that droll interior, beat a heart! And that's what kept Frank going through thick and thin, through several walls, through the front of a restaurant, even through a two-thousand-year-old handmade Japanese screen.

Certainly people laughed at Frank Drebin, but they stopped laughing when the picture ended. Because Drebin had proved that there was a madness to his methods, and that while Ms. Justice may indeed be visually challenged, she could still play those scales of fairness she carried in her hand—although sometimes she tripped over the piano because of that blindfold she insists on wearing.

For my portrayal of Lt. Frank Drebin, the Academy of Motion Picture Arts and Sciences awarded me my second Oscar as Best Actor, an honor of which I was extraordinarily proud. "I couldn't have done it myself," I said gleefully as I accepted my Oscar, "particularly the love scenes."

Costarring with me in *The Naked Gun* were the legendary Oscar winner George Kennedy, the great Dicko Montalban, the brilliant Oh Simpson, the utterly superb Nancy Marchand, and the gorgeous yet glamorous Priscilla Presley.

During the brief time we worked together I became extremely protective of Priscilla. As the former wife of the best-known popular icon of our time, Mr. Elvis A. Presley, she was constantly barraged by questions about him. In particular, scientists working on government-funded Elvis projects were desperate to ask her about the ridiculous rumors that Elvis was sharing an efficiency apartment with John F. Kennedy in a remote New England whaling village.

Naturally I was sensitive to her feelings. In fact, to try to make her feel a little more comfortable with me, when we first met, I sang several verses of the Canadian favorite "Are You Lonesome Tonight?" However, I refused to sing my version of how that song would sound if Elvis had been a Canadian: "Are You Lonesome Tonight, Eh?"

Certainly I was curious about Elvis. Who isn't? But I never asked her a single question about him. The most I ever asked were questions like, "You happen to see anyone with long sideburns wearing a sparkling velvet jumpsuit walking around here last night?" Or I'd sing the harmony to "Blue Suede Shoes" and listen to hear if anyone sang the melody. But I found no evidence to support the theory that Elvis was still alive. That proves nothing, of course. I didn't find any evidence to prove that Robert Culp is alive either. I know Priscilla appreciated my sensitivity to her feelings because this was when she confessed the fact that Elvis had been consumed with jealousy after I'd won the role he so desperately wanted to play in *Tammy*. And when we parted, she gave me a photo of Elvis, which he had personally autographed to me.

When we wrapped *The Naked Gun,* the legendary producer-director Barry Levinson offered me the lead in his new medical thriller, but I didn't want to do a docudrama, so I turned him down. Instead I went to Montana to work with my friend Kevin Costner in his epic western, *Dances with Wolves.*

Although it isn't widely reported, quite often we megastars in the film industry will work for free in projects we believe in. De Niro, Cruise, Harry Ford, me, Madonna—if the project is worthwhile, we'll turn down other offers worth millions of dollars and at our own expense fly anywhere in the world to lend our names and talents. *Dances with Wolves* was such a film, an exploration of the difficult life of the American Plain Indian, or, as the politically correct people prefer, "Men Who Wore Pretty Feathers." These were the people who discovered the vast riches of the North American continent, secure in the knowledge, "If we find gold, they will come." In the film Kevin played an American cavalry officer who became known to the Indians as Dances with Wolves, while I played the small but wonderfully written role of an Indian brave named Spits Without Provocation. It's probably incorrect to call Spits Without Provocation a brave; he was actually more of a practical. For example, when my chief wanted to attack the fort, I was the counselor who pointed out to him that there were a million soldiers with guns in there and suggested we should go around.

Costner is one of the most even-tempered, talented actors I'd ever worked with. The only time I ever saw him upset was when he had to leave the set to attend a Madonna concert. Ironically, in Madonna's controversial film *Truth or Dare,* Kevin was shown coming backstage to congratulate her, and after he'd left she made a pouty face and a nasty remark. Well, the truth is that Kevin didn't want to go to the concert at all. I remember him telling me, "The last performer in the world I want to see is Madonna, but my people gave my word to her people." Then he corrected himself. "That's not true at all. The last performer in the world I want to see is the winner of David Letterman's Stupid Pet Tricks contest. Madonna's second."

"I wouldn't tell her that," I replied, "she doesn't like being second."

The result is film history.

It had taken me a long time, but my life was full. Complete. Once again I was being offered the most prestigious roles in the motion-picture industry. Bob Redford was being offered the scripts I turned down. When the gossip columns wanted to promote a restaurant, they claimed I'd eaten there. Instead of going through my garbage, the *National Enquirer* had new garbage delivered to my home. I received some seven-figure offers to become the spokesperson for products, although admittedly the first three figures were zeroes. NASA wanted me to pilot a space shuttle. Both the Arabs and the Israelis asked me to negotiate a peace settlement. I had a new home and a woman I loved very much, although when Joyce found out about her I willingly gave her up. And I had my yodeling.

I was in the position dreamed about by every person who ever picked up a script and put on stage makeup and a leotard; I could pick and choose projects I wanted to do without fear that a failure would end my career. I was an actor!

When those fine boys the Zuckers and Abrahams decided to make a sequel to *The Naked Gun* in hopes they would become very rich, they begged me to bring back to life the enigmatic Lt. Frank Drebin. Having won the big prize, the Oscar, for that role, I agreed to reprise it.

Alas and aladdie, I didn't win the big O again, but *Naked Gun 2½* grossed almost $375,000,000 worldwide, becoming the most successful motion picture ever made. And when it is released on video, I am assured by the studio it will go into profits.

How do you define career? For some people, it means little more than the back of an automobile. But to me it means everything I've ever done, the great and the moderately great. And in a career filled with honors, including my two Oscars and the coveted Nobel Prize for Good Acting, I am most proud of the fact that the good and wonderful Paramount Pictures, the greatest motion-picture studio in recorded history, the studio's studio, decided to make the motion picture about my life. Very few Americans have been the subject of a big-screen biography, among them Al Capone, Bonnie and Clyde, Doc Holliday, Louie Lepke, Machine Gun Kelly, Jimmy Hoffa, Dutch Schultz, Al Capone again, Ma Barker, Leona Helmsley, Frederick Krueger, Bugsy Siegel, Meyer Lansky, the Elephant Man, Billy the Kid, Gen. George Custer, and my old pal Frank Sinatra.

When I was first approached, I wondered: Who could really portray me? While there was tremendous competition for the role, I wanted it to be someone who was just as I was before I became known, an unknown.

Actor: The Leslie Nielsen Story opened to numerous reviews, starring . . . We had searched everywhere, but couldn't find an unknown. Perhaps that's why they are known as unknowns—no one knows them. So I had no choice but to play the role myself. I was a natural for the part, I knew all the lines. Playing myself as a young actor was quite difficult, though, because I had to act as if I hadn't learned to act, which requires tremendous acting ability. And certainly one of the nicest things that happened was that my old friend Robby the Robot, with whom I'd worked so long ago in *Forbidden Planet,* came out of retirement to put on the greasepaint, or in his case, the grease, one final time.

The most difficult part of playing yourself, I learned, was determining who wins. Playing me served to remind me how incredibly lucky I've been, how many wonderful people I've worked with, how many great movies I've made. I'm often asked what it's like to be considered America's greatest living actor. I always respond being at the very, very top isn't as easy as it looks. To those legions of actors looking up at me, it probably looks incredibly glamorous and exciting, but to those pigeons flying overhead, all I am is a big target.

I'm a very fortunate man. And I'm extremely grateful for the opportunities I've been given and the experiences I've enjoyed. And I've tried to remember those words of wisdom spoken by the legendary Notre Dame football coach Knute Rockne, who once said, "It's better to kick off in the first half than receive." So it is with great pleasure I'm proud to announce that I have endowed the Leslie Nielsen Chair of Good Acting at the Yale Drama School, in New Haven, Connecticut.

Actually it's not a complete chair; it's the Leslie Nielsen Folding Chair of Good Acting at the Yale Drama School.

Perhaps it's not an official folding chair. Officially, it's the Leslie Nielsen Stool of Acting at Yale Drama School. And I'm very proud of it.

All right, it's really the Leslie Nielsen Hammock of Acting.

My life is now an open book. And it will remain so for at least a few more paragraphs. Through it all, what have I learned? I have learned the price of fame. Fame doesn't come cheap. Fame is a bitch goddess; believe me, I've known her in many disguises. Fame is tall, and she has a little mustache and she wears too much cheap perfume, and she's very arrogant, always demanding reverence. Fame grants wishes and adulation and respect to those she kisses, fame gets you the boss table at trendy restaurants; but she is a thief, robbing you of your privacy, your freedom to walk those mean streets or drive an old car or wear silly hats. Fame steals the very basic freedom to be yourself.

The price of fame is steep. Many people are desperate for it, they crave it, they pray for it, but they don't know how expensive it is. And for those people, I've gone back over all my old tax returns and figured it out. Including the cost of all lessons, management and publicity fees, minor plastic surgery, transportation and communications, and incidentals, the price of fame, adjusted for inflation, is precisely $264,744.88. (New Jersey residents add 3½ percent sales tax.)

And that is the Ultimate Naked Truth.

(NOTE: Some individuals appearing in this book may not appear in the index. Some individuals appearing in this index may not appear in this book. Page numbers may not directly correspond to specific entries. Appearance in this index does not constitute an endorsement of this index by the individual. Michael Jackson appears in this index through the courtesy of MikeMoney Productions. Mr. Nielsen's wardrobe for this index was provided by TopStyle 350 in return for this credit.)